DRAWING INSPIRATION

Visual Artists at Work

MICHAEL FLEISHMAN

Visual Artists at Work

MICHAEL FLEISHMAN

DELMAR
CENGAGE Learning

Australia • Brazil • Japan • Korea• Mexico • Singapore • Spain • United Kingdom • United States

Drawing Inspiration, *Visual Artists at Work*
Michael Fleishman

Vice President, Career and Professional Editorial: Dave Garza

Director of Learning Solutions: Sandy Clark

Senior Acquisitions Editor: Jim Gish

Managing Editor: Larry Main

Associate Product Manager: Meaghan O'Brien

Editorial Assistant: Sarah Timm

Vice President, Career and Professional Marketing: Jennifer McAvey

Marketing Director: Deborah Yarnell

Marketing Manager: Erin Brennan

Marketing Coordinator: Jonathon Sheehan

Production Director: Wendy Troeger

Senior Content Project Manager: Glenn Castle

Art Director: Joy Kocsis

Cover Artist: David Bowers

For product information and technology assistance, contact us at
Cengage Learning Customer & Sales Support, 1-800-354-9706

For permission to use material from this text or product, submit all requests online at **cengage.com/permissions**. Further permissions questions can be e-mailed to **permissionrequest@cengage.com**.

Library of Congress Control Number: 2009933907

ISBN-13: 9781418052256
ISBN-10: 1418052256

Delmar
5 Maxwell Drive
Clifton Park, NY 12065-2919
USA

Cengage Learning is a leading provider of customized learning solutions with office locations around the globe, including Singapore, the United Kingdom, Australia, Mexico, Brazil and Japan. Locate your local office at: **international.cengage.com/region**

Cengage Learning products are represented in Canada by Nelson Education, Ltd.

To learn more about Delmar, visit **www.cengage.com/delmar**

Purchase any of our products at your local college store or at our preferred online store **www.CengageBrain.com**

Printed in the United States of America
1 2 3 4 5 6 7 X X 13 12 11 10

Dedication

To Joanne, to the boys. To the cats, to the morning.

Table of Contents

Preface

Who Is This Book For?

I've had a one-track mind since I was a little kid—it's all about drawing. As a student I was fortunate enough to be trained by teachers who considered drawing to be important. For many of my instructors and contemporaries, drawing was all encompassing. Some were down right zealots. That mindset—really learn to draw and you can do anything—invades my thinking and pervades my classroom strategies to this day. This book is for folks who think that *drawing is important,* that drawing connects it all together.

The Audience

So I talked to the everyday experts about drawing—not coincidentally the same folks who just might have a real need for such an aide: current (and former) teachers and students, students who are now pros, and many who are—not surprisingly—now teachers. Folks like you.

We chatted with students about teachers, the teacher about the student. Indeed, *Drawing Inspiration: Visual Artists at Work* seeks to unravel the string between academic and professional product and process. And, as such, philosophy and opinion, as well as concept and technique, are fair game for our discussion. Illustrator and teacher Rick Sealock says he teaches by that example. "Most illustration today still encompasses that 'in the trenches' attitude," he comments. "Students need those instructors who not only can talk the talk, but walk it too."

Bottom line: Students taking an "Intro To Illustration" class are the primary target audience for this book. But *Drawing Inspiration* was written to maintain a longer hang time than just freshman year. It also boasts a wide reach above the first floor of the art building, and could also be used as a companion book to a variety of art classes throughout the curriculum (as well as creative endeavors beyond formal education).

Why I Wrote This Text

I assert that drawing is the core—the root activity—of most, if not all, visual arts. We're all students, and we should be lifelong students, at that. The rudiments of drawing lay the groundwork for a lifetime of exploration. I wrote this text to explore the concept that drawing—like life itself—is an immersion exercise, a hands-on event.

Drawing (even for "fun") demands determination and direction. This book provides heaping helpings of both.

And when people ask me what this book is about, I always reply: "This is a book about *connections.*" The soul and substance of "connections" may be many things. You can obviously connect through networking or mentoring, or inspiration and influence—definitely. But making a connection could also be about good feedback that enables you to turn the corner on a cranky composition, a high-energy marker sketch that elegantly segues into a powerful digital final, or one process deftly morphing into a related technique. In simpler terms: interaction and relationships. For instance: take business seriously. But also know how to relax, have fun, but still be passionate about what you do. Know your process, but don't forget to enjoy it, too. Connection. Relationships. Another example: regarding schooling as an apprenticeship because your entire art education is certainly about making some kind of *career* happen. And that career is all about *you.*

What a Trip

To begin your journey, you must start at, well, the beginning. But where you start isn't necessarily where you end up. "Fundamentals are crucial," says illustrator Matt Kindt, who, as a student, didn't take any classes in cartooning or illustration. "I took graphic design, figure drawing, sculpture, paper-making…everything else."

Kindt is the Harvey Award-winning writer and artist of the graphic novels *Super Spy* and *2 Sisters* and has been nominated for four Eisner and three Harvey Awards. At school, Kindt knew he would be illustrating and drawing graphic novels *eventually.* He wanted to learn anything and everything even tangentially related to that goal. Ultimately, this facilitated a deep background that brought more to his work than a strict focus on one narrow subject.

Keep that in mind, because the book you hold in your hands offers a rather original conceit. *Drawing Inspiration* is a bonafide multi-tasking drawing tool. I use the process and product of drawing as a general springboard to address the creative act whole cloth. Thus, we explore techniques and formats that are not traditionally classified as pure drawing (whatever that may be) but are definitely drawing-based, drawing-related, or drawing-augmented (for instance: painting, collage, 3-D, fabrics, printmaking, etc.).

Organization of the Text

The book is organized into three sections. Twenty-one chapters divided over these three major sections both inspire and reveal *how to* inspire through the creative connections of drawing:

1. Connections. This section explores the under-pinnings: the "why" part of our drawing equation. 2. Tools. Here we examine the foundations of drawing fundamentals. You might say the "how" of it all. 3. At Work. In which we discuss the "who" and the "what" of drawing process. And by the way, no identity crisis here. In the spirit of that bigger picture (the connection thing again) we deliberately—and liberally—cross-reference chapters and info. Cool—the book is joined at the very hip. The chapters:

Section 1 Intro: "The Connections"

Chapter 1: Ideas: Why We Draw. This chapter reconciles the mechanical with the intellectual processes and asks the basic questions: What encourages an artist to make a drawing? What inspires you to draw? Where do you *start*?

Chapter 2: Subject Matter: What We Draw. For many, *what* we draw—*subject matter*—may well be the major focus of the whole exercise. Here we look at various subcategories of picture making—better yet, make that subject-making: opportunities to address that million-dollar question posed by Chapter 1.

Chapter 3: Sketchbooks. We look at the roots of drawing and begin with another basic question: where do ideas come from? This chapter considers sketchbooks (and by extension, journals, diaries, and scrapbooks too) as creative outlets to record relevant answers to this question and play with those solutions.

Chapter 4: The Process. This chapter discusses the core of drawing methodology, where the art and act of drawing begins. We'll again address the central question: where do ideas come from?

Chapter 5: Concept. Let's talk about what many consider *the* key element of the creative process: concept, the big *idea*. We'll consider what that illustration is really about; what you are trying to say, and how you go about saying it (conceptually *and* technically).

Chapter 6: Composition. This chapter discusses a key foundation that is all about both communication *and* foundations: composition—the ordered arrangement of visual elements within the picture plane.

Section 2 Intro: "The Tools"

Chapter 7: Line. This chapter begins a discussion of the core foundations of the drawing process: the fundamental element of *line* and how line informs the root of that process.

Chapter 8: Color. This chapter continues the discussion of the core foundations of the drawing process: the key element of *color,* in concept and practice; how color works, and how the viewer perceives that function.

Chapter 9: Value. This chapter explores another core foundation of the drawing process: the crucial element of *value,* an important building block regarded by many artists as *the* most critical link in the artistic chain of creative command.

Chapter 10: Texture and Pattern. Dots and dashes, dabs and scrubs. Drip or dribble, flick and splatter. Squirt and spray, skim and comb, smear or wipe. Sponge and scumble, cluster and repeat; group, repeat.

Chapter 11: Shape and Form. This chapter looks at shape and form: shape as the *overall* visual perception of the parts of an image; form as the rendering of that organization.

Section 3 Intro: "At Work"

Chapter 12: Drawing in Character. While ostensibly about portraiture, caricature and cartoons, this chapter is more about rendering and description: character (internal interpretation) and characters (external representation).

Chapter 13: Drawing Is Provocative. This chapter is about how drawing sparkles with emotion, mood, and personality to make a statement or send a message; to instigate and incite thought or action.

Chapter 14: Old School/New School. This chapter explores education: drawing educators and how drawing educates; how drawers are educated.

Chapter 15: Drawing Imagines. From realism to the surreal, from fantasy to science fiction; from the bizarre to the fantastic…how drawing can lead the viewer on flights of fancy and imagination.

Chapter 16: Drawing Observes. People watching. World hopping. Communication and observation. Visual thinking and conceptual insight.

Chapter 17: Drawing Takes Off. This chapter expands the scope and idea of "drawing." Artists you'll meet here begin with drawing, and then spin it off—literally and conceptually. The chapter talks about how drawing practice is at the root of process and how the act of drawing extends the reach of concept (both 2-D and 3-D).

Chapter 18: Digital Illustration. This chapter explores what it means to be a "digital illustrator." Here we'll discuss the relevance of digital illustration, and examine the connections of digital illustration process to traditional practice.

Chapter 19: It's Just Business. It's called "commercial art" for a reason, but this is a *business* of people, potential and opportunity. Many illustrators complain that if there is one thing they never learned at school, it was, well, the *business* end of the business. This chapter seeks to address that.

Chapter 20: Words and Pictures. This chapter discusses the relationship between letterforms and visuals, calligraphy and art, typography and illustration; how words and pictures combine to link people, techniques, tools, and concepts, and offer creative opportunities.

Chapter 21: Drawn Together. Here we look at teams, collaborations, and, yes, *connections*: how a simple sheet of paper bonds the creative act; the relationships behind a shared space; and the human connection of common experience.

Features

Via relevant text and pertinent visuals, each chapter thoroughly addresses the topic at hand, reviewed with an end summary and capped by a portfolio of relevant projects. The in-class activities (titled "Working It Out") and at-home exercises (labeled "Home and Away") supplement text information and are designed to spark continued concepting and promote hand skills. A note here: it is not intended for students to complete all the at-home exercises, these supplemental projects simply give them an opportunity to practice what they have learned and grow as artists. Also look for each chapter's *Checkpoint* section, a succinct hot list of items to further push critical thinking.

An Illustrative Showcase

Just a word about the art you will find inside. By the numbers: 188 international creatives (including the author) graciously showcase their ideas and skills in this book. We offer roughly 500 illustrations. *Drawing Inspiration,* indeed! All the artists took this book title literally. The art is purely beautiful and incredibly eclectic: truly inspiring, even breathtaking. This book offers a unique and diverse gallery that is both visually lush and technically encompassing. Every day was a giddy Christmas when collecting the art for this book—I was continually humbled by the kind generosity of my contributors and the jaw-dropping talent of these wonderful artists.

The artists whose work is featured in *Drawing Inspiration* also munificently agreed to forego permissions fees. Instead, they join myself and Delmar Cengage Learning in making donations in support of the visual arts to a variety of charitable organizations, including the Society of Illustrators Student Scholarship Fund and The Ohio State University Cartoon Library & Museum.

Instructor Resources

And complementing the written word, our Instructor Resources available online, continue the rich offerings of the text. These resources, which will assist instructors in implementing their instructional programs, with these following features.

- Sample syllabi for both 11 and 15 week semesters
- PowerPoint slides highlighting the main topics of each chapter
- Quizzes and practical tests for each chapter
- Additional class projects
- Additional resources

About the Author

Michael Fleishman was a zombie extra in George Romero's *Day of the Dead* (but if you blink, you'll miss him). His real day job is as a freelance illustrator, writer, and teacher. Drawing inspiration out of Yellow Springs, Ohio, Mike

is an Associate Professor of Commercial Art at Edison Community College in Piqua, Ohio. He's been honored there with a regional SOCHE Excellence in Teaching award, as well as a national teaching excellence award from NISOD.

Fleishman has written for a variety of arts publications, and is the author of five books, most recently: *Exploring Illustration* (Thomson/Delmar), and *How to Grow as an Illustrator* (Allworth Press). He's presented at How Magazine's DesignWorld, the NISOD annual conference, and the national Illustration Conference, ICON 4 (currently serving on the board of directors for ICON 6, to be held in Pasadena, California, July 2010). Fleishman has also been a visiting artist at Kendall College of Art and Design, Savannah College of Art and Design, and Minneapolis College of Art and Design.

Mike is married to the award-winning documentary filmmaker, Joanne Caputo. They are the parents of Max (19), and Cooper (21). All are endlessly entertained by two knucklehead cats, Tilly and Simon.

Acknowledgments

The author is indebted to the gracious artists who generously contributed to *Drawing Inspiration: Visual Artists at Work.* Their art is absolutely stunning and extraordinarily diverse; their commentary truly resonant and enlightening. Working with this international collective was a sheer delight—a delicious trip to the creativity candy store everyday. Without these talented artists' commitment to (and enthusiasm for) my project, this would be a decidedly different book. Thanks to MaryAnn Nichols. And a special "thank you" here must go to David Bowers, our cover artist.

THANK YOU (in big, loud capital letters) to my family and friends for your care and support over the many years, particularly during the incredibly intensive last leg of this journey. I am blessed: Joanne—I married *so* well. You're the rock. Cooper and Max: you were a big help (plus you make me proud).

A tip of my hat to the folks at the helm, principally Meaghan O'Brien, Glenn Castle, and Tintu Thomas—who are all super sharp, efficient, and a complete joy to work with—and especially Jim Gish. Some years ago, Jim and I got together (at Young's Dairy, right here in Yellow Springs) to hash out ideas for our next project. We didn't quite realize the long and winding road this book would take. And here it finally is ... amazing what gets started with a good country breakfast! Jim: I could always count on your guidance and counsel, input and expertise, so thanks for leading the band.

Finally, if I've left anyone out, my sincere apologies; you are certainly here in spirit and definitely in contribution. I got you covered next time round.

Questions and Feedback

Delmar Cengage Learning and the author welcome your questions and feedback. If you have any suggestions that you think others would benefit from, please let us know, and we will try to include them in the next edition.

To send us your questions and/or feedback, you can contact the publisher at:

Delmar Cengage Learning
Executive Woods
5 Maxwell Drive
Clifton Park, NY 12065

Attn: Media Arts and Design Team

800-998-7498

The Connections

What It's About

Drawing! I can't help myself; I *gotta* do it. It has been this way since I can remember. As a student, drawing was a sheer joy—my thing. And *teaching* drawing is the shared, continued joy of that rich, multi-layered (and incredibly satisfying) experience. As a teacher, I tell my students that drawing is *the* thing.

The relationship between the worlds of academic and professional art making is real. Yes, some artists, like Philip Burke, have no formal training; it's all intuitive—it's more instinctual, impressionistic. But there's a real process with Burke's work, annealed and hammered after 30 years of painting his wonderful caricatures: *a lot* of drawing.

So, in writing this book, I never considered a direct student/teacher connection any kind of an issue. Likewise, the time line between school—any schooling— and the pro life was never a contract breaker. I quickly realized that I could simply talk to every artist as a teacher—someone with knowledge, insight and wisdom to offer. Indeed, I eventually saw that every artist *was* a teacher—and the studio was a universal classroom (no virtual about it).

This book focuses on the creative connections of drawing. But we'll also look at media and techniques that are "simply" drawing-based. And that, to my mind (and it's a grand that, at that) can be anything. No, make it: *is everything*. I believe drawing to be the heart, if not the root, of most visual artistic endeavors. Being able to draw what you think (or see in your head)—if only to visualize the concept on paper—is true creative power.

© Philip Burke

1

Chapter 1

Ideas: Why We Draw

© Dan Krall

Reconciliation

It's important to reconcile the mechanical with the intellectual process. A teacher's real job is to show students how to make their own marks from personal observation, particularly not to mimic the instructor and certainly not to ape the current hot illustrator or popular art trend.

As a professional, you will reach for something more. You must, or you're not tracking a basic definition of the word *professional* itself.

Reaching

Scott Campbell, a freelance illustrator based out of San Francisco, knows exactly how far he must reach, mechanically and conceptually. "I love the *life* of the line; it can have so much feeling to it. My favorite step in my painting process is when I get to lay in the line work. I like my lines to be very loose and imperfect—they feel more vibrant to me. It isn't until the lines go down that I am happy with how the painting is looking."

Telling Stories

Campbell is adamant that concept is the most important of foundations. "It wasn't until I started telling little stories and portraying moments in time that I really felt satisfied. It's very important to tell the story, but the more you leave for the viewer to figure out, the better—I like to empower my audience."

Figure 1-2: And if line is the spark, Campbell feels that value contrast is the flame—the passion—behind a painting. "With a limited palette, I can pop important areas with more vibrant color," he says. "Color swatches on scraps of paper let me try combinations that feel good. When I decide on a color scheme, I try to stay to that palette. Sometimes I can't hold back, but it's alright."

Figure 1-3: You must make the art *you* are meant to do. Strive for meaning and relevance by getting to the marks directly, through open reflection and hard work. Case in point: the work of Dan Krall, a production artist for the movies (as well as a freelance illustrator), working out of Los Angeles, CA.
© Dan Krall

Where Ideas Come to Work and Play

What encourages an artist to make a drawing? As a kid, a box of crayons and a blank sheet of paper were probably all you needed. You didn't have to work at it. But today, drawing may be your work.

I can speak to what makes the vocation of illustration a perfect job for me—it's the *joy* of it. If this job isn't enjoyable—first and foremost—why do it? There are other ways to break a sweat, save the world, or just make money (and, yes, more money than an illustration gig).

Resources

Let's talk about where we go when we want to draw. I'm not necessarily referring to a physical location (or studio space), so let's look at some other likely haunts—where we go in our head, and where the heart of the process takes us.

Figure 1-4: What inspires you to draw? Where do you *start*? While drawing for Hallmark Cards, illustrator Jenny Kostecki-Shaw learned a simple, elegant mantra that is all of two wonderful words: *Begin Anywhere.*
© Jenny Kostecki-Shaw

Cinema Verité

Matthias Lechner is an art director, production designer and visual development artist, living and working in Vancouver, British Columbia, Canada. He points out that you don't have to come from classical training to find your voice as an illustrator, you just have to dope out what drives you. Lechner illustrates for animated movies. "This is what I have always wanted to do," he says, "and this is what satisfies me to this day."

Figure 1-5: "The key to good production design is asking the right questions," Lechner says. "I can't tell you much about where the ideas come from—and I don't worry too much about it either. There's just a *spark*. And you can only ignite a decent fire by working hard at the drawing board."
© A.FILM A/S

Checkin' It Twice

Lechner discusses his process:

1. Use broad reference. Know and appreciate the object you are going to draw.

2. Grasp personality. "Everything has personality. Every house, tree, or cloud."

3. Avoid clichés in your composition. Look beyond textbook solutions.

4. Create a believable and original space. Solid perspective is essential.

5. Draw! And rough it out first.

6. Lighting has a profound emotional impact on the picture. Direct the shadows to promote interest (and help transport a two-dimensional drawing into a three-dimensional space).

Figure 1-6: Stay open. "Since this is a game of relationships," Lechner advises, "don't necessarily stick to your plan. If something else works better, go for it."
© A.FILM A/S

Needs

"I create art because I *need* to do it," illustrator Avram Dumitrescu says. "It's so easy to *not* challenge yourself and rust out."

Raised in Belfast, Northern Ireland, Dumitrescu currently lives and works in West Texas. He ponders what causes you to create in the first place: is it a certain combination of textures on an old metal grate, the quiet drama of that knockout sunset at the beach?

Maybe it's the challenge of a tricky concept: now how do I draw *that*? Perhaps it's the routine, or conversely, the excitement of something new. Or do you simply appreciate creating art and getting paid for it (don't discount this great basic motivator)?

Figure 1-7: "I create art because it's a calling – I need to do it," says Dumitrescu. "I've always done art, so being paid for it is very motivating. It's also nice that my work will eventually end up in print!
© Avram Dumitrescu

Wants

Christopher Nielsen works in a beautiful old warehouse studio in Sydney, Australia. He once asked a colleague what it took to be a serious, full-time illustrator. To which this gentleman replied, 'It's easy, if you want to . . . you will.'

"It's as simple as that," Nielsen states. "It's really a case of self-realization— knowing what you want and going for it."

Mind Games

Need some inspiration? Well, okay— drawing is just plain *fun*. Fun is certainly a great motivator, but even the most enjoyable gig can beg for inspiration. Don't discount the inspiration of sheer *energy* and *work*—blood, sweat, and tears—plus *passion* (another critical muse).

Rianne Lozano will talk with you about passion. Lozano is an art director for a pharmaceutical advertising agency. It's a good gig, but with a sly smile, she'll quickly tell you, "My true passion, however, is creating my own world of little creatures. Ever since I can remember, I was always sketching these guys. The characters were always doodles, and never digital. I didn't show them to anyone. It was just for fun; something I did when I got bored."

Figure 1-8: Nielsen's retro images, scratchy surfaces, and itchy characters are inspired by vintage design and advertising from various cultures.
© Christopher Nielsen

Her characters really started to come to life *after* college—after she got out into the "real" world. "I am learning to let go and have my imagination run wild," she says. "It just lets me be who I am, with no restrictions, no set guidelines."

Figure 1-9: At the end of the day, Lozano looks for that feeling of accomplishment that completes the creative cycle. "For me my most important building block is my imagination," she says. "Without it I wouldn't know how to start my illustration."
© Rianne Lozano

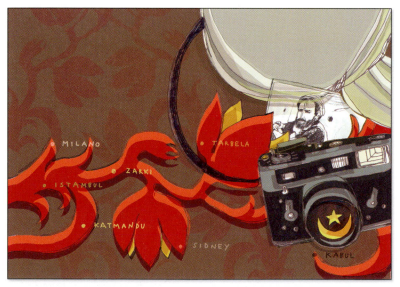

Figure 1-10: Agliardi works her pleasing magic in illustrations like this.
© Allegra Agliardi

"Often times there's really no concept; nothing too deep," Lozano points out, and then pauses for a beat. "Maybe it's simple inspiration that's my actual concept," she considers.

Live Wires

Don't think twice about a good *challenge* (and don't duck it). *Think* (about anything). *Look* (everywhere). *Listen* attentively. *Feel* it—whatever "it" is—and feel it fully. *Learn* from there.

And get tuned up. "Line is magic," smiles Italian illustrator Allegra Agliardi. From her studio in Milan, this award-winning young artist finds working in line "an immense pleasure." And every time she picks up a pencil, wields a brush, or just uses her fingers, the artist says she magically *rediscovers* line and creates a new dialogue with her art.

Scare Tactics

British illustrator Michael Renouf states that the frightening uncertainty of getting ideas can often make you wonder, "Where the hell did that come from? And you can't bottle it—if you try, it disappears."

Even now, the illustrator keeps a bulletin board plastered with words like "play," "experiment," "exaggerate," "shapes," "muscular thinking," and "curiosity."

"In the end," he comments, "it's about trusting your brain to get on with it and not getting too upset when it doesn't."

Figure 1-11: Trust. Action. Grace (and forgiveness). More great daily affirmations courtesy of Renouf, whose smart, playful work is shown here.
© Michael Renouf

Expression

Yuko Shimizu is an illustrator and fine artist living and working in New York City. "Artists must express something about *themselves* through their art," she says, "and students aren't generally told that everyone is different."

Family and friends. Childhood experiences. Individual interests and personal growth. Culture and society. The environment. School, of course: All factors in the development of that personal voice Shimizu emphasizes.

"As artists we must grow," Shimizu states. "But there's a core part of you that never changes, that makes *your* work your work. It is about who *you* are."

Pump You Up

If one is working on an interesting project that inspires great passion, you may not need much *motivation*. Adrenaline and excitement are prime movers and shakers. But if you can't connect in some way, it might be a totally different story.

Celeste Rapone, a 2007 RISD graduate, regards the subject of motivation: "There's no way to motivate me to do something I'm disinterested in," she

Figure 1-12: "You are different from everyone else, and your personal voice should already be within you," Shimizu advises. "Learn to let that come out in your work."
© Yuko Shimizu

Figure 1-13: Rapone's work often focuses on Catholicism and targets a child's understanding of religion, and the effects that knowledge has on personal development.

© Celeste Rapone

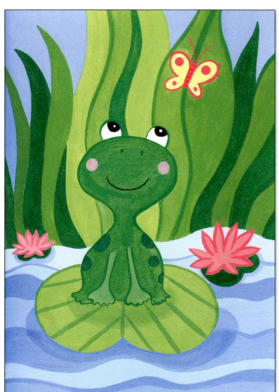

Figure 1-14: "Learn what you want to do," says Jin, "but what you *don't* want to do, as well."

© Susie Lee Jin

says. "I may mope about the assignment until the day before it's due, then pump out an unsatisfying piece I'm, at best, indifferent to as a direct result.

"Find *some* aspect of a project that excites you," Rapone concludes, "figure out how to incorporate yourself into the piece, and work up from there."

Yin/Yang

Fortune can also be a factor in this mix. But maybe you don't believe in serendipity (or fate, karma, whatever). What's that saying . . . "luck is when timing collides with opportunity"?

Susie Lee Jin was on another career path, but the arts beckoned her and she took a permanent detour. Arriving in New York City, she applied to various art schools. "When I left for my interview at SVA," she relates, "I was unforgivably late for my appointment. I imagined that I would just be thrown back out, but I actually received a warm welcome."

"On the subway home was actor Matthew Broderick who, during our conversation, asked if I was a professional artist. I said, 'Yes, I'm working toward it.'"

"When I was ultimately accepted to SVA, I quietly said 'thank you', but I jumped up and down for minutes—I was *that* excited."

Field Work

After playing the mental game, it's an actual hop, skip, and jump to "real world" scenarios. Healthy doses of exercise, diversions, hobbies, outside interests, events and activities, all stimulate and inform the creative process. If you're open to it, inspiration is likely everywhere.

Figure 1-15: Kroik's stimulating and informative illustration is a great workout for both mind and eye.

© Jenny Kroik

Originally out of Boston, comes freelance illustrator Jenny Kroik, who feels that the illustration process is a total workout: an exercise for mind, hand, *and* eye. "And I think that art is always *an exchange* of ideas," she adds. "Understand that, and your art will be successful."

Research and Reference

Research and reference, plus professional development and fieldwork, also promote inspiration and motivation. We must mention the library (and it doesn't have to be the art section) and bookshops. Again, do the whole store (not just the art section). And if the place sells coffee, forget about it, I'm on-site for the afternoon. Of course, there's the Internet. Are you of a certain age to even remember a creative life without this incredible resource?

The scrapbooking business is a big industry these days. But beyond nostalgia and keepsakes, the maintenance and organization of one's vital inspirations and motivations is a very solid concept. Academics label it research and reference. In the old days before the Internet, we called it maintaining a picture file (otherwise known as a photo morgue).

What? An actual physical picture file? Huh? Use a real bulletin board? Yep, even in our digital age, there's still something soul-satisfying about tacking a snipped clip on a slab of cork.

Jimmy Gets Along Well with Others.

The practice of illustration is a business of people. Networking cannot be underestimated. Your professional and personal relationships—both formal and informal—are fountains of wisdom and inspiration.

Accept guidance when you need it. Welcome the feedback. Make contact. Socialize (and reasonably party hard, dude). Actively seek input and other opinion (but learn to discern). Schmooze unabashedly. Compare notes wisely, and without reservation when it's right. Communicate. Stay in touch. Bring the doughnuts.

It's easier than ever to talk shop and stay in that proverbial loop. The explosion of websites, blogs, and forums has created an unprecedented, all-access pass to a universal community center.

And here, the basic tenets of traditional networking will (or at least, *should*) never change. You've known the ground rules since preschool: play nice. Make friends, be a friend. Listen more than talk. And don't forget those doughnuts.

A Beautiful Day in the Neighborhood

Penelope Dullaghan wanted a better portfolio. Dullaghan lives and works in Indianapolis, Indiana and found herself lonely at home. "I'm used to having critiques and being around people to help better my work," Dullaghan says.

So along with her partner, Brianna Privett, she started *Illustration Friday*, an online neighborhood of like-minded artists. "It's a place to experiment

Figure 1-16: One of Dullaghan's favorite posts on her blog is this simple, but powerful, declaration: *You Are Good.* Think about how right she is. Here's her good work.
© Penelope Dullaghan

and find your natural self in art," she explains, "with no art director telling you it doesn't look right."

Every Friday brings a new topic, and folks have a week to illustrate that concept. Then they post on the site. Participants get comments or give feedback on the work. "Anyone can do it. You can be a five-year-old and contribute," Dullaghan smiles. "I think it gives people a reason to create."

Influences

Why we draw is often *what* we draw (or vice versa). Some folks say that the *world* is the only real subject matter. But as it is also often said, location is everything—you must build a unique home for yourself in that world.

Blatant imitation or mimicking a popular artist is an ethical (and aesthetic) dead end. Visual gimmicks (even when it's *your* innovation) or exploiting the hot trends soon turn cold. Personal vision and individual voice, spun by your character and imagination, are the keys.

However, we are all products of our research and reference (both historical and contemporary), consciously and unconsciously. We don't live in a social, cultural or historical vacuum. Has it "all been done before"? There's a good argument there, probably tempered by the snappy comeback, "and it will all be done again."

Figure 1-17: Alex Bostic lives in Glen Allen, VA, and teaches at Virginia Commonwealth University. "I don't want to look left or right," he says, "and I don't want my students looking at the kid in front of them.

"I look at *myself*, because I'm in enough trouble already," Bostic laughs. His students laugh with him, but realize this is sound advice.
© Alex Bostic

The Pool

Look to the future by studying the past. Art history is both cumulative and ongoing. Every era has its "modern artists," bold concepts and "new" techniques that rub raw against current, conservative craft.

But time is funny. Mavericks may become the establishment, and make way for younger iconoclasts who reject, rethink, and reshape the status quo as they perceive it.

And style? Don't chase your tail, for *real* style—*your* style—comes from within. That means: a healthy ego, an affirmative lifestyle, conceptually pulling from *your* resources; mechanically remodeling your reference as only *you* see it.

I won't have you throw out your black clothes (or disregard that hard-earned outsider's persona), but you're not in this alone. Other professionals hopefully help you reach higher and stretch further. Look to family and/ or friends as folks who actually reflect your potential audience.

Figure 1-18: Nielsen says, "Go ahead, be a sponge; but the verb 'appropriate' is far classier. If you have any identity whatsoever, your influences will filter out on the page as yours. By the time you develop a fledgling style there may be no traces left—all that remains is *you*. It's no fun recreating what someone else has done anyway."

© Christopher Nielsen

Forward Motion

I assert above that "modern" art—as history, in practice and theory, via education or commerce—is really an extensive chain of substantial links. We make the point all through the book: art is all about *connection*.

"Art"—or "Illustration," or "Craft," or whatever—is a rich fabric of interwoven strands, a particularly sturdy tapestry. The thread of history is the spool of all art. To me, "inspiration" and "influence" are nicely in synch with "learn" and "grow." Properly influenced, truly inspired artists usually stay educated. The next play is to then "pay it forward," so the string never unravels.

The Long Haul

"Understand that you don't live in a vacuum," Brooke Cameron says. "Many people read endless art reviews; I prefer seeing it for myself." Cameron is Professor Emeritus of Drawing and Printmaking at the University of Missouri–Columbia. "One learns from one's own work," she says. "Your career laid out reveals patterns that never occurred to you previously. Be a visual thinker. Know that every artist must have his or her own voice."

"As a teacher, I'm only successful if my students can find *their own* vision of what their art should be. And if that vision can evolve from their life experiences (and thinking), then they will be artists for the long haul, not just while they are in school."

Figure 1-19: Cameron's work successfully illustrates the idea of thinking visually.
© Brooke Cameron

✔ Check Point: Buds

Artists are not really born with a silver pencil in their mitts. You *want* to draw. You *have* to draw. You *go for it* and draw every day. You *improve* over time. Here's what illustrator Lizzy Rockwell and her fellow illustrator (as well as colleague and former student) Susanna Pitzer say on this subject:

1. On a personal level, you should draw for *you*. And by the way: professionally, that statement isn't an oxymoron.

2. If you love it, then someone else will.

3. The job of drawing shouldn't be taken lightly. The idea of "hard work" eludes most people.

4. So many of us fight our style—who *we* are: "I want to do what *she's* doing." "*Your* stuff is so much cooler." "*His* work is really better."

5. The terrifying little fact is that you might be right.

6. *Our* style clings to us, wanting to be seen and brought to the forefront.

7. Odds are, you may get a rough critique, hear discouraging words, or you'll make comparisons and lose heart. You might even be tempted to put away the pencils, crayons, and paints (and you'll totally miss the fact that everyone puts lines on a page in a different way).

8. You may wonder, "What was I thinking . . . can I really do this?" The answer is a loud "Yes!" The secret to being able to do some-thing is in saying "Yes, I can." And yes—*you* can.

9. Artistic perception forges technique and influences the tools. Give a class the same assignment, same tools, same colors, and all the projects come out completely different.

10. This is what we love about art. *Everyone is right*. Art is speaking your own language, letting go and being who you are.

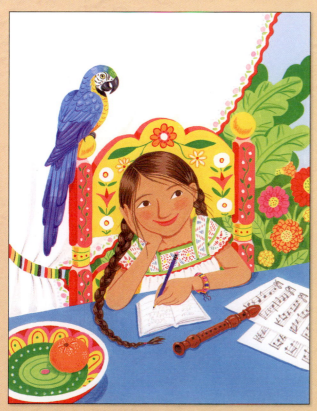

The work of Lizzy Rockwell.
© Lizzy Rockwell

The work of Susanna Pitzer.
© Susanna Pitzer

CHAPTER SUMMARY

In this chapter we discussed motivation: why we draw, how we learn through inspiration and influence, and grow via resources, research, and reference. We talked about the importance of an education (and why it's critical to stay *educated*). We looked at the practice of illustration as a business of people, discussed the advantage of networking and why it's necessary to pay that forward.

Working It Out

1. Buzz Me

In class we'll spend time leafing through magazines. We will channel surf some TV, and listen to the radio. In our discussions, pay attention to the conversations. Find (or listen for) buzzwords or catch phrases that resonate with your process on both conceptual and technical levels.

We'll compile samples and discuss this list in class. Next, we'll write and/ or cut out a series of these words and phrases—you choose the number. We're going to splash these on the walls of the art room, around your workspace (or on the bulletin board).

For Michael Renouf, it's words like "play," "experiment," "exaggerate," "shapes," "muscular thinking," and "curiosity." Your list should be personal and meaningful for you.

Use your buzzwords to visualize a particular word or the feeling associated with that word and draw the first thing that comes to your mind. Next we will link words or extrapolate from your first word. Here we will establish a train of thought or sequence of emotions sparked by building on the original word (or the chain reaction of combined words).

2. Toned

Do a painting with muted colors on toned paper. Do the same painting with vibrant colors on white. Do the same painting in black on white. Do the same painting with white on black. Working the same concept/composition in a variety of color/tone combinations facilitates a number of things: a true perception of that theme, a better understanding of the nuances of the design, and a more studied grasp of the lighting of the piece.

3. To Each His (or Her) Own

Everyone in class will get a different assignment, and you will receive your assignment privately via email or a "secret" handout. *Don't talk about your particular assignment.* Take your tools and materials and do the assignment during class, but away from your classmates (and if need be, the classroom itself). Let's see what you/we come up with independent of peer influence.

A variation: everybody receives the *same* secret assignment.

Home And Away

1. Field Day!

Going to where the drawing is makes artistic sense. Drawing from observation sharpens the eye; working on location heightens a sense of contact with your subject matter. Grab your sketchbook. Maybe take a bus drive on a back road; get on your bicycle and head down the bike path; go for a short walk around the block or a long hike in the woods.

2. Road Trip

Go to where the *inspiration* is, including (but not limited to): museums, art shows, art stores. Music shops and bookstores. Hit the gym and dive in the pool, play some ball (or other activities). Volunteer at a Senior Center. Play in a band—rock out. Go online. Go off line and watch movies (and more TV), attend lectures and workshops, visit the library, stroll the mall. Start and maintain a picture file. Actively use a bulletin board. *No drawing on-site*, however! Just use your senses and trust your memory; soak it all in and record (and create) later.

3. Copy That

Study books and magazines, watch TV, surf the 'net: identify several hot visual trends or popular gimmicks. Pick a current topic. Consciously work from a concept, in a manner, or with a technique you consider overdone or overblown. Now do a separate drawing based on your vision and thinking, that speaks with your voice. Compare and contrast. Analyze both process and product.

Chapter 2

Subject Matter: What We Draw

© Giovanni Da Re

Looking at It Subjectively

For many, *what* we draw—*subject matter*—may well be the major focus of the whole exercise. Whether an illustration hawks bottled water, whips up emotion, or pushes opinion...even if the drawing is simply a mechanical workout or an exercise in pure concept..."What's this picture all about?" is indeed a core issue.

But just talking "subject matter" means we are examining a big picture in a wide frame. Let's look at various subcategories of picture making—better yet, make that subject-making—as opportunities to address that million-dollar question above.

We'll Always Have Paris (Part 1)

From Los Angeles, Akiko Stehrenberger says simply, "Substance overrides technique."

Approaching a caricature, this illustrator finds as much online information and picture reference as possible (and this certainly works for non-figurative assignments as well). Through intensive study, she gains an insight into the *substance* of her assignment. She'll use little hints of personality to establish a likeness—a vital focal point in the artist's work.

"Some years ago, I was still trying to get a handle on my own style, while being heavily influenced by Eric White and Sebastian Kruger. The contrast between work from those days and *Paris* (**Figure 2-1**) is that she's not merely a style study, and inspired by fashion with a touch of 'Cholo' art."

Easy Reader

From his studio in Castelbellino, Italy, Giovanni Da Re says, "I live for the chance to synthesize concepts with simple shapes, unobtrusive textures, and catchy color." But the artist also cautions that *readability* is important. If you only have a few moments to catch the reader's attention, you must be a strong communicator. Characterization, imagination, and resulting visual translation work to amplify—or clarify—the text.

"That challenge always teaches me something *more*," says Da Re. "You never know where new projects will bring you. The opportunity to create beautiful environments or reconstruct history makes every new assignment a sort of test."

Figure 2-1: "Cholo" art refers to the Los Angeles Latino graffiti that actually inspired Stehrenberger to first draw as a preteenager. A major influence for the budding artist throughout junior high and high school, Stehrenberger says that this Cholo flavor is, "a blast from the past for me, and much fun to bring back into my art now."
© Akiko Stehrenberger

Figure 2-2: "I consider new assignments as a sort of challenge that I confront with my computer," says Da Re. "I look at each job as a learning opportunity."

For some years the illustrator's method has been just about completely digital. "Sometimes I work on projects that take a long time," he tells you, "hundreds of sketches and illustrations. Illustration can be tedious, but there is always a euphoria that brings me back to my Mac to draw again; to experiment, to push forward."
© Giovanni Da Re

Flip That

The equally valid flip side here is that you often will get the opportunity to disturb your reader's equilibrium and disrupt the status quo of conventional beauty.

One of the most prolific illustrators in the business, Bill Mayer works in many different styles (including the great airbrush stuff he's justifiably famous for). "In *Bed Bugs* (**Figure 2-3**)," Mayer tells us, "the art director couldn't decide between two ideas, so he ended up doing both illustrations, making room for one as a full-page inside."

Ed and Ad

"Editorial" translates to books, magazines, and newspapers, electronic media, novelties and greeting cards, et cetera. Advertising agencies (and public relations firms) solve a client's marketing problems by communicating—a.k.a. *selling*—concepts. Both editorial and advertising are historically big markets for art.

Conceptual and Narrative

Concept spins both composition and mechanics—design and illustration—as well as process and product. Conceptual skills are all about communication and problem solving. The "conceptual" in "conceptual illustration" is an

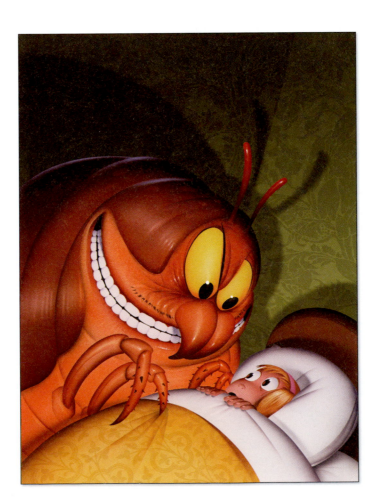

Figure 2-3a and b: Sometimes you can get attention with uncomfortable images that "make people itchy," as Mayer says—and shows us—with these wonderfully biting *Bed Bugs*.

2-3a © Bill Mayer

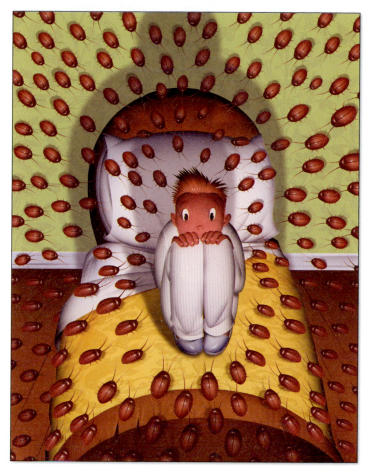

2-3b © Bill Mayer

umbrella term of creative expressionism—both intellectual and technical. You might say it's a visually active idea (whoa—what a concept).

"Narrative" literally means "story." So, logically, narrative illustration tells a tale, sets the stage, describes action, or establishes character. It's no accident that illustration and illumination—as in illuminated manuscripts—share the same root. As illustrator, painter, and teacher Robert Brinkerhoff says, "I tell my students working on editorial content that they are as much the author of the reading experience as the writer."

"The best illustration challenges interpretation," Brinkerhoff asserts, "often offering insight and meaning even the author of the text did not anticipate."

Give and Take

Maybe it's a pure dedication to your task. Or a consistent commitment to doing very finished work. If your technique and imagination are sparked by the challenge of finding the best way to make a statement, you'll seldom be out of synch with your teacher.

Teaching at Rhode Island School of Design (RISD) since 1997, Brinkerhoff instructs his students to tell him something he doesn't know. "You teach me something," he says, "open my eyes to those discoveries made through your process and critical observation."

Figure 2-4: The main objective of quality art instruction just may be to challenge and be challenged. The type of assignment Brinkerhoff loves to throw at his students is deceptively simple, but getting to the point is the real fun.

And don't play it safe. Shock value—in the right measure and exact spot (and particularly when juxtaposed by humor and wit)— can be terribly exciting. Here's Brinkerhoff's engaging—and challenging—work to make that point.

© Robert Brinkerhoff

This academic philosophy eloquently reflects his own practice of illustration. "I find real pleasure in sharing the excitement of problem-solving," he declares. The (not so) trick questions are: "What's the picture all about? What are you saying?" And while a student's illustration may radically differ from his own, Brinkerhoff may share a common use of metaphor and narrative, or the distillation of ideas.

Pathways

"Arguably, the nature of my illustration is to get an idea across with minimal, effective language," says Brinkerhoff's student, Jamie Allaire, who knows that saying too much (or not saying enough) can lessen a viewer's interest in a work of art.

Through her work with Brinkerhoff, Allaire has learned that editing and condensing ideas are difficult but vital steps down what she calls the "right path."

"I try to intrigue my audience," she says. 'What is this thing?

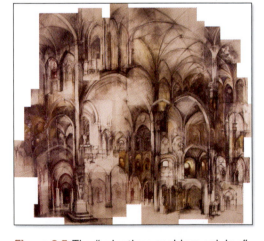

Figure 2-5: The "relentless problem solving" Brinkerhoff advocated prompted Allaire to take chances and challenged her ideas— even if "it meant starting completely over."

© Jamie Allaire

Why is it here? Am I supposed to notice it? The 'perfect' solution takes time and effort," Allaire says. "The end result might seem effortless, but even the most straightforward answers can involve an exhaustive process.

Scratch That

Just a special shout out to scratchboard: a venerable, demanding medium that still thrives to this day. Patrick Arrasmith lives and works in Brooklyn, New York, and as he explains it: "Scratchboard is a thin layer of white clay, machine-applied to a base of illustration board. The clay is coated with black ink. A blade not unlike a scalpel is used to scratch off lines of the black ink, revealing the white surface below."

Scratchboard is yet another classic process where many practitioners spin a dynamic technique digitally. Tim Foley, a former typesetter and art director, works primarily in a semi-traditional scratchboard style that is actually *100%* digital. All color in Arrasmith's illustrations is applied on the computer.

Figure 2-6a-d: The classic process of scratchboard, as interpreted by Arrasmith and Foley.

2-6a © Patrick Arrasmith

2-6b © Patrick Arrasmith

2-6c © Tim Foley

2-6d © Tim Foley

Classics

Landscape and still life are venerated and long-popular creative pursuits. You should also explore architectural rendering, travel illustration, and cartography (signage, maps, and charts—which could also include directional and informational graphics).

Are you drawing food and product illustration (not to mention animals, vegetables, and minerals) all the time? If so, do look into the technical, scientific, and medical venues as well. And from there you can warp space and time to check out the Science Fiction, Horror, and Fantasy genres, too.

© Fernanda Cohen

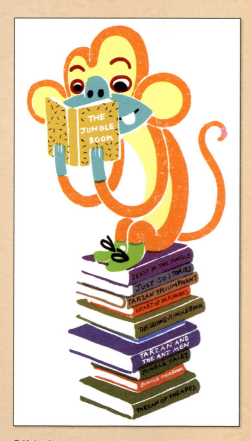

© Kaksplus

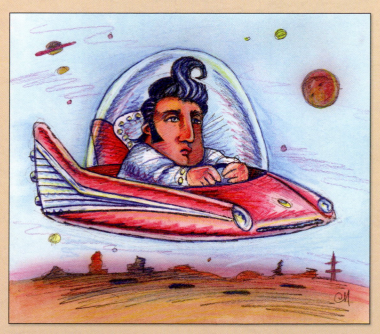

© Benton Mahan

© Avram Dumitrescu

© Douglas Klauba

© Dan Krall

© Jacqui Noll

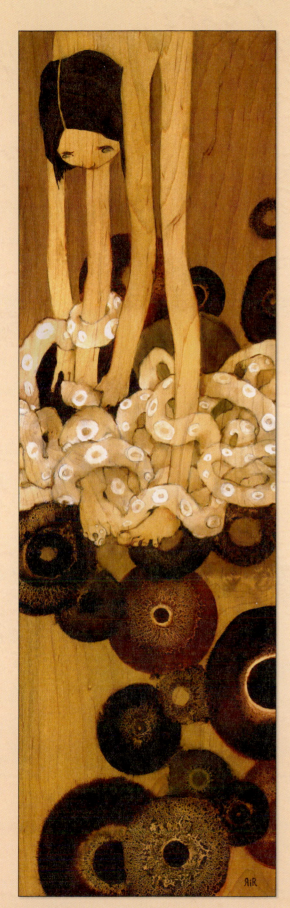

© Bill Russell

© Rachel Reinfurt

© Gabi Swiatkowska

© Shaun Tan

© Edwin Ushiro

In the Abstract

Subject matter is linked to pre-planning as well as perception (you hand off inspiration to concept, and segue composition into technique). Without these interactions we could argue that abstract (or non-objective) art is not so heavy on *representation*, but more about *interpretation.* Thus non-representational art can simply target one's intellect, hit you in the gut, or tickle your fancy.

Perhaps you're just exploring the *stuff* of it: the tools and materials. You fool with concepts and play with rules, but the work ultimately begs only one relevant question: "What did we *learn* here?" Remember, on his way to turning on the lightbulb, Thomas Edison regarded each failed experiment as simply what not to do again.

Figure 2-7: Trained both in China and the United States, Lampo Leong's inky blacks, dense color, and radiant lighting speak to his fascination with process. Through digital imaging technology, he transcends the challenge of integrating a dual artistic heritage.
© Lampo Leong

Let's Face It, It Figures

Portraiture and figurative art are esteemed subject concerns. Drawing the figure and face are at the very core of nearly every creative enterprise, and considered by many (this writer included) *the* most demanding—and rewarding—challenges of pictorial expression.

Art chops not withstanding, everyone knows intuitively when a figure drawing is "off" or a likeness isn't quite "right." But of course, fidelity is *not* the only benchmark of a "good" figure study or portrait. However, we are hard wired for drawing from life—regardless of style, technique, or the difficulty of the task.

In any event, life drawing is a marvelous exercise guaranteed to tweak those critical mind to eye to hand mechanics.

You're In There

"I imagine what the character is feeling in that moment," says Zina Saunders, who's been a writer-illustrator for more than 15 years. "This begins the process for me of connecting emotionally with my subject—even if that person is made up. Even if that person is me, striking a pose in the mirror for an assignment."

And Saunders considers just how much she inserts herself into every portrait. After all it is her vision of what they look like. "But," she smiles, "they look exactly like that inside themselves."

Saunders didn't set out to make intensely colored portraits; it was a natural outgrowth of her interviews with the people she was painting. Her very

Figure 2-8: "I visualize their energy while I'm doing their portrait," Saunders says of the folks she paints. "I almost hallucinate those hues in their faces—I perceive these vivid flashes of color as another way for me to convey their bright spirit. I'm very interested in joyousness."
© Zina Saunders

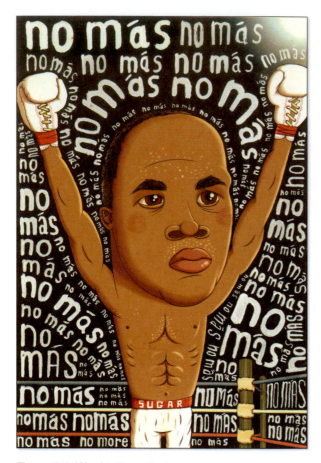

Figure 2-9: Ward tells us that *No Mas* started out life as an editorial illustration and was then adapted for use in an apparel line. Like that infamous cry of defeat itself—the type shouts out; it cannot be lifted off the context of the page. So, concept and composition are truly integrated: look how the type echoes the V shape of Leonard's upraised arms and underlines the piece in both design and idea.

© Andy Ward

personal and extremely transcendent reportage experience resulted in an enduring (not to mention, endearing) series called *Overlooked New York*.

These seriously fascinating portraits are affectionate character studies of the human condition—real folks, with all their exciting enthusiasm and unique perspectives, actual fragilities and vulnerabilities (plus egos) right out there.

Bohemian Rhapsody

Andy Ward is an expatriate Englishman living (and illustrating) near Venice, Italy. "I'm somewhat editorial," he comments. "Figurative. With a narrative, slightly darker—yet still commercially appealing—edge or mood.

"I struggle on everything I do," says Ward. "I never find anything easy, at all. It's an intense process, especially if you seek to expand your boundaries—balancing concepts, composition, and color. It's a thrill to begin a job and it's exciting to close a piece, but the middle can be laborious, difficult."

"I'll jump at a job that takes me in a different direction," says Ward. "It's important to push yourself and the possibilities (and the doors that may open as a result)."

There is an interactive quality to Ward's art. Illustration is design; design is illustration. "This stems from when I started out, trying to be this Bohemian painter," Ward laughs, "I segued into becoming an illustrator, and thought that you had to do anything and everything. Design. Paint. Draw. Type. Paint or hand draw type."

Mixmaster

So Ward mixes it up. His creative repertoire is varied and he keeps it off the cuff (as much as possible): "My calligraphy is not rehearsed," he will tell you. "While digital, it's direct and liquid, hand-lettered via a Wacom tablet. It translates quite easily from what I used to do before I started working digitally."

Mas Appeal

No Mas (**Figure 2-9**) boasts hand painted letterforms on a digital, scanned image. Ward hand painted the words; he then reworked these letterforms in Photoshop, printed that out again, repainted back in, and scanned this back into the computer.

"Type is extremely critical to this piece," states Ward, "just as the power of those words were terribly important to the context of the event." As you boxing fans may recall, this is the infamous Leonard-Duran middle-weight title bout where Duran throws up his hands, gives up the match and cries, 'No Mas!'"

Figure 2-10a and b: These two illustrations are near and dear to Ward's head and heart. He broke out of his comfort zone to successfully push his process, design, and concept in a different direction.
© Andy Ward

Bird Calls

"*Charlie Parker* (**Figure 2-10a**) and *13 1/2* (**Figure 2-10b**) are some of my favorite pieces," says Ward. About *13 1/2*: "I tried something different on this one," he says. "I built a tension by balancing the standing figure on one foot—you don't know if she's going to fall or fly. I pushed a deeper, flat plane perspective through composition plus select color and value. Pinks drop the background; the darks pop the foreground."

Funny Papers: Cartoon, Comics, Caricature

Cartoons, comic art, and caricature are enjoying a renaissance. Outlets and markets for adult and juvenile animation, graphic novels, video games, as well as computer-generated graphics are booming. See for yourself: at general bookstores and comics book shops; in magazines; at libraries; on television, at the movies or video store, on the Web. Don't forget the traditional avenues of newspaper cartoons and comic strips, comic books, advertising venues, and editorial outlets.

Figure 2-11: Like many budding cartoonists, Kevin Huizenga began drawing comics in high school, but not many are ultimately named "Minimalism Cartoonist of the Year" by the Comics Journal (this, in 2001). Huizenga, as *Drawn and Quarterly* tells it, "[delves] into mythology, belief, and spirituality. [His] familiar characters [confront] the textures of mortality in unique and sometimes peculiar ways."

© Kevin Huizenga

✔ Check Point: Comic Relief

Illustrator Jonathan Edwards' strong line and punchy color set the stage for his inventive characterization and quirky humor. He provides our hot list for this chapter.

1. It's immensely tough to write about drawing without actually resorting to drawing!

2. Line defines the shape and the weight of any drawing.

3. Most of my drawing is done with a brush now. When I started using a brush to draw, it seemed almost impossible to draw an artless line with it—I've since proved myself wrong.

4. Line works differently in comics. A traditional comics page features panels and borders, word balloons and lettering. The most successful comic pages have a continuity between all of these elements.

5. Pure black and white can be stunning, but the key is balance. Add and subtract until you get it right. Consider the negative space as a result of that process.

6. I like to look at each illustration or comic panel as an individual composition in its own right. As well as being a representation of whatever

you're trying to draw, each panel should also hold up compositionally.

7. Consider each element within a panel as a shape (rather than a figure or a building etc.); make every component work together as if in an abstract image. This can be a subtle way of drawing the eye across the comic page.

8. A limited color palette can heighten mood, push temperature, and strengthen composition (and

help you jump space and time without resorting to text or obvious background changes). It's far more effective than using every hue at your disposal.

9. In general, self-imposed creative restrictions produce interesting results. It's like solving a puzzle; artistic challenges help break a drawing block or provide inspiration during a period of low creativity.

10. A commissioned illustration is always about communication.

© Jonathan Edwards

© Jonathan Edwards

© Jonathan Edwards

You'll Get Stuck: Collage/Montage

The word "collage" comes from the French. According to the dictionary, it means *gluing*—"An artistic composition made of various materials (as paper, cloth, or wood) glued on a surface." A good, right-to-the-point definition there.

Let's stay with Webster's. *Montage* describes an artistic association of juxtaposed elements, combined side by side (or one after another) to create a series of images.

Cut Up

When asked about her collage process, Jenny Kroik tells you, "I truly enjoy gluing things together. But besides that, I like using parts of images and making something new out of them, something they weren't meant to be."

Digital technology has made this exploration a little easier for Kroik; she worries less about mistakes and feels more relaxed about her collage process. "Collage technique corresponds really well with the computer," she says. "It opens up a lot of new opportunities to combine different media. I can paint elements on separate pieces of paper, in different sizes, and make them all look like they were painted on the same surface."

Dedicated to collage, Kroik still tries to draw every day. "Drawing is never a purely mechanical action," she wants you to consider. "It's always the result of some concept, whether it's subconscious or deliberate."

Covert Operation

Chris Covert's work has been labeled as "folk" or "outsider" art. But as he says, "All I ever wanted to be was original. What I seek to accomplish with my illustration is to leave an impression—good, bad, indifferent, but remembered."

Covert has clung to the dream of being an artist in small chunks. As an adult he took on what he tags arty "side jobs…nothing to write home about," he says with a shrug.

"And then it happened," he declares. "While checking out at the local food store I spotted a goofy tabloid magazine with the headline 'Elvis Alive!' The connection raced quickly through my mind: collage Elvis out of the tabloids!"

That big "ah-ha!" moment led to three months of creative labor and discovery. Covert literally divided his time between his full-time job and his art, confessing he actually slept very little. "When I applied that last cut and stepped back, I knew that I had something here."

The idea of creating portraits using a medium relating to the subject was killer. 50 plus pieces later, his journey continues. Covert has rendered Donald Trump out of 285 dollar bills. His collage of Jesus Christ was made from 14 Bibles. By the way, the artist's intention was always to create a religious portrait in good taste. Yes, some would say that the very idea of cutting up bibles borders on the sacrilegious, but the work has received praise from people of all denominations and walks of life.

Straight Forward

Susan Farrington was co-owner of a small rubber stamp company when an art director friend suggested she show her work around Boston.

She feels her process is fairly simple. "Most of my work has been editorial," she says, "So when I get a text, I read it and do tiny thumbnail sketches in the margins. I'll pick the two or three strongest ideas and develop them into larger sketches."

"From these, the art director will choose the one that she likes best, sometimes combining elements from one of the other roughs. Then comes the construction. I cut out basswood, gesso and paint it, add fabric, wheels, buttons—whatever is needed. Once the piece is glued into place I have it photographed and send a 4x5 to the client."

Figure 2-12: Kroik puts it all together in her vibrant collage work.
© Jenny Kroik

Figure 2-13: Chris Covert created this portrait of the author by collaging passages of actual text snipped directly from copies of my books.
© Chris Covert

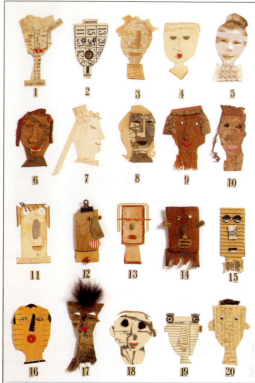

Figure 2-14: For her personal art (as in *20 Faces,* shown here), Farrington works without a sketch and adds elements as the piece develops.

© Susan Farrington

Something New Every Day

"I use color with conviction and I tend to allow it to unfold unconsciously," says Katherine Streeter (Figure 2-15a, and b) from New York City. "I have a new favorite color every other day, so that helps me experiment and get excited about new combinations."

"And when I draw," she continues, "it is about tapping the unconscious and shutting off the thinking part of my brain. You know, there are certain ways most people will look at something. We look for sense, by intuition. We aim for a story or a pattern as our minds take in information and dissect it. There is reason to method."

"My style has been driven by metaphor, as much of contemporary illustration has."

"It's true that concept influences technique, but the bigger picture (for me) is that we all have a certain style. Any commission based on that style assumes that part of our process is to use a certain language to inform (or suggest or relay) a certain mood or emotion."

"I use collage because I am attracted to the factual information given by a piece of photography. My own drawing and painting is inspired by that existing element. It is about striking the balance to play off of that, to show both reality and dream, with fact and fiction, together."

Figure 2-15a and b: "I think drawing is as direct as speaking," Streeter tells you. "It came before words, so I suppose it can even be more direct than speech sometimes. Drawing is rather a process of thought: brain … hand … line on paper.

"Drawing is immediate, and I believe it can communicate hidden thoughts and a deeper human connection. Drawing takes on a personality and although some of us are trained, absolutely everyone can draw and there is a certain universal connection to that."

© Katherine Streeter

CHAPTER SUMMARY

In this chapter we considered *what* we draw: *subject matter* was the major focus. "What's this picture all about?" was a key question; "how it was done," a connected concern.

We spoke in both general and specific terms about looking at the "big picture." That means frame and all, so we examined details of the various picture-making settings and subject-making opportunities. We evaluated all this in terms of meeting market needs and providing creative challenges, simply diversifying your artistic diet, or mixing up your daily routine.

Working It Out

1. Look Alike

For this unit, we're going to do portraits—specifically portraits of your classmates, 1+ a day, every day for two weeks. Media and technique will be announced for each class session (see general supply list and be prepared).

2. Word Jam

For our next two-week unit we will work relatively in the same vein: pick or create a number of themes from a string of nouns, verbs, and adjectives (for instance, good robots at work; bad vegetables I've known and loved; friends and enemies dance together). We'll fully explore this for the next two-week section.

3. Fame Game

In this unit, we will do four collages of famous personalities. These pieces will each have a bit of a catch: on one, facial and figurative components must *not* contain any actual elements of the subject's real face or figure. One will be done with nontraditional materials. One will be mixed media. One will be digital.

Home And Away

1. Look Alike

Do a self-portrait every day for a month. Accentuate the challenge by juggling style, media, and technique. See how long you can go before you repeat yourself in any manner. Want even more of a test? Do a daily self-portrait for a year.

2. Word Jam

Expand on the in-class Word Jam, but target a bit more. Pick or create *one* theme from a string of nouns, verbs, and adjectives (choose one…for instance: hopelessly lost at the psychedelic laundromat). Limit your media. Explore your concept for an extended period (a month or more).

3. Senior Project

Do a family history of your grandparents in 32-page comic book (or graphic novel) form.

Chapter 3

Sketchbooks

© Steven Hughes

From the Incept

We're going to look at the roots of drawing and begin with a basic question: where do ideas come from? Sketchbooks (and by extension, journals, diaries, and scrapbooks too) record relevant answers to this question and play with those solutions. These creative outlets document the give and take between imagination (bright ideas) and information (input/output) and are an inspired means to identify what the drawing job is really about: figuring out how to express oneself visually.

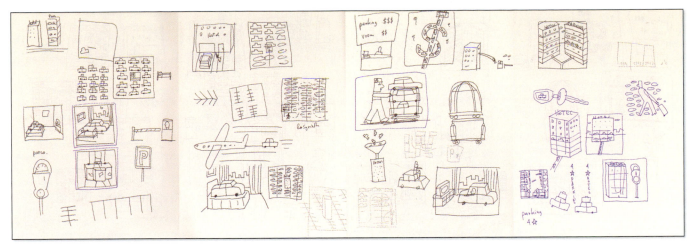

Hands On

Do you carry a sketchbook wherever you go? Is it always handy—a personal, onboard resource of inspiration, observation, and reference? Maybe even therapy?

Indeed, sketchbooks are frequently creative *diaries*—an emotional release or intellectual steam valve, justifiably private and strictly personal. Sketchbooks can be graphic travelogues that showcase the eye and mind (as well as highlighting the journey) of the artist/correspondent.

For some, the *act* of daily journaling simply provides needed *discipline*—the key to self-control. And for many, sketchbooks can actually be a bit of a benign addiction, a creative "fix" that rounds off the edges of an angular day.

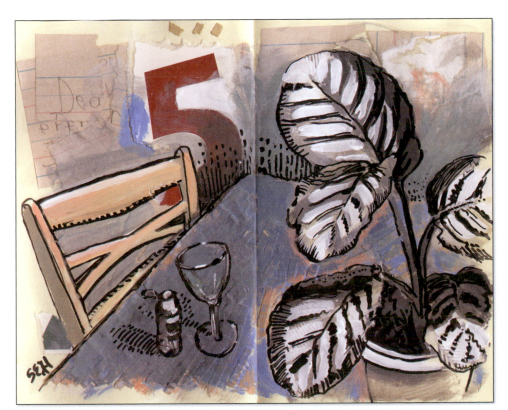

Figure 3-1: Luc Melanson is a Quebec illustrator with a whimsical, engaging style. Here are two pages from one of his sketchbooks. "If I learned something over the years," says Melanson, "it's to let my hand go, let the line think, let the concepts just flow. Give your brain a break."
© Luc Melanson

Figure 3-2: Two pages from a sketchbook by Steven Hughes. Hughes, out of Kent State University, says, "I always do sketches on whatever paper I have on hand—usually plain computer paper because it's cheap and smooth. I have a hard time working in sketchbooks, because of their cost; I can't loosen up. I get too precious with them, like each page has to be a fully realized work of art. I'm constantly amazed by people who aren't challenged by this limitation."

But while this part of the process may challenge Hughes, he'll tell you that sketchbooks let artists search for the truth about themselves and visualize any thoughts or concerns on the page. "There's a cathartic benefit. In a financial sense it could even turn into a published memoir of sorts and an additional source of income. Of course, if you're popular enough to attract an audience for your sketchbook, you may not be dependent on every paycheck anymore."
© Steven Hughes

It's Handy

"I am a snob about good drawing," Melanie Reim admits, "especially drawing from observation. Drawing from life is the underlying foundation of the creative process."

And it is why a sketchbook is never far from her side. For Reim—a full-time professor and chair of the MA in Illustration program at the Fashion Institute of Technology (FIT)—sketchbooking teaches a heightened sense of observation and enhances one's memory and experience better than any camera.

"My sketchbook is where my stories as an illustrator first unfold," she tells you. "I much prefer to use my books as a visual diary. It keeps my skills fresh and evolving, but it's also my history: the travels, people I meet, the culture, patterns, and parades.

"There is no better way to enhance one's proficiency as a draftsman (or a storyteller) than to constantly record what is around you," Reim considers. "The more you draw, the better you draw."

Reim insists that your obligation as an illustrator is to develop an opinion and a point of view through one's drawings. She adamantly maintains that there is no better way to discover this perspective than through your journal. "Journals provide a living memory of what you were thinking about, how your hand was working, what medium you chose to express

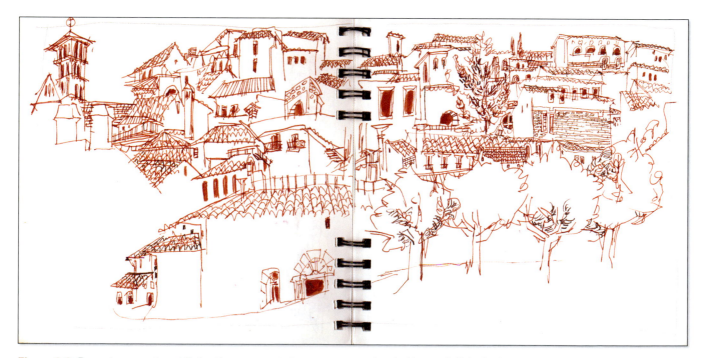

Figure 3-3: Reportage captured Reim the moment she was exposed to it. How so? "It's the immediacy," she says, "the command of the figure. The fluidity of line. It was the feeling of being present in a space. This unbridled action and spirit still remains invigorating for me."

© Melanie Reim

the experience. My sketchbooks are treasures, as much a part of who I am as my family photos."

Moleskinner Blues

An artist keeps a visual diary for a variety of reasons, and the format is a real means to actual ends; inviting regular participation, helping you organize, brainstorm, and practice. Indeed, you may have more than one diary project going at a time, generating work on a range of subjects.

A sketchbook is like your Grand Central Station of creative input/output. You may actually delight in the very process of journaling, and explore different aspects of the diary experience itself.

"My regular visual diary goes with me most places," Margaret Huber tells us. Huber, a senior lecturer at the University of Brighton, uses this diary to take notes, observe, develop ideas, and reflect on the day's events. "My diaries aren't just pictures. There are lots of words and sometimes those words are images in themselves."

"I enjoy the methodical approach of a visual diary," she says. "Being able to turn the page to start again opens up the potential for new thinking."

All Aboard

"Day Return to Brighton" is Huber's ongoing diary project of drawings done on used train tickets from her daily commute from London to Brighton (England). Now close to a thousand drawings on, Huber started the series by setting a few ground rules to help her remember what was important in the work:

1. Huber limits the drawing materials to pencil, pen (black and blue ink only), and white correction fluid. This kept the project portable.

2. She never throws tickets away. "If I make a mistake, I keep working on it until I'm left with something I like or can use," she says. "I try to work with the mistakes, remembering that I'm allowed some less than wonderful tickets over the long haul."

3. Every ticket used in the series must be hers—and it's only those tickets used for that daily commute to Brighton. The objective is to find a positive way to acknowledge the time and money invested in commuting. As Huber says, "Each ticket represents one day of my working life."

Whispers Become Shouts

Aurelia Lange is Huber's former student, a recent graduate from Brighton. "Her drawings are very interesting," says Huber. "You can tell they're personal, even the more abstract work inspired by nature: the earth drawings and animations." For Lange, concept informs the tools (as well as color and tone). It strings everything together, places emphasis, and sets the scene.

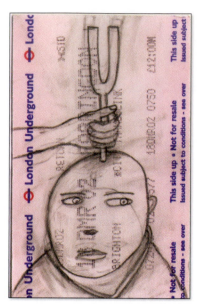

Figure 3-4a and b: Pages from one of Huber's sketchbooks, plus a sampling of her ongoing diary project, "Day Return To Brighton."
© Margaret Huber

Figure 3-5: Lange thinks that an illustrator's color palette and value system reflects as much of their style and personality as any drawing technique. "I went through a long stage of just using pastel colors," she says. "I couldn't physically bring myself to use anything but egg shell blue! I am becoming better at leaving my comfort zone, which is important to do as it challenges me to try new things. Look out … neon pink one day soon!"
© Aurelia Lange

But Lange laughs when she points out that an original concept doesn't have to be rocket science. "It could be simple, and lead to incredible things," she considers. "Drawing can be as much about interpretation as it is communication. It's rather like the party game, 'Operator,' where a whispered phrase gets exaggerated or distorted through the process of conversation. Drawing's like that—it's a big exploration."

Lange's personal sketchbooks often challenge the viewer to guess the original source of her abstract lines and obscure shapes. "I like that mystery to create an innovative structure, drawing as a visual language in itself: translating the environment around you, making it new, telling fresh stories."

Slip Case

Matt Hammill is a freelance illustrator, animator, and game developer who uses his sketchbook for thumbnails. As a piece progresses he'll slide doodles and test art between the pages (as well as movie tickets, newspaper clippings, and business cards). "Eventually, when enough paper keeps constantly spilling out of my book," he sighs with a grin, "I go back and glue things down."

When he starts a drawing, Hammill does numerous thumbnails over the course of a couple days. "As many as I can," he says. "I don't give special treatment to my first idea. I like it when, after drawing a bunch of roughs, I can't remember which one came first."

Figure 3-6: "I do sketches with a pencil and paper, and try to play around with different versions of various ideas," says Hammill. "Sometimes I add grey tone digitally later. And I can never come to a conclusion about 'style'—I just go back and forth considering its pros and cons."
© Matt Hammill

Practice

You must have a curiosity and drive to make this all work. Just as no one should have to tell you to get up and paint in the morning, nobody should make you keep a sketchbook; it's just part of the process of creativity, of moving on to the *next* idea.

As pointed out to me, you don't want to spend all your time rendering an idea. You want to come up with the idea—and then render. This may be a struggle, but sketching can help you understand composition, design, and lighting without the stress of filling up a space (as in: "Oh no, what the hell do I do now?"). Trust me, life can be infinitely easier if you have a plan when you sit down.

Be spontaneous, ready to change it up on a dime. Notice I said life "*can be*" easier. I also believe in chaos theory and certainly appreciate a little yin and yang.

Alex Bostic always says to consider the *task* at hand. You have this big sheet in front of you—and your charge is to fill it up. Consider that doing a *job* well can simply be all about *practice*.

And to my way of thinking, the final is not the place or time to practice.

Figure 3-7a and b: Two progressive pages from one of Pitzer's sketchbooks. Here, everything's possible, and anything goes.
© Susanna Pitzer

Jack

"My sketchbook is a jack of all trades," Susanna Pitzer says, "my best friend. A secret room, my business partner, my therapist and confidant."

Pitzer carries that sketchbook wherever she goes. Here she draws, jots down notes, captures ideas, and develops stories. Pitzer's sketchbook is her cherished safe haven, a vital steam valve. "No one judges you in a sketchbook," she tells you. "You are mentally and creatively free to write, sketch, and say whatever comes to mind, try things any way that pops into your head."

"This freedom affords me the gift of an abundance of ideas. The sheer act of validating and honoring an idea by writing or sketching it causes more ideas to flood my way. It's amazing! Plus, this habit of working so freely in a sketchbook carries nicely into all other work."

Take Two of These and Call Me in the Morning

Afraid to commit to—or worse yet, "make mistakes" in—your sketchbook? There's a strong argument to be made that if you suffer from perfect page syndrome (or common journalitis), you actually defeat the heady air of exploration and experimentation the sketchbook experience offers.

✔ Check Point: A Deep Well

Rob Dunlavey is an illustrator from the Boston area, and an inveterate doodler. His sketchbooks incorporate all the elements of a robust art-making habit—color, content, diary, line, texture, and so on—and he has several *feet* of sketchbooks built up over the past few years. "They are the well," he says, "the ever-fresh spring that keeps me sane (debatable) and happy (definitely)." Here's Dunlavey's Sketchbook Checkpoint:

1. Work *every day*. Dunlavey usually works very early in the morning for 1-2 hours.

2. No holds barred.

3. Any blank book will do. Quality is negotiable, but mark-making and honesty are not.

4. He rarely works on assignments in his sketchbooks. "Most of the time it's just for me."

5. Dunlavey's weapons of choice: ball point pen, watercolor, and collage. Lately he's been using house paint.

6. Sketchbooks help delineate his personal vision, which subsequently might find expression in

© Robert Dunlavey

more finished commercial projects. Content may include life and landscape studies, diary comments, to-do lists, etc.

7. Dunlavey says he often apologizes for a lack of substance, but realizes that most folks will have no idea what propels him to carry that book around. "For me, it's probably a desperate attempt to catch a fleeting scrap of something original out of the humdrum."

8. "I look at the world around me and I fail to see the art that I most wish to see: *my own*. The images I encounter are all great and inspiring, but it's not me. Mine are locked up inside my brain somewhere. My sketching habit attempts to fix tangible form to that."

9. "Sketchbooks are the intersection of my thoughts about life and art, various mark-making techniques and many different formal and critical analyses.

10. "I hate the thought of dying and having left no record of the activity in my verbal/visual brain."

11. "This is a *big* also—once the work is fixed outside of my consciousness in the sketchbook, it becomes available to be refined, polished, and turned to other uses."

Collected sketchbooks (and a sketchbook page)

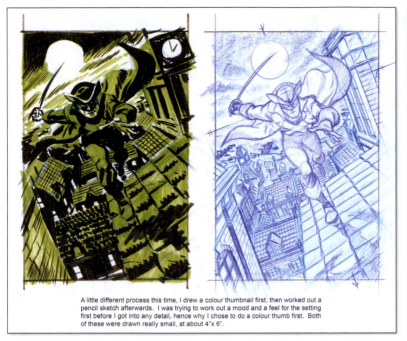

A little different process this time, I drew a colour thumbnail first, then worked out a pencil sketch afterwards. I was trying to work out a mood and a feel for the setting first before I got into any detail, hence why I chose to do a colour thumb first. Both of these were drawn really small, at about 4"x 6".

But no judgments here. Michael Cho, a freelance illustrator, cartoonist (and an occasional writer), is based in Toronto, Canada. He has some simple wisdom to get you over the hump (or past the gutter of the second and third pages). "Sketch on loose paper and collect only 'the best' of those pages in a binder later. Now, screw around without fear or guilt."

Special

And speaking of fear and guilt, just how precious and sacred is the sketchbook process? Is it all too heavy an idea to promote the exercise? If so, consider Ric Stultz's realistic outlook about the sketchbook concept: "My sketchbooks get piled up downstairs and sometimes I'll go through these big piles of paper and find something that I totally forgot about," Stultz tells you.

"Some work shines," says Stultz, from Milwaukee, Wisconsin. "But I have thrown out tons of imagery because it didn't make the cut, and that's the operative mindset here. In the back of the mind is the idea that I don't want to die and have all this stuff showing in some show or hanging on someone's wall."

Understand that Stultz (Figure 3-9) isn't telling you to raze your house or burn bridges. Nor is he suggesting you sacrifice your children. What he's saying is that cleaning house (metaphorically, emotionally, or physically) is a good thing. And he's right.

A Fine Mess

"I draw incessantly," says Scott Bakal. "Sometimes I draw for drawing's sake and other times I draw because I need to draw." Bakal lives in Boston and teaches at The Massachusetts College of Art. "Of course the

Figure 3-8a and b: Super heroes are frequent warm-ups Cho will do at the drawing board before kicking off his assignments for the day, or, as he says, "If I'm working on something really, really boring."

Here's a little end run around the sketch process for you: On *The Blackcoat*, Cho drew a color thumbnail first, then worked out the pencil sketch *after*. "I was trying to develop a mood and a setting before I got into any detail," he explains, "hence the preliminary color rough. And both of these were drawn really small, about 4 inches x 6 inches."

© Michael Cho

Figure 3-9: "Much of my work comes directly from my sketchbook; I am a constant sketcher," Stultz says. "I think that's really one of the main ways to develop ideas and images. I'd be practically lost without my sketchbook; I draw daily. If I put the pen down for a couple of hours and come back, I'm rusty. And I usually sketch beforehand. It actually takes about an hour (of drawing) to get to where I am lucid and what I want to draw is what I draw."

other side of all this is drawing because I have to. Life studies, things made up, decorative patterns (both observed and imagined); notes, comments, charcoal, paint, collage…all that stuff. All steps to a new idea and inspiration."

"Often, throughout a course of a sketchbook, a particular image pops up again and again—but slightly different. That's me working out a visual stuck in my head. I won't think about it in between jobs. But then maybe on a train, I'll start drawing it again until it gets to a particular place where I can move on to a final."

Whatever It Takes

Bakal says that his line enhances a personal interpretation of ideas that "come from all over." Often it just takes a mark on the paper to inspire him. But sometimes it takes days of research, sketching, and thinking.

Allowing his mind to wander in odd directions also blazes a path to new concepts or reveals how to communicate an idea in an interesting way. "Other times," he comments, "all it takes is a sketchpad and a pencil; sitting on the couch with my feet up watching TV, just letting it flow."

Let's Get Physical

Bill Russell lives and works out of San Rafael, California. He feels that an illustrator needs to be a keen observer, and that illustration students must develop a personal vision, a unique point of view, and an ability to translate what they are seeing onto paper.

"Learning drawing is like physical training," Russell explains, "like exercising a muscle. It's actually something students can develop. There's no big secret to it. It simply requires you to draw...a lot."

From Day One of any semester, Russell makes it a class requirement that each student carry a sketchbook all the time and that they draw whenever they can. "They make that pledge and must be willing to honor it," Russell informs.

Then, once this foundation is established and students begin to develop their drawing "muscles," Russell asks them to take it "outside." "Now," he says, "students are ready to come out of themselves and start functioning as 'illustrators in the world.'"

"Literally go outside with your sketchbooks and draw everywhere," Russell says. "In cafés, at the mall, to a courtroom. Take chalk and draw on

Figure 3-11: "Develop a feeling or empathy about what you are drawing," Russell says. "So, when drawing a floral arrangement, line qualities would reflect the variety, texture, shape, color—even the smell—of each flower."

"If you're drawing from a life model dressed as a football player, I would expect there to be a gusto or energy in that drawing," he states. "I ask students, 'what's your response to what you're seeing?' Then I suggest they try to incorporate that into the piece."

© Bill Russell

the sidewalk. Get to know and draw people (even interview them).

"Even if you're shy, it's important that you look outward; even working in uncomfortable situations—like at a baseball game or at the circus—where people might be looking over your shoulder. Produce drawings in an environment that is problematic and constantly in motion and your work will be better for that sense of urgency and immediacy."

"This kind of reportage is not easy," Russell points out, "but it helps inform your art, sharpen your drawing skills, and lets people know you are a public artist."

Doodle Bug

"Sketchbooks let the artist search for the truth about themselves," Steven Hughes comments. But truth be told, the sketchbook process doesn't click for every artist.

Perhaps you don't keep sketchbooks per se, but—like me—are an incessant creator of doodles. During quiet contemplation, often in deeper thought; at a meeting (and particularly on the phone), I am in deep doodle.

I collect much of these squiggly masterpieces in a folder, and/or tack 'em directly on a bulletin board. I have recurring themes, but some stuff continually (and naturally) morphs into something else—wonderfully impulsive, and oh-so stream of consciousness.

I never really know who's going to pop out, and I don't often see where the lines are going until I get there. Such drawings rarely look forced and are usually *very* fresh. Thus, my doodles are invariably a delightful little surprise (no wonder I keep so many).

To begin, I simply immerse myself in line quality and characterization. Here anything goes; no "mistakes," no "right"—and definitely no "wrong"—ideas yet; no supposed misdirections. It's all quite spontaneous, almost unconscious. The exercise is completely relaxed and unrehearsed, free flowing; it's rather Zen-like, actually.

Focus, Fleishman

The illustrations shown in Figure 3-13 are part of a series of extended sketches, actually doodled during the interview sessions for this book! Each interview ran approximately one hour; each drawing took multiple interviews to accomplish.

The problem I ran into was that, while I do these drawings on autopilot, I needed to pay sharp attention to the ongoing chat. When my scribbling took an interesting turn, I had to stop drawing (and *concentrate*, as my teachers always told me). However, the stop-and-start development of these particular

Figure 3-12: I love to doodle. Some assorted scribbles from the archives of *Advanced Crayon Research*, the tongue in cheek title I gave my binder of collected drawings.
© Michael Fleishman

squiggles proved only a negligible hardship. The herky-jerky process actually got me to continually come back to a fascinating exercise.

I was hooked in and tuned up, constantly experimenting with technique and revisiting the drawings beyond the interviews. Later, I even explored the motif via digital and other traditional media.

Figure 3-13a and b: "Mere doodles" inspired art I've sold through our local gallery, plus a great assignment I adapted for the classroom.
© Michael Fleishman

CHAPTER SUMMARY

We've been looking at the roots of drawing process: where the art and act of drawing begins, and specifically the basic question, where do ideas come from?

This chapter discussed sketchbooks (and by extension, journals, diaries, and scrapbooks too) as a vital way to record relevant answers to that question and a great way to play with those solutions.

Sketchbooks are creative outlets that document the give and take between imagination—your bright ideas—and information (input/output). They are an inspired means to identify what the drawing job is really about: figuring out how to express oneself visually.

The chapter talked to artists who carry a sketchbook wherever they go, as creative *diaries* or graphic travelogues. For others, the *act* of daily journaling provides discipline and a key to self-control. And for many, sketchbooks are a healthy mental, intellectual, or emotional steam valve.

Working It Out

1-3. Routine x 3

Buy a sketchbook for class sessions (separate from your at home journal, these will be kept in class). Keep this sketchbook small: it's up to you, but no bigger than 9 x 12 in. Your instructions are to take the first few minutes of every class and draw. Ostensibly, it's anything and everything, but see the options below. Hand in your sketchbook when called in for an ongoing cumulative score (see handout for grading criteria).

You can mix and match: choose three or more exercise options for this ongoing class project. Here are some spins on the basic assignment (see other handouts and listen up in class for further specs): some days this will be an ungraded assignment; other days you will grade your work; there will be days when you grade your classmates' work. You will also be switching sketchbooks with other students and adding on to another person's drawing (each week starting with a new sketch).

  a. Media Jam (mixed-media)

  b. Line Hunt (explore and experiment)

  c. Words and Pictures

  d. Visual (Personal) Diary

  e. Fact or Fiction

  f. Fact *and* Fiction

  g. Comic Book

  h. Free Choice

Home And Away

1. Continued Routine

Buy a sketchbook. The size of the sketchbook is up to you, but for the sake of argument, I'd keep it somewhere between 4 by 6 in. and 11 x 14 in. For one month, draw in your sketchbook *every day*, at the same time, for the exact same length of time everyday. How long? 30–60 minutes, minimum. The exercise is not about how many pages you do each session (that challenge is coming up); this go-round we're establishing a sketchbook *discipline*. Subject matter and media: free choice.

2. Old Hat

Write the numbers 1–10 on 10 slips of paper. Put them in your artist's beret and mix 'em up. Pick one. Whatever number you fish out, that's how many complete pages you must do per day (and we're talking 7 days in a week). Wait, we're not finished: Select the numbers 4-8 from your slips. Replace these in the hat and choose one. That's how many *weeks* you will be doing the exercise. Now, have at it, and have fun!

3. Street-Wise

Time to "take it outside." Head out into the world with your sketchbook. Venture out with sketchbook in hand, draw *everywhere*: in coffee shops, at stores, on public transportation, at secluded spots or private places. Go to a ballgame or the zoo. Think off the page, too: draw on the sidewalk or a wall (hopefully with permission). Draw it in and draw it all, and capture people, places, and things away from home and studio.

Chapter 4

The Process

© Fred Lynch

How We Begin

This chapter discusses the core of drawing methodology, where the art and act of drawing begins. We'll again ask the central question: where do ideas come from? To get to the heart of the answer, we will examine:

1. Style and technique as underpinnings to the drawing event. Fundamentals are also linked to all this.

2. Brainstorming as the place where the *vision* of a drawing materializes, the first step—where the artist revs up his thinking and gets her creative juices flowing.

3. Roughs and thumbnails (and followups called comprehensives). Roughs and thumbnails could be tagged as the place "where the ideas live." These preliminaries kick off the life cycle of most illustrations. A drawing begins, takes shape, and gets refined here.

4. Finals. The journey completes. How an illustration goes from a loose, spontaneous product *in concept*, through progressively tighter approximations of the bright idea (comps—comprehensives—as a cap to the sketch stage) and ultimately the finish (as covered throughout this book).

Figure 4-1: "Things that work, work," says Peter Arkle. "Avoiding the fundamentals is like trying to tell someone that you don't care about fashion—not caring is itself a fashion statement." Arkle lives in New York City, where he's a freelance illustrator of books, magazines, and ads. He occasionally publishes a newspaper, *Peter Arkle News*, containing stories and drawings about everyday life.

Figure 4-2: Braught's work confidently takes wing here.
© Mark Braught

Everything is Everything

"Line is the foundation," says Mark Braught, as he considers process, "the skeleton to hang the meat on. And composition? The plate to serve it up." Braught knows that the better the foundation—established first through the gesture of line and placement of those strokes, then fine tuned through the clarity of your message—the better the possibilities for successful communication.

And there are many tools available to help further that communication. Value. Color. All the basic skill sets? "With technical ability, you gain control," he tells you. "The more expertise, the more control you can exert over the image at hand (and the more likely you will be able to successfully express yourself through your media)."

"The more skills you control, the more choices you have when it comes to solutions. Less is left to random luck. And yes, experimentation keeps things lively. Creativity is about going places unexplored. Exploration is for the courageous—and we have to be prepared to try a number of times. Whatever it takes to get it right."

The Puzzle

"Composition is my favorite part of illustration," says Whitney Sherman, "and I admire those artists who deftly employ white space (or negative space) along with a fine eye for design. I have a compulsion to discover ways to have one line or shape serve two or more design elements—a bit like a puzzle, a little Design 101; a lot of distillation.

Figure 4-3: Sherman's attractive and colorful work.
© Whitney Sherman

Line is an essential component of Sherman's art. In her work, line is complimented by color values. Often it plays out in small shifts that suggest detail without literally delivering detail. "The search for the edge not only defines the process of drawing," Sherman points out, "it can also establish value: a quasi-crosshatch effect—in print production terms—creates a halftone-like effect."

"At its best," says Sherman, "color can imbue an image with cultural meaning and power. At its worst it can be gratuitous. I like to use color to determine mood, and use a limited palette. I have a real attraction to colors that look like old cement and tree moss, muted tones that complement touches of vibrant colors."

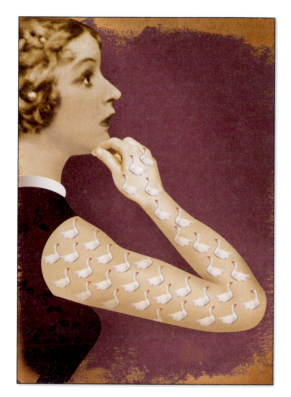 

Figure 4-4a and b: "Color in my work either sets a mood or makes a scene more realistic," says Weinstein. "An interesting thing is that, by using color in a more natural way, the viewer can focus on the unnatural elements to get what I am saying."
© Ellen Weinstein

A Capital Idea

Illustrator Ellen Weinstein lives and works in New York City. When considering process, Weinstein's alphabet starts with the capital letter "C." "Creativity is about Color, plus Concept and Composition," she says. "Concept is the key element of the creative process. It always starts with the idea. The viewer is active and engaged in that process, and an illustration is a dialogue between the artist and the viewer. It comes down to what you are trying to say and how you say it; you have only a limited time between someone 'not getting it' and 'hey, I get it.'"

A Four-Point Program

Freelance illustrator Shanth Enjeti teaches at Rhode Island School of Design and Montserrat College of Art. He says he critiques (and builds his own work) based on four criteria. You may want to do the same.

In order of importance:

1. Composition: how elements are arranged on the page. If this isn't right, *nothing* about the piece will work.

2. Value: does the range—and contrast—of tone communicate space…where the eye is directed?

Figure 4-5a and b: How about this for process? (a) was painted on the perfectly good punch out of a circular mat (and actually found in the trash bin). (b) was an old bulletin board cut down to a comfortable working size (18 in. x 26 in.) to eliminate the battered frame and grubby outside edges of the cork. The surface was very compromised, but I wanted to retain these gnarly chunk holes and myriad nasty bits as the painting's base layer—that was the whole point!

© Michael Fleishman

3. Hue: how color supports value and the way the eye moves.

4. Draftsmanship: how well you draw is not as important as authentic mark making ("technique," by the way, only comes later).

Funny, You Don't Look Stylish

From Pittsburgh, Pennsylvania, Ilene Winn-Lederer creates original imagery that navigates the delicate bridge between the mundane and mystical theaters of human experience. "Is it all a question of style?" she asks you.

In a measured response, Winn-Lederer makes a strong argument that *style* is all about *us*—who we are, where we've been, where time may take us. "Having said that, style is also about research and perseverance," Winn-Lederer says, "developing a process that becomes your own. Style reveals your understanding of concept while technical skills clarify that understanding to your viewers."

Figure 4-6: "Today's market pigeonholes illustrators into a specific saleable style," Winn-Lederer says. "But I think it's necessary to have an array of skills. We must be flexible when times change."

"One size doesn't fit all. Conceptual skills and mechanical skills are not mutually exclusive; together they enhance a great message or story."
© Ilene Winn-Lederer

The Top of the Box

Bound by what he calls a "never-ending curiosity," freelance illustrator Nathan Walker currently lives near Boston. For Walker, technique is style. "I paint the way I want to see the world," he says. "I tend to paint the happy stuff just a shade dark, and serious things a little bit fun."

Figure 4-7: "Students should be forced to go *inside* themselves," Walker states. "Focus on becoming artists *and* thinkers; the only truth being that which you can defend. Make the world a place to explore and leave your mark."
© Nathan Walker

"Style should be the last thing you worry about," Walker chides good naturedly. "If at all, fret about the strength of your ideas, or whether your picture making skills are up to snuff. Style will come whether you want it or not. Your style will speak for itself soon enough."

Luc Of The Draw

Luc Melanson's Bachelor's degree is actually in Graphic Design, but he's devoted himself to illustration, winning accolades from the publishing world and corporate clients alike. "Style is something that concerns art historians, not artists," Melanson states.

"I'm an illustrator who never really learned how to draw," he says modestly. "I don't consider myself a great draftsman. But I'm a good problem solver. Drawing and concept are inseparable," he firmly continues. "An artist must communicate to serve his work (and audience) better. But it's a very personal matter."

Stay Informed

Scott Bakal says to draw regularly. "And keep informed about what's going on in the world, especially in social contexts. It's one of those things I like to pay attention to," he tells us. "Because I am focused here, I'll get hired for that type of work simply because I'm able to visually connect a particular emotion and social situation."

Figure 4-8: Melanson advises you not to chase style. Find your comfort zone, and navigate towards work you love—*that* will end up as your style. "Surprise yourself," Melanson says. "Trust your instinct. Just please *you*. Stay balanced. If you put your heart into your work, people will feel it."

 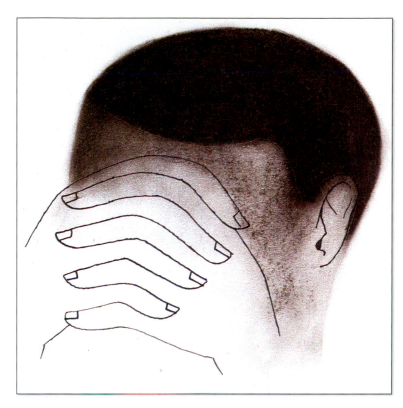

Figure 4-9a and b: "People naturally gravitate towards their distinctive process," says Bakal. "Knowing that personal process is a step toward knowing yourself as an artist."
© Scott Bakal

Process: Off and Over the Top

For many illustrators, process is reliable, and may be the only *consistent* part of illustration. It is for Steven Hughes, who went to Kent State University and discovered illustration during his first basic drawing course. "Illustration is very process-oriented," he says. "Some students never get it; others are born with more of an artistic eye. School helped *me* focus and see the everyday in a new way."

Something Hughes learned from Sterling Hundley (at the Illustration Academy) was how to look for those unexpected connections, to make lists and link interesting combinations of items. "Basically it's all about relationships," Hughes explains.

Hughes will also tell you that he goes through four well-defined stages with his process:

1. Crap

2. Discovery

3. Exploration

4. Overworked (boredom) or conversely: overconfidence (doing *too* much)

Figure 4-10: "During school a lot of my ideas came at the last moment when my back was to the wall," Hughes remembers. "There are times I look back and wonder, *What was I thinking?* But I believe it's just the maturity factor."

© Steven Hughes

"And of course, I next curse the acrylics for drying too quickly," Hughes sums up with a grin.

Scratch That

Art Grootfontein lives and works in Paris, France. He was an illustrator for about ten years when he realized that, "I never really paid attention to how I was drawing and why. I had no real personal style."

Grootfontein yearned to take his art to that next level. So the illustrator—an art director as well as a typographer—took three serious steps: "1. Every day, I fed my brain with all the art resources and references I could handle. 2. I returned to my (visual) roots. 3. I started over from scratch: no lines, no curves, and no realistic color palette! Everything opposite to where I was at the time; I had to think different, and I learned a lot."

Poster Boy

The look of 19th century posters attracts Grootfontein. "Their restrained color palette was actually a strength," he says. "That's why I often design with fewer colors. A tighter palette and balanced shapes help stabilize the composition. Color is a challenge. I'm always learning."

Figure 4-11a and b: The tight palette and balanced shapes of Grootfontein.
© Art Grootfontein

"The computer enables you to achieve perfect, solid color," says Grootfontein. "But digital images are often too cold and synthetic. I usually use textured brushes, a little grain or a bit of noise to offset this. That hand-made, slightly aged effect is warmer, and I like the idea that new illustrations can appear to have been done years ago."

It's Routine

Peter Cusack has lived in and around New York his whole life. "I love living and leaving here," he smiles. Drawing has always been Cusack's greatest pleasure and he finds sharing "the experience" with other artists to be deeply fullfilling.

"My process?" he considers with a laugh, "usually starts off with panic and anxiety. To move through this stage I need some time to just muse on the subject matter and uncover the elements that interest me. After which, I move to honest interest and a deeper personal involvement in the assignment. I begin working in my sketchbook; toying with characters and ideas, organizing the important aspects of the narrative and boiling it down to the simplest composed statement."

Figure 4-12: "When working on the final painting," Cusack says, "I like to have room to paint directly and fresh from reference; building the composition in terms of detail and color, as if working directly from life or, as they say, en plein air."
© Peter Cusack

Figure 4-13: Higgins' focused work is anything but routine.
© Sean Higgins

Every Day

A graduate of Kent State University, Sean Higgins works from a simple premise: you devour good food, cherish great music, revere solid design, and absolutely treasure illustration. Higgins appreciates that staying ahead of the game translates to the practice of his craft. "As a freelance illustrator," he says, "you must focus on the 'here and now' in order to keep on top of this job."

"You really need to get a daily illustration routine down," Higgins advises, "drawing every day—even if you are busy or have another job that drains you. You have to keep with it, that's the only way to grow. Make drawing a big part of your *everyday* life."

The Think and Do Thing

Prior to graduating from Ontario College of Art and Design with a degree in Illustration, Huan Tran already had a diploma in *another* field. After OCAD, he knew what he wanted to accomplish and set milestones (and a timetable) to achieve these goals.

"I'm often asked how many hours I work a week," Tran tells us. "If I quantify the actual time that I sit and create something tangible, the hours are not that great. But how many hours do I spend *thinking* about work? That's a full-time gig—I am *constantly* brainstorming. Eventually something clicks and I will have an image in my head."

Figure 4-14: Tran's well-thought illustration simply clicks with his audience.
© Huan Tran

Communication

Jesse Kuhn received his BFA in Graphic Design and Illustration from Missouri State. He currently resides in New York City. As he says, "There is never a time when drawing does not communicate. After all, the most abstract drawing is open to interpretation. Even doodles communicate one's thoughts or subconscience."

"Knowledge is power; it always will be," Kuhn considers. "Exercising the rules enables you to speak confidently, intelligently, convincingly. Understanding the fundamentals authorizes you to possibly break that set of rules and creatively upset the balance (and to know when that makes your good work even better)."

Brainstorms

Brainstorms provide the raw materials of concept. Brainstorming is an excellent source of artistic fiber, and is rich in creative proteins. Goofy dietary metaphors aside, brainstorming should be fun, loose, and informal. It's the kind of activity that can be done solo, with a partner, or in a group. No pressure, no wrong answers; hey—*anything goes.* Doodle (especially on autopilot), fool around with wordplay (or be a wordsmith). Free associate, work out pencil games or futz with puzzles; maybe charts and outlines are your thing—whatever primes the pumps of inventive thought, discovery, and production.

Figure 4-15: Kuhn breaks the rules convincingly, with confidence and intelligence.
© Jesse Kuhn

Figure 4-16: Illustrator Steve McInturff has been teaching at Columbus College of Art and Design since 1987. "There are any number of ways to develop ideas," he says.

"Sometimes I'm in a restaurant and I'll grab a napkin, do a fast sketch, stuff it in my pocket. Back at the studio, I'll take the napkin art and photocopy the bits that work. You can then piecemeal the image back and forth until it finally starts to take shape."

This sample of McInturff's work may or may not have been developed on a napkin—only the waiter really knows for sure.

© Steve McInturff

All Thumbs

Thumbnails, as you've heard previously in this chapter, are the raw shape of the concept. You may or may not be asked to show thumbnails at the preliminary stages—it might just be part of one's process to get to a rough.

But designer/illustrator Buddy Hill points out that going to your end design too soon means you are making composition changes within the final piece itself. These are solutions better worked out in the thumbs (and sketch) stage. By doing that, you focus less on process and more on the work being generated by that process.

Fred Lynch has a notebook comprised of *only* thumbnails. In this particular sketchbook, these thumbs are only an inch by an inch. Lynch always works with a ballpoint pen; he tries to do as many variations of the assignment as he can, and all are on one sheet of paper.

Figure 4-17: The drawings are deliberately small, purposely quick, and, "I draw in pen so I *can't* erase them," Lynch tells us, "so I don't get into any details. No digging for reference, no searching on the Internet. At the beginning of a project, I want no limitations; only possibilities."

I Swear

Some illustrators swear by the idea of doing "thumbs" and roughs, others swear at it. But thumbnails and roughs only make good sense and are invaluable on many levels (in fact, thumbnails and roughs are mandatory when I assign a school project). Visual—if not conceptual—organization should not be overrated.

Andrea Wicklund's sketchbook is actually half drawings and half words. "I'll make a list of words and associate them with other words until I narrow it down to those that are the strongest," she explains. "Then I try to come up with an icon for each of those words; something simple and obvious." The goal: to establish how those icons relate to each other (visually and conceptually) and work them together like a jigsaw. Then the Seattle-based illustrator starts drawing.

Figure 4-18: "I research, gather reference, learn more about the topic, and find my visual sources to put the puzzle pieces together," Wicklund says. "After the drawing is on the board, I contemplate my color palette and what medium I'd like to use where. Then I just go for it, and cross my fingers."
© Andrea Wicklund

Sketches and Roughs

You then refine and upgrade your thumbnails via scaled roughs and/or a larger sketch (or sketches). Look at this rough and finish for *Ghostland Observatory*, by Kyle T. Webster. We included the sketch to show the artist's thinking before a final direction was chosen by the art director. "Some of my roughs are nearly identical to the final," Webster comments. The sketch is low-res, because that is how Webster draws and sends them out.

Figure 4-19a and b: Hot off the sketchpad and nearly identical to the final.
© Kyle T. Webster

Figure 4-20: Webster's work moves with a frantic energy here.

© Kyle T. Webster

In Deference to Reference

"I drew the Swedish band, 'The Hives,' while watching their video. This inspired me to create an image meant to feel like it is moving with frantic energy," says Webster.

"The art director really liked the result and I learned a new technique in the process of creating the image. I reproduced my line work and layered it over the original strokes in a lighter color. I next rotated that by about 1 degree, adding a sense of movement or a 'ghost image,' if you will."

Finally!

You may be doing a comp (comprehensive) next. Comp art can get kissin' close to a finished illustration. Your little gem will have some coarse edges to polish—sort of the diamond in the rough. Think, "what you see is—*just about*—what you get."

A client (or instructor) may not require this step to get to the finished piece, but comps may simply be a stage in *your* process. And in any event, from here, it's usually on to the finish.

You Shoulda Seen the Sketch!

Usually, as far as commissioned art is concerned, the final is certainly the main event. In some instances, however, that may not be the case (at least for the creator of the piece). In the process of turning a sketch into a final, it's just a fact of the artist's life that a piece can lose some verve in that transition. Noboutadoubt it, sometimes a sketch *is* more spontaneous. There's a vitality that may be lost in the translation to finished art. Plus the fact that the rough is not judged by the same criteria as the final often allows you to be looser and less self-conscious.

Anthony Freda's delightful, thought-provoking illustrations are a mashup of modern and vintage, classical and antique artifacts plus relevant social commentary. "You can lose some of the passion for the image itself as you revisit the same territory," Freda considers. "The desire to create a beautiful finished piece can be nerve-racking and may make an artist overwork the piece, stomping the life out of it."

"The best thing about a tight deadline is that it keeps you from muddling stuff," Freda states. "You just don't have time."

Figure 4-21: Freda's vital, thought-provoking illustrations are relevant mashups of classical and modern motifs.

© Anthony Freda

✔ Check Point: You Might as Well Jump

Here are some not-so random thoughts about process, as brought up by Derek Gores.

1. Line is the most economical mark you can make. Most people think of line as the *where*—as in "where things are"—but it's often overlooked as the "how" things are.

2. People know 15,000 words or more. It takes that vocabulary (perhaps more) to hold an interesting conversation, to read a good book, and certainly to write a great book. And in drawing, you'll need 15,000 ways to make a mark (a line) if you hope to create a compelling image.

3. I love ambiguity in line and shape. A dynamic (but contradictory or) ambiguous space is certainly not the same as "flat."

4. As a late teen the German expressionists got me. Franz Kline, too (and maybe Eddie Van Halen's guitar).

5. Make sure you see Seurat's drawings, and definitely Rembrandt's too. Too many folks see things as just line or tone, and don't bridge the possibilities between. Rembrandt's drawings show you there's an infinite range in between.

6. Learn to make space in interesting ways. A hint: think "form!"

7. I enjoy all black and white, and also "high pop" colors. I admire but have little interest in chasing down subtle differences of a color across light and shadow. At least for today!

8. I hesitate to say drawing is about communication. To many, that would mean a drawing is the execution of a *preconception*. That doesn't excite me much. Drawing can be the tangible manifestation of an experience. Schiele and DeKooning were monsters of drawing, and I wouldn't say they were communicators primarily.

9. A friend calls my approach to concept "zen narrative." I let it flow. I let it happen. I trust that the process has the potential to add up to a more interesting dynamic than if I just illustrated a literal scene, or a simplistic concept.

10. I'm wary of symbols in art. Symbols engage the intellect; we understand because of our memory—as opposed to a genuine, fresh response you *feel*. These days, symbols can be used with irony; that's fun.

11. There is no Cliff's Notes® of universally "good" compositions—only compositions that help or don't help the idea. The relationships of shapes have tension, or they have release of tension. They have *thrill*, or they have *calm*. Figure out your mood and purpose, but beware of "balance." Instead of harmonious distribution, may I suggest searching for the thrill of being on the edge of falling apart?

The calm thrill of Gores' fine work.
© Derek Gores

No Alternative

Erin Brady Worsham was diagnosed with ALS (Amyotrophic Lateral Sclerosis) in 1994, and creates her art without the use of her hands. Working on the computer—through a painstaking process with a sensor taped between her eyebrows—she says this is "a small price to pay."

For Worsham, there is no alternative. She is an artist, and her art has given her an identity above and beyond her physical limitations—as art does for any other artist; as it does for even the "temporarily abled" folks (as my friend, disability advocate, Greg Smith, puts it).

Figure 4-22: An effective illustration knows its audience, as shown here in this work by Worsham. Along these very lines, the artist was once commissioned by the DaVinci Awards in Dearborn, Michigan to create a piece for their annual fundraising dinner (the DaVinci Awards honors technology that improves the lives of people with disabilities). She decided to use Leonardo's famous *Mona Lisa*, but with a twist. "The edge of a wheelchair headrest protrudes from behind her head," Worsham says. "I can't tell you how many people looked at that picture and didn't see the headrest at first. Then they looked again—a true 'Gotcha' moment!"

© Erin Brady Worsham

CHAPTER SUMMARY

In this chapter we discussed the roots of drawing methodology; you might say, where the art and act of drawing begins. We began by asking the core question: where do ideas come from? To get to the root of the answer, we examined style and technique; brainstorming; roughs and thumbnails (and followups called comprehensives); and finals.

Working It Out

In Class

1. Roughin' It

In class you will pick one object from a box. It will be something simple—an apple, for instance. We will do 25 thumbnails, then refine these further by doing another 25 roughs (quarter-sized would be about right). Media: Pencil, ink, digital, marker. Color and/or b&w; mix it up.

2. Object Lesson

Do a new drawing each class period for our two-week time frame. We're working in black and white from a "limited" box of tools; choose *one* media: pencil, marker, ink, or charcoal. Don't mix and match. Portray this subject matter in one style or multiple styles.

3. Word Game

Here's an exercise courtesy of illustrator John Hendrix: find an article (or book passage, whatever). Narrow down the three main concepts from the article. Make a short list of *visual* solutions to those ideas. For example, under the idea of "Astronomy," you might write: stars, telescopes, planets, constellations, satellites, observatories, etc. Once you have three or more columns of visual ideas, start, as Hendrix puts it, "slamming them together" to create your illustration.

On Your Own

1. Mix and Match

At home, research a number of related topics that intrigue you intellectually or stimulate you emotionally (for instance, big government, welfare, and tax reform). Visually, you will now portray this subject matter in *multiple* styles and techniques: a different method and/or material with each rendering. This is a long term project, so the sky's the limit: experiment, mix and match. Try new media. Explore a manner you've always admired; better yet, a style you never cared for!

2. Simple and Elegant

Can you get to the essence of your subject matter? Pick a general topic: fruit, for instance. Do a drawing a day (think one week to one month, at least) and explore it *fully*: visually, conceptually, and technically.

Your first drawing can be as complex, detailed, or nuanced as you wish. But each subsequent drawing must be simplified. The work should become progressively more simple and elegant; simply elegant would be cool indeed. Meet with your classmates after class hours to discuss and evaluate progress, philosophy, and product.

3. Trashed

Take your general topic and do another drawing: one per day (again, for one week to one month, minimum). Explore it—with appropriate gusto—from the opposite end of this spectrum: trash and grunge.

Your first drawing can be clean, simple, elegant. But each subsequent drawing should progressively get busier, messier, more complicated (visually, technically, intellectually). Compromise line and color quality at will.

How is readability (in terms of both the visual and the concept) on such a piece? Meet with your classmates after class hours to discuss and evaluate progress, philosophy, and product.

Chapter 5

Concept

© Martin Wittfooth

Concept: Communication. Message. Explanation.

Like all artistic endeavors, drawing is about communication. A drawing communicates when it sends a pertinent message to the viewer. This live connection may spark on many levels (visceral, emotional, intellectual, whatever).

Let's talk about what many consider the key element of the creative process: concept, the big *idea*. We'll consider what that illustration is really about; what you are trying to say, and how you go about saying it (conceptually *and* technically).

We'll discuss how artistic perception forges technique and influences tools (and vice versa). We'll examine how ideas dictate content, and how content then determines composition and impacts fundamentals (line, value, color, pattern and texture, etc).

First Up

"Concept comes first and foremost," Akiko Stehrenberger says. "I can't begin an illustration without a concept. It's a waste of time to start without a clue of where to go. So, concept first, and composition next—*then* I look at technique and likeness."

Stehrenberger's "Pervert 2" (**Figure 5-1a**) is really called "Your Fingers Taught Me How to Dance." It's a self-portrait, the second one in a series. It's a very personal piece for the artist, "my absolute favorite illustration to this day," she states. "I constantly love mixing cute with creepy, beautiful with ugly, masculine with feminine." In this one she also mixes acrylic and ballpoint pen.

"*Kurt*" (**Figure 5-1b**) was done for *Filter* magazine. Later, the image was used as promotion for the movie "Last Days" by Gus Van Sant. Again, this piece is acrylic and ballpoint pen. "I wanted to focus more on the concept of *character*," Stehrenberger says, "Kurt as a character, rather than getting a 'perfect' likeness. I thought it would be as effective showing certain characteristics as it would be if I would have shown his face."

Figure 5-1a and b: As shown here, concept comes first and foremost for Stehrenberger.

© Akiko Stehrenberger

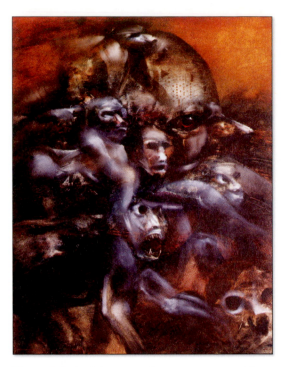

Figure 5-2: As Arisman points out, you provide the expression, concept provides the outlet.
© Marshall Arisman

Figure 5-3: Stahl tells us that getting your concept across is an art in itself. As you can see here, she makes that case quite eloquently.
© Nancy Stahl

The Root

"Drawing is an act in itself," Marshall Arisman emphasizes. "Van Gogh said this: 'Drawing is the root of all art.' *What* you draw is another matter. As Charlie Parker put it, 'Music is my wisdom, my knowledge. If you don't live it—it won't come out of your horn.'"

"If you have nothing to say, your drawings will be limited to observation," Arisman observes. "Now, there's nothing wrong with observation (look at any master drawing). But the problem in illustration is that you must choose between decorating a page or saying something with it. I have chosen to use illustration as an outlet for my own thoughts. That is not a style issue but a content issue."

The Good Fight

Nancy Stahl's painterly pixels and retro-style vector work are the calling card for this pioneer of digital illustration. Stahl says she still struggles with concepts. "Mine are usually subtle and maybe too personal," she states candidly. "The tangents that my brain takes when sorting out a concept lead me away from the easily communicated. Finding clear, direct visual solutions to a verbal, abstracted idea is really difficult. It's very deceptive; conveying ideas is an art in itself."

"I'm trying to work more conceptually," she says, "now that I have decades of experience behind me and many art directors who hire me have much less. The balance has shifted and I finally have the confidence to pare things down to a kernel of an idea. (And I can finally talk my way through a concept. Yes—you shouldn't need words; but working in visual symbols requires verbal translation on occasion.)"

Positively Giddy

At this writing, Martha Rich is relocating to Philadelphia. For Rich, line expresses her thoughts and feelings at the time she is creating a piece. "Even if you don't know what you are feeling," she says, "you will, when you look at the line when you're done."

"Value is a minor factor in my scheme of things," she continues. "My building blocks start with what's in my head and how I am feeling. I come from an intuitive place and don't consider value until after I have started. Value helps emphasize what I want the viewer to see, where I want the eyes to go. It balances an image out—or makes it awkward—whatever mood I am trying to capture."

"Color is good for manipulating. Put a couple of odd colors together and you can feel happily angry or sadly annoyed. I love color; color is fun. I like to be weird with color…color makes me giddy. I love using color to be disobedient and daring and rule breaking."

Yes and No

Rich is mixed as to whether drawing is really *all* about communication. It's a toss-up for the illustrator, who says she often draws to express herself rather than communicate. "But if I *show it* to someone, then it will communicate whether that is the intention or not. If someone is looking at a drawing, the piece is communicating."

"For me drawing is a diary. Instead of writing in a journal, I draw. Sometimes there's something specific I need to get out and sometimes I let intuition take over and see what happens."

Figure 5-4a and b: Is concept a key element of the creative process? According to Rich, this will depend on the goal of that process. "If the goal is pure expression or experimentation, then the concept is important but fluid," she says. "It can evolve and grow and take a different direction during the creative process."

And technically, Rich likes that process as loose as possible and to make mistakes. "Too much time is spent trying for perfection," she says. "The mistakes are just as important as the successes, maybe more so because people are so afraid of making mistakes. I don't use pencil—ink is more committal. You can't erase it, so you are forced to go for it. Ink has some stones."

Say What? (Concept and Composition)

For some illustrators the act of drawing means the flash of technique. Others reflect that technique is really directed by subject matter—content. And for many artists it's all about design—composition is the thing. But if you think about it, concept obviously establishes content, and content is certainly integral to composition.

I'm a "best of both worlds" kinda guy. I'll go to the mat to argue that drawing skills are key. However, I also believe that we have to float some earlier (and important) questions immediately: *conceptually* what *are* you saying…what is this illustration about?

The act of drawing is a bit like pitching practice. If your delivery isn't complemented by the curveball of good ideas, you only have your fastball to get you through the inning (and ultimately keep you in the show). Conceptual and technical skills need to be developed in tandem.

Did You Hear the One About…

Some artists, like Jill Calder, ask if drawing is just a process that *enables* communication. Calder lives in the United Kingdom, and is a lecturer at Edinburgh College of Art.

For Calder, concept communicates the theme, like a classic one-liner. For many illustrators, concept may be the toughest bit, worked out through the freedom to arrive at better ideas; filtered to the best and brightest; but a long

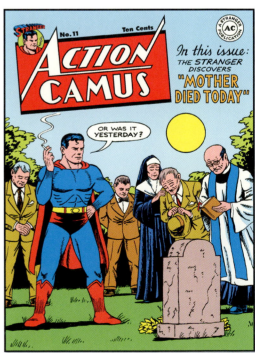

Figure 5-5a and b: R. Sikoryak is a cartoonist and illustrator, based in New York City. His work blends technique with concept to morph culture and cartoons in a smart homage to comics history and literary classics.
© R. Sikoryak

and painful process. Maybe your light-hearted approach simply camouflages the serious business of pinning down a good concept: it only looks simple and witty; clever while short and sweet. However, getting to that is anything but.

Like Calder, maybe you work by instinct when putting together an illustration: what is really needed for content? Does too much detail here detract from the idea? Do you need to use less color to get the point across more effectively?

If you are passionate about good, strong composition, that well thought-out (and executed) design can make a good illustration great. And at some point it may become a largely subconscious process. Here's what Calder tries to do:

1. Place a "first" object (a face, a hand, a plant, whatever) off center.

2. Play with scale and perspective. Use the edges of the paper, crop, tilt, twist.

3. Create drama: enhance the power of the concept by applying compositional challenges—lead the eye around the page or screen.

4. Tinker with the order of things (for instance, layers in Photoshop), and arrange elements, crop and flip; scale up and down.

5. Eventually she arrives at the "perfect" composition. "Or at least," Calder says, "as good as it's going to get (and do listen to your gut feelings here, too)."

Figure 5-6: Practice what Calder calls an instinctive application of line—which, over years could possibly become somewhat subconscious. Deciding when a line weight should be heavier or thinner is to some extent the byproduct of the tools you use and random quirks of a particular drawing instrument. Enjoy this serendipity, let it inform your 'style.' These extra marks and blobs bring an added dimension and immediacy to Calder's work. "I choose to keep these in, unedited," she says. And so might you.

© Jill Calder

Feel What? (Concept and Content)

Peter Cusack understands that a clear concept is an excellent host for a solid composition and that a painterly, vigorous manner can easily convey detail.

Good organization of content simply amps up your ability to communicate. So Cusack also knows that a well-organized concept can broadcast emotion in any technique. "Emotion is the main focus of my work," Cusack says. "I try to create stirring images that carry a quiet power and a mood that draws viewers in."

Don't try to drill a concept down to a single emotion driving the piece. Combine a number of narrative devices to build emotional content. "Often," Cusack explains, "I'll assign one element of the painting to carry the emotive or poetic quality. Other elements take care of the narrative or action—the business end of the piece. This way the *overall* expression of the piece should be evident—organized, straightforward, and (most importantly) never overstated."

Threes

Along these lines, here are a few tips, tricks, and theories from Cusack:

Figure 5-7: The work of Cusack.
© Peter Cusack

1. Don't explain everything, leave something out (and put something in).

2. Work in threes. Three narrative elements. Three major compositional elements. Three basic color notes (but only one at full chroma). Three clouds, three windows, etc.

3. Don't make everything perfect. Strive for 80%. Leave the last 20% for the next painting.

We Don't Mean to Nag, But...

Conceptually what are you saying...what is this illustration about? Visually, your answer must be right there on the page (or screen)—not too obscure, and not necessarily that obvious (or even immediate). But the ultimate payoff—that little "ah ha!" moment of understanding—should be a lock. And remember, a satisfying illustration experience is all about audience participation (despite the long distance and time delay).

Nail the concept first. The other foundations—line, value and color, composition; texture plus pattern; shape and form—can next come into play. *Now* have fun with those creative building blocks to develop your process, technique, and yes, style, too.

Keep it Simple, Sarah

The best advice Sarah Mantell has heard about balancing concept and style was something Fred Lynch always said in class: "Something about this image has to be simple!"

Lynch encouraged Mantell to tap into less complicated ideas, and to really have fun with the look of the piece. Other students got the opposite advice: scale down the image and let your concept do most of the work. This relays the same message: artists work in very different manners. Feel free to play up your strengths—and what you love.

"What appeals to me first is the way a remarkable perspective, unusual cropping, or unexpected juxtaposition look." Mantell says, "I often make my way to the best conceptual choice when I think I'm just playing around with the look of the piece."

The Mechanics of Concept

Conceptual skills are forever important. Mechanical skills are absolutely essential. It's kind of a no-brainer to me—there's no way to execute good ideas if you can't draw them out.

You know this guy: the student who can render anything—but when asked, "Do you have any *ideas?*" has no clue. Conversely, another student comes in with design chops and great concepts, but weaker rendering skills.

Both of these students can thrive. "And drawing helps you see what you are thinking," Alex Bostic supports, "but we often struggle between mechanics and concept."

From Dayton, Ohio, Paul Melia chimes in: "To make the concept click, you have to develop those mechanics," Melia says. "It's like going cross-country by automobile. For a sweet ride, the whole car has to work. Everything has to be there."

And so it is with conceptual thinking: it's gotta be there, Jack. Thus, the question looms large: how do you bring a concept to that mechanical (the visual) place where it works?

Art's a Goofy Guy

"Well, you put in the time," Melia starts off, "Although it's not clocking hours like you're working for some company."

"And you don't make it a labor. There has to be a certain *joy* there. Joy is practicing and practicing (and drawing and drawing), and all of a sudden someone says, 'Hey, you're better than you were!'"

Figure 5-8: The work of Mantell.
© Sarah B. Mantell

"You're losing yourself in your art and doing what it takes to develop those creative skills. But art is a little goofy…one guy can put 60 minutes in and do a better drawing than another guy who invests 20 hours."

"However," Melia concludes, "I do know that joy comes out of any hard work that's constructive."

Balance

Martin Wittfooth studied at Sheridan College in Canada and the School of Visual Arts in New York, and now lives in Brooklyn. This artist's productive illustration and gallery work often pits the industrial complex against the natural realm, frequently mixing the two—as if by a bizarre matter transporter malfunction—in remarkable and unsettling juxtapositions.

To Melia's comments above, Wittfooth adds: "Generally, concept balances out mechanics. One skill set *may* outweigh the other in specific instances. Think New York Times Op-Ed versus a children's picture book.

"Some artists create highly conceptual, clever, or humorous work that looks—deliberately or not—'badly' drawn. Yet, the art functions perfectly fine. On the other hand, many illustrators simply craft their work with incredible technical skill. And this works for its purpose, as well."

Figure 5-9: "You can have all the ideas in the world, but if you don't develop the foundations and mechanics of bringing that about, it's never going to happen," Melia says. "Concept is terribly important, but you need to bring that concept to a visual place where it works!"
© Paul Melia

Figure 5-10a and b: "Most illustrators fit somewhere in that middle," Wittfooth says, "where both conceptual skills and drawing skills play a fairly equal role."
© Martin Wittfooth

The Weight of It

Douglas Goldsmith is an Assistant Professor at Kent State University. He understands that concept can't outweigh the image (and vice versa). That relationship of meaningful purpose and visual intrigue makes for a strong marriage.

"Some students have considerable difficulty with drawing," Goldsmith admits, "but they have great ideas. And there's the child-like self who tries everything in all media and gets head-to-toe covered in paint," he smiles. "Then there's the processor/thinker," he considers. "This artist strives to strengthen the concept as well as the craft of drawing."

Figure 5-11: "I don't expect all students to fall in love with drawing," Goldsmith points out, "but you need to know how to draw if you're going to do *anything*—especially if you process and sketch for a client."
© Douglas Goldsmith

Figure 5-12: In an interview with *Idea-Illustrator* magazine, Tran says, "I wouldn't say my problems stem from the technical side, but more from the conceptual side. Most times, I'm not only producing the final art, but also coming up with the concept for the image as well, so coming up with ideas is usually half the battle. Unfortunately, sometimes it takes longer to nail down a good concept then others, and at times it seems like no good idea is coming at all. In these cases, I usually go for walks, read news, and generally stimulate my brain, hoping something will spark an idea."
© Huan Tran

A Quandary

"The conundrum of conceptual versus drawing skills is too black and white," Huan Tran insists. "The question boils down to what you prefer to do and where one excels. The logical step is to market to the demographic that will love your work."

"Drawing skills come with practice—outside of school, on your own time," Tran says. "Growing concepts, however, is not an easy thing to do on one's own. Exploring your conceptual skills is very important. This is where a good teacher can enable you to see new perspectives; to generate fresh ideas and help you gauge your strengths; to figure out what kind of illustration you want to pursue."

Surprise!

Geneviève Kote graduated with a design degree from Ontario College of Art and Design in Toronto. Kote appreciates that communicating a message entails attracting the eye; finding a new twist; nailing that element of *surprise*.

"You can actually do something both fun *and* conceptual," says Kote, "but I'm not a big fan of brilliant ideas that seem to be drawn by a four year old. I need more than just an idea—I need to love what I see."

Figure 5-13: Kote's funny characters and vibrant colors combine to create images jam packed with a real joie de vivre. And she wants you to know that practice is good for you. "However," she smiles, "after work, there are other things I am interested in. I'd go crazy if I'm *only* doing art. You need a break; it's too easy to just stay inside when you work at home."
© Geneviève Kote

✔ Check Point: Murphy's Law

Kelly Murphy teaches at Rhode Island School of Design, Massachusetts College of Art, and Montserrat College of Art. As a student (at RISD) she grew to appreciate the myriad ways of making and describing line. Here's our chapter checkpoint, courtesy of Ms. Murphy:

1. The very first day of college, I was instructed to *throw* the charcoal at the newsprint. I thought to myself, "Oh god, I'm in a room of lunatics. The inmates are running the asylum."

2. Invite line in from the outside. My drawing instructors at Montserrat College of Art were constantly telling me that and I'd ask: what does that mean…

3. It means that it really isn't about holding a piece of charcoal at a precise angle; it's more about getting a 20-second figure pose down with a few perfect swooshes of that vine…

4. It means that it was about a sophisticated eye that could grasp the key elements of weight and angle to interpret an object in 2-D space…

5. And, of course, it was *very* much about concept.

6. Concept gives meaning and drive. Fred Lynch taught me how solve a visual problem; that concept is the reason your artwork exists.

7. Concept does not need to be a life changing revelation. Successful concept can be direct and simple. A successful concept can have a sense of humor as well as engaging characters.

8. Line creates a skeletal system and structure. Value acts as the circulatory system (tone is crucial to composition).

9. Tone propels concept and narrative, plus delivers mood and atmosphere. Tone holds the piece together on many levels. The only way I can approach the actual physical act of painting is through a thorough tonal underpainting.

10. According to Lynch (who described it perfectly): "Illustrators live to communicate, to express ideas to the world." Fred was the first teacher to make me understand that I was entering a noble profession.

On a very remarkable first day of class (see above), Murphy remembers, "Fred gave a daunting assignment for first timers: illustrate 100 apples. No other instruction but that.

"Around apple 20, it became pretty clear that there were no limits. I still approach every assignment in this fashion. Upon reading a story or article, I compile a list of keywords and central characters. At this point, I ask myself if I can substitute or simplify any of these with a shape or a symbol.

"It's safe to say," Murphy considers, "that if I did not have the 100 Apples assignment, I might not have fully grasped the level of research and exhaustion of ideas that is necessary."

© Kelly Murphy

Capable

Finally, a last word about a peripheral concern when considering concept. Shanth Enjeti doesn't think you'll find a wholly original work anywhere. Which would mean—if we adhere to Enjeti's notion—that there are no original concepts either. That's a debate for another time (and another book), but it's worth your attention (regardless of "right or wrong").

I do know that Enjeti firmly believes in the absolute importance of *authenticity*. And that's only a good thing. You don't have to draw like everybody, you just have to draw like yourself—to be real. Work from simple confidence and personal honesty. Understand what you bring to the drawing table. And as Enjeti will remind you, "You are the only one capable of manifesting this."

This can be both liberating and challenging. And it weeds out a bunch of excuses, as originality can thus derive from *content,* not execution (and content derives from concept…get it?) There is no shortage of master technicians out there (you may even be one). But factor in a superior grasp of concept and you can actually eliminate competition.

© Michael Fleishman

CHAPTER SUMMARY

In this chapter we discussed concept: how drawing is about communication, and that drawing communicates through concept (a.k.a., the big idea). We considered what an illustration is "really" about—what you are trying to say, and how you go about saying it (conceptually and technically). We looked at how artistic perception forges technique and influences tools (and vice versa). We examined how ideas dictate content, and how content then determines composition and impacts fundamentals (line, value, color, pattern and texture, etc).

Working It Out

1. Keep It Simple

Giovanni Da Re says, "I live for the chance to synthesize concept with simple shapes, unobtrusive textures, and catchy color." That's your assignment here: illustrate a complex concept—self-esteem and self-image, for instance—just through rudimentary shapes, simple textures, and a limited color palette.

2. Don't Tell Me

Concept and composition are integrated. Create an illustration where the concept is advanced solely by the composition of design elements—no figurative components may be used. So, for example, an illustration done for an article about the physical stresses of driving too fast must *not* show cars or people.

3. Double Trouble

"The best illustration challenges interpretation," says Robert Brinkerhoff. The job: create an illustration that can be interpreted any number of different (or contradictory) ways.

Home and Away

1. Like Wow

Do a long series of illustrations based on a metaphor or simile. For those of you who are green at this, such an assignment may be a battle for you (two metaphors for the price of one). But I trust you'll get it done like clockwork, and quick as a wink (two similes).

2. An Apple a Day

Illustrate 100 apples. No other instruction but that. No limits.

3. Smack Down

Do a series of illustrations that alternate your time/energy investment. For instance, do a drawing in 60 minutes, now do one that takes 20 hours. Subject matter: pick various paired opposites that are at odds in some way (for instance, organic/mechanical; simple/fancy; rich/poor). How critical is your deadline in fully realizing and rendering your concept?

Chapter 6

Composition

© Tina Sweep

Visual Balance and Order

This chapter discusses a key foundation that is all about both communication *and* foundations: composition—the ordered arrangement of visual elements within the picture plane.

I'm careful to use the term *ordered* and not the adjective *orderly*. Putting design components in the "right" place, in the "correct" order (while establishing a "good" balance of artful mechanics) is specific to *your* particular picture and that picture's unique concept. It doesn't

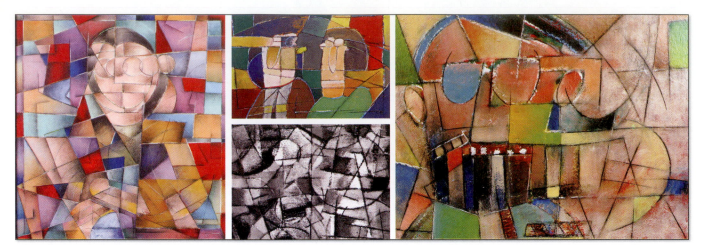

necessarily mean an "orderly" composition. A frenzied or chaotic design—if duly considered and measured—could simply be considered an active composition—all part of the master plan behind your concept, content and message.

Thought and Action

To understand "how to create" you might want to emphasize drama through contrast. This could be taking your cast (and their serious conversation about the affordability of fixing up the house) and moving them from an interior room to the great outdoors. Or you go from a shady character barely seen via a limited light source to full light.

How about a subtle and unsettling shift in perspective? Tap into movement; utilizing sequential (and/or color) elements to depict a life change, mood swing, slow metamorphosis, or sudden switch—devices that carry characters (and character traits) through a real *story*.

Figure 6-1: I'm kind of a closet cubist. But I guess I've done enough of these that I'm truly out by now. Cubism fascinates me: the geometry of the compositional form and its various incarnations as the style progressed over time; the cast of characters (sure, Picasso's a big player, but I'm more of a Braque n' roll kinda guy); the concept, and its pervasive influence to this day. Talk about legs; cubism was red-hot fresh in 1909!

You know, there was cubist sculpture, and guys who actually wrote cubist poetry and plays! How wild is that?

© Michael Fleishman

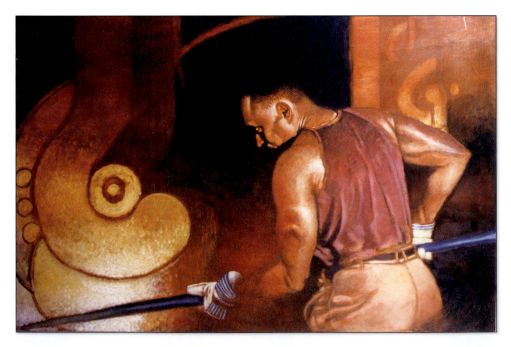

Figure 6-2: "View composition as just simple problem solving," says Alex Bostic, "or a fresh way to approach a particular drawing situation. It's much like shooting a mini movie. Don't talk about the story arc … *show* me—now I know what you're saying."

© Alex Bostic

I Really Want to Direct

Illustrator Boris Kulikov trained in theatrical costuming. So on his pages, you'll notice dynamic staging, dramatic color and lighting, and exquisitely staged page composition. You'll also see a highly tuned sense of color, texture and pattern, and characterization.

Kulikov tells you that what composition comes down to is *expression*. "Sometimes you can say *everything* in just a couple of lines," he asserts.

Push come to shove, Kulikov considers composition as the base. Line, color, and value are the important building blocks. It's these raw materials that develop an interesting and expressive composition and the very concept (of the illustration) itself. "Great skills with line, color, and value mean little if your composition is weak," Kulikov insists. "And pictures must reach a viewer—the art must stir up emotion. If a reader feels nothing at all, the artwork fails in its construction."

"If we talk about illustrating picture books," Kulikov states, "it's more interesting to illustrate a 'visual dialogue' based on an author's text and ideas. The goal is to capture the spirit of the words, to reach and touch a reader."

Kulikov loves playing with a story. As Bostic says earlier, "It's like a movie where you embrace the screenplay, but feel free to interpret it (within the designated boundaries, of course)."

"I feel I'm the writer and director, the cast, crew, and cameraman all at the same time," Kulikov smiles. "So I design sets and dress the costumes, develop histories and flesh out personalities, work out camera angles."

Figure 6-3: "Every detail counts," Kulikov says. "And I believe if an artist has fun with these details, readers will enjoy it too."

© Boris Kulikov

Get Back

Kathy Moore earned her BFA in Painting from Wright State University. Two of her former instructors are Diane Fitch and Glen Cebulash. Working with Fitch, Moore learned to measure forms in space, and how form and space relate to an edge. Fitch pushed structure that stems from drawing ability—in thought and action.

Moore's drawings are really a separate thing; they don't necessarily lead to paintings. And her drawings aren't preliminaries for paintings, either—a drawing is a finished, complete work in itself. All these efforts stand on their own merit.

"Maybe a third of my work is drawing," she estimates. "Large drawings. These don't *have* to so big, it's just how I like to work. My drawing board is probably 4-5 feet away—which is the way I do large paintings as well."

"I like to keep physically active. I'm getting back, looking at my motif and then walking up quickly to the drawing board. I make my marks and then get back again. Back and forth…working fast…it's almost like a dance, keeping my body physically engaged, my mind alert."

Figure 6-4 a and b: Approaching her subject slowly, Moore might hover close and look down. Perhaps it's simply backing up—a few feet left or right and you'll have an entirely new point of view. "I'm visually cropping as I study," Moore says, "positioning and measuring. This is a physically tiring exercise—much harder than just being the observer. "Sometimes I'll make thumbnails, usually black and white, acrylic tonal studies. Not exact compositions of the work in progress, but tone exercises that lend themselves to the development of the actual work."

6-4a © Kathy A. Moore

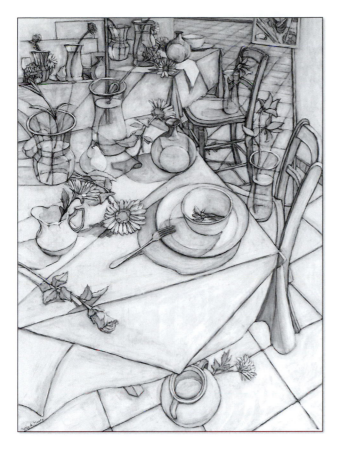

6-4b © Kathy A. Moore

On Purpose

Moore is resolute about getting her spot and keeping it. "A slight turn and you can lose the perspective," she explains. "I'll often mark my placement on the floor with a strip of tape."

Moore builds a work with purpose, and she works responsively. Thus, she is immersed in the yin and yang—the counterpoint—of her process. The focus is on composition. "I want to place the viewer in a hopefully interesting context—my immediate and intimate viewpoint," she tells you.

Direct Results

Sarah Mantell finally succumbed to the siren song of the reference photo. It happened in Fred Lynch's *Style and Substance* class.

Mantell went to college convinced she would do realistic oil paintings, even though, she says, "This didn't quite match the way I actually worked." So she spent her first two school years bouncing around between mediums and influences—a new way of working every week, never getting *really* good at anything, hoping to hit upon something that felt right. "I was trying to find a way to combine bits of all the artists I loved, *all at once,*" she smiles.

This proved to be slightly difficult. Captivated with the reference photos she took, Mantell loved rendering faces and hands, but felt compelled to reduce objects and spaces to lines and shapes, and to leave certain elements open-ended. "I liked unfinished *better,*" Mantell says, "but I didn't know how to balance 'resolved' and 'unfinished' at that time."

So, heeding that dusty art school catchphrase, but with a new spin—eventually it hits Mantell to *literally* work off of the reference. "I pasted it down on my board and set to work," she tells us. "Something about that just felt right. I liked that the things I loved in the photo were already there to be *edited* instead of recreated."

"Once I started using the photos, other stuff got easier too," she comments. "My favorite teachers always stressed thumbnails, and I couldn't do it. I would spend forever trying to get the twist of the body or some expression when I was supposed to be doing quick, tiny little sketches."

Mantell realized she was working backwards, and eventually stopped fighting the natural order of things. Using Photoshop to play around with her photos as thumbnails, she discovered the flexibility to juggle picture elements and trust her instincts. "The details are already there. I can take away, add on, tear off, attach and re-tear, layer my paint and paper—it feels really right. It's much more of a 3D process. I'm not working purely on a surface but working *with* the surface."

"My teachers were absolutely right about where I needed to be going," she concludes, "I just had this strange way of getting there."

Figure 6-5: "The physicality of the art is very important to me," Mantell will tell you. "Artists don't blink an eye regarding taboo subject matter, but we'll cringe if someone tears their work down the middle. This makes me laugh! It feels, just for a moment, like I am doing *extreme* art."

© Sarah B. Mantell

✔ Check Point: Geometry Lesson

Paul Melia embraces a linear approach to design that grows a composition geometrically (and if it's not a contradiction in terms, somewhat organically, too). All his paintings reflect this distinctly linear, geometric tendency. Even portraits. Here's his method:

1. Focus on the rhythm of shapes. "It's just my particular way of doing it," he says, "I'm a 'geometric kind of guy.'"

2. Melia usually commences with a charcoal pencil drawing, and subsequently layers with color.

3. He invariably begins with the eyes and works out from there. "This is a fun, logical place to start," he says…

4. …which, according to some artists (Melia included), may classically be the "wrong" way to do it.

5. Traditional training dictates that you draw the *head* initially, seeing the basic mass first (so on a portrait, you rough in the shape of the head, and *then* go back and pull out details—a rather tried and true methodology).

6. But Melia builds all the shapes *out* from the eye until it fashions a head. He looks for any kind of shape that defines a facial plane—the myriad triangles and squares and circles that ultimately form noses and eyes and cheeks, etc.

7. To Melia, this is a clear and simple process (and if you think about it, it really makes a lot of sense). "Everybody's face and figure share the same basic shapes," Melia tells you.

8. Every figure, each face, is individual and slightly different. However, these unique spatial relationships *always relate to each other*. "It's a wonderful way to draw," Melia states, "difficult at first, but worth the practice."

9. Melia works and plays with line and geometric composition to craft a canny likeness. Lines inform the basic design, while color (and, of course, tone) sandwiches in between.

10. Learn to isolate shapes. For instance, pulling shapes together to create a nose. "So, around that eye—anybody's eye—is the eyebrow and the socket," Melia tells you. "That's a definite shape. And between the two eyes, on the top of the nose is another specific little trapezoid that fits everybody's face. However wide that is determines where you place the other eye, and so on."

11. The human figure is arguably the most difficult thing to render, but Melia applies this geometric intuition to make the figure, too.

© Paul Melia

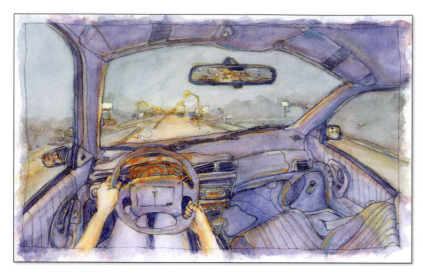

Figure 6-6: Intuitive artists like Sweep know that value is *the* key to composition. The darkest dark next to the lightest light will draw the viewer's eye. The object with the most value contrast brings you right there. Spatial distance is established through a progression of values. A full range of values from dark to light helps to define all objects.

© Tina Sweep

The Line on Value

"Composition is intuitive," Tina Sweep tells us. And for Sweep (who, as a student, was selected as the Society Of Illustrators' very first Zankel Scholar in 2007), the key to a good composition is value structure. Whether it's a dark shape on a light field or a light figure on a dark background, values define your content.

"Depending on the artist," Sweep says, "the purest blacks and whites are established first; after which, mid-tones are created between the two. Other artists block in a midrange of values and apply those pure blacks and whites last."

It's not so much the order of these events. It's that the events are all in good order. So instinctively, line must also be a big part of this mix. But, as Sweep states, "A consistent, flat line is boring…there's no information! Variation in line weight adds interest, engages the eye; expresses space, weight, movement (and rest). Line itself can show value structure: for instance, multiple lines will show a build-up of darker value and form, establishing the light side. A break in a line will indicate a highlight; weight can be created through pressure; with added interest through a tremor in the movement of the pen."

Can You See It?

Allegra Agliardi lives and works in Milan, Italy. She won the 2009 "Young Illustrator of The Year" award at the Festival of Illustration in Pavia, Italy. Back in her student days, Agliardi recalls that color was "just something to add to line." It's different for her today. "I play with the potential of both line and color," she says. "Each has a different role, depending on the image."

Agliardi understands that pure color can often be the main event, or "just" decorative support. Line and color will work together and translate into the suggestion of space. Color and line play an emotional game of relationships and combinations. But while line practice and color theory are key, *observation of value* is really your first move.

"Value, for me, is often bound to realism," Agliardi comments, "an instrument of shape, space, and place. Value is technical—a means of understanding; a method of study and observation. When I need to do a realistic or descriptive illustration, value steps in to simplify that process."

And real or abstract, it's about study. Research. Focus. *Then* you make decisions about line, color, and value. As Agliardi puts it, "Concept and emotion are actually the true starting points—even before you consider tone and color, technique and composition.

"The goal is to keep *all* that in mind so the job can flow naturally. Focus on the feeling of the piece and the quality of the image. *Communicate.*"

The Long Unwinding Road

Agliardi tells you that composition follows concept. You show what's important in an image by creating a "roadmap" for the eye. Color helps, but color can't do it all (especially if the composition isn't working).

"A complex composition calls for simple color," she advises you. "A simple composition needs interesting color and line. Saying that, a simple composition of multiple elements creates an image that can be viewed at length and discovered slowly."

Saying *that*, try using fewer elements but make them count. Be strong (and more precise) with less or more—but make it *your* critical choice.

Accentuate the Positive (and Negative)

Whether it's thinking about form or deciphering your composition, concentrate on positive and negative relationships. And although it might be the easiest pos/neg combo to dope out, it's not so much about black and white. It's really more about what's labeled figure/ground (foreground figure against background). Structure negative space to sort out the positive shapes. By nature's law, negative space creates positive shape (and vice versa). It's definitely a symbiotic thing, a give and take relationship.

Big (But Not) Easy

Susan Loeb was classically trained in oils to draw and paint from direct observation. About 30 years ago she transitioned into painting with watercolors (still from direct observation). Longing to use her art to deal with a nagging dissatisfaction about her work (and problems with her home, New Orleans), she began experimenting with photographs.

Enlarging and cropping the pictures to get to a satisfactory composition, the reference image is drawn on Arches paper and painted with black paint. "The white is the paper," she says, "the black is the paint."

"Black and white represents my feelings about losing New Orleans on so many levels," Loeb tells you. "Traditional rendering (and color) is much too romantic, sort of like an Andrew Wyeth. Something about the black and white was very powerful. And after much experimentation—ink, collage, acrylic, charcoal, working small (the paintings have grown to be quite large—up to 8 ft. tall)—I decided to try watercolors, and it worked!"

Figure 6-7: "Keep it vital; not so studied, not too perfect," Agliardi sums up. "Make sure your illustration is quite alive; with all the natural imperfections—like life itself—right there. Like life itself, it's more interesting that way."

© Allegra Agliardi

6-8a © Michael Cho

6-8b © Rama Hughes

6-8c © Kevin Huizenga

6-8d © Gwenda Kaczor

Figure 6-8a-d: It's not always so black and white, but point of fact, positive and negative relationships actually form shape and dope out composition in your drawing (negative space actually establishes positive shape). Dynamic figure/ground provides a dramatic visual hook that can enhance character development (as well as tone of voice). Case in point: these terrific illustrations by Rama Hughes, Kevin Huizenga, Gwenda Kaczor, and Michael Cho.

A word about the two illustrators we haven't met previously. Gwenda Kaczor is a freelance illustrator based in Denver, Colorado. Rama Hughes currently resides in Los Angeles, California.

3-D or not 3-D—That Is the Question?

Why talk about working 3-D in a drawing book? First, realize that there's usually a *drawing* behind all creative and crafty endeavors. I strongly suggest you do *some* kind of 3-D stuff—your sense of 2-D composition will only benefit. But there's even a more compelling (and related) rationale: for "visual people" of all persuasions, drawing is simply another life function (like eating, drinking, breathing, etc.).

By Hand

Freelance illustrator Bob Selby was a staff illustrator at the Providence Journal, and taught college courses at a number of institutions; he lives in Vermont. Margaret Cusack graduated from Pratt Institute with a BFA (cum laude) in graphic design. She creates stitched and dimensional artwork/illustration, is a graphic designer and folk artist, and even worked as an art director from 1968 to 1972. Aliza Lelah attended the University of Vermont, received her MFA in Painting from Savannah College of Art and Design (SCAD) in 2007, and now maintains a studio in Washington DC.

"The artists I know all seem to think with their pencils," smiles Selby, "as if it were a logical extension of their thought process. When they're creating or even discussing a project, the first thing they seem to do is to reach for a pencil. I know I do."

"In contrast to traditional 'flat' artwork," Cusack chimes in, "dimensional illustration blends fine art, illustration, and sculpture into a single image. And that's what grabs the attention and stops you from turning the page. Dimensional illustration's '*unusualness*'—if there is such a word—makes the image intriguing and more memorable."

"Especially," she continues, "if that art has obviously been created with the human hand, as opposed to illustration that *looks* dimensional but is actually computer-generated."

Figure 6-11a and b: Illustrator Ken Meyer, Jr., out of Savannah College of Art and Design, says that a sculpture class helped him see things "in the round," and not just contour shapes bounding objects (the focus of many artists who draw exclusively). He's right. 3-D mechanics and design can greatly benefit your 2-D sense of composition.

Look. Study. Jump in. Dig below the surface layer of your art. This may even lead to you illustrating dimensionally! You may even find you *love* the unique technical challenge and creative point of view. Case in point (and *needlepoint*, at that): these works by Cusack and Lelah.

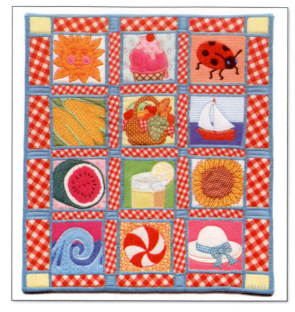

6-11a © Margaret Cusack

6-11b © Aliza Lelah

Lelah says she "draws with thread," sewing by hand cautiously, but using the sewing machine in a way that is both free and passionate. Her stitches tell the story of her characters. "Of all of us," she smiles.

Muck it Up

I admit it: I'm big on the idea of a rounded, interdisciplinary education. I'm not necessarily talking about a formal program. It can be the simplest of self-studies: actually *look* at a thing, then get your hands in there.

"Getting your hands dirty" provides the understanding that dives you (and the viewer) below the surface of your paper or canvas. There are considerable benefits to working from observation (life drawing, still-life, drawing right on the spot). It's beneficial to take a sculpture or ceramics class, maybe even *build* something—any of which usually starts with drawing up a plan or a technical drawing anyway.

The Fine Print

Just a little FYI: photos are certainly traditional and standard reference tools and layout devices. But a photograph doesn't replace real anatomy, true perspective, and actual light. And often, a photo sports poor lighting and/or mediocre composition that compromises creative vision and mechanical structure.

Direct reference can be essential to establishing an image (and ultimately a successful piece). So if photo reference is a big part of your process, heed Steven Hughes' good advice: "It's good to exercise a different muscle," says Hughes, "get out and find the needed reference yourself. Think it through *before* you lean on a photo too much. Maybe something else presents itself; you don't want a photo to be your sole impetus."

To which Sweep adds, "In my own work, I am always affected by the reference that I create or find, but I consciously do not allow the reference to dictate the piece. In other words, I use my reference, but I don't marry it without reason."

CHAPTER SUMMARY

In this chapter we continued our discussion of drawing as communication and how fundamentals play a critical role here. This chapter discusses composition—a key foundation that is about both communication *and* foundations.

We examined the terms *ordered* and *orderly* in terms of composition, concept, content, and message. We talked about drama through contrast, composition as problem solving, how compositional structure stems from drawing ability.

We explored composition from a number of different angles: the use of reference, research, and the importance of study; geometric design and spatial relationships; how value works to focus composition; the path from concept to composition.

We looked at 3-D composition and the relevance of a rounded, interdisciplinary education.

Working It Out

1. Vary Nice

Try to avoid clichés in your composition. Look beyond the "textbook" solutions. Think variation. In class we will do an illustration where you only use decidedly non-traditional shapes—no simple squares, rectangles, circles, ovals—and we won't use the same shape twice.

2. Off the Cuff

Pick a concept or topic to illustrate (for instance, steroid use amongst small town librarians is running rampant). Create an illustration that is composed on the fly, as you go—right on the board. No prelims!

3. On the Cuff

Take that same concept. Now, brainstorm, do thumbnails and multiple roughs (both color and tone) before you commit to the final.

Do this finish, and compare/contrast both versions (#2 and #3). Consider your process and both experiences. Which is the better illustration—why?

Home and Away

1. Comic Relief

Do a visual narrative (high brows may call this a graphic novel; but if you're a proud-as-punch low brow you probably still call them comic books). Design each comic panel as an individual composition in its own right (as well as being a complete representation of whatever you're trying to draw—in style, technique, and concept). Each and every panel should also hold up as a mini-masterpiece that can stand alone from its generic page.

2. Of Course

3-D mechanics and design can greatly benefit your 2-D sense of composition.

Take a class (or work at home for a semester) in a 3-D discipline: sculpture, pottery, metals (which could be jewelry), fabrics. Look, study, and learn. Jump in. Get your hands dirty. Dig below the surface layer of your art.

3. Observe, Please

Take a *figure drawing* class or find a studio that offers sessions with a model. This should *not* be a general drawing class; work exclusively from the figure (and observation) only. No reference! Do not work from photographs, please.

Option: try Melia's geometeric compositional method as he outlines it above.

The Tools

Lift You Up

Section 2 is all about the basics. The rudiments of drawing lay the groundwork for all that. But maybe I'm gilding the lily here. It's also very true that drawing just simply "makes you feel good"; no fancy college words required or metaphysical ramblings need apply.

"I don't think about what I do or why I do it," says Drew Struzan, "because it's become just a function of my ability to do it. I draw out of my training, my experience, and my creativity."

Students may not know what Struzan is talking about here. What Struzan is saying is that you train your eyes and your hands, you hone the ability to see and comprehend (and then translate). "Ultimately," he states, "a practicing artist concentrates more on that creativity, what you're trying to achieve emotionally or intellectually. The tools serve *that*. The tools are just a means to reaching an end.

"It has to be about what you are trying to say, what you're trying to emote, what you're trying to communicate," Struzan advises. "That's the point of it—that's the stuff that lives. Talk to people's hearts.

Nothing is 'wrong' with a great technique, but have something to say to back it up."

© Copyright Drew Struzan

Chapter 7

Line

© Paul Hoppe

The Gift of Language

If you've ever heard someone remark, "That drawing *speaks* to me," then you understand what Peter Cusack refers to when he says, "Drawing is indeed *my* language." The language of drawing has guided him on an adventure to discovering his truest self. "Drawing is a gift," he smiles. "It's given me a means to communicate with the world."

A younger Cusack loved doodling cartoons in his school notebooks. As an adult, he cites the influence of Watteau and Rubens, Hopper and Messonier. Their work "spoke" directly to Cusack, and he praises these artists as "amazing teachers for me."

Figure 7-1: The work of Cusack.
© Peter Cusack

The art of such consummate draftsmen crackles with life, keen observation, and unique characterization—all hallmarks of Cusack's fine work, as well.

Lay It on the Line

Teachers speak the language of drawing. Terry Shoffner, who teaches at Ontario College of Art and Design in Toronto, also holds firm to that idea and says, "Drawing is the foundation of visual vocabulary."

"Line is both ancient and modern," illustrator and teacher Whitney Sherman says. So line has history. (Art history?) Drawing is the most direct way to put some order in your creative world; it's the express lane to that visual language we're talking about.

Thinking about drawing as a language may be somewhat abstract. But drawing itself is somewhat abstract, for, as Diane Fitch points out, "The world isn't made out of lines; we don't exist in black and white, our 'edges' aren't readily defined."

Thus drawing is about translation; in other words, *abstraction*. Your first marks force you to deal with the picture plane and the illusion of reality. Translating three dimensions into two rubs you right up against the push and pull of visual perception and actual organization—the language of volume and dimension, positive and negative, space and structure.

Naturally

Marshall Arisman points out that there are no lines in nature. What can be perceived as a line—a hair, a spider's web, etc.—is, upon magnification, the edge of a form or mass. "When I work in line," Arisman says, "my brain is visualizing the form *separating* the lines. My hand then considers the width

Figure 7-2: Shoffner's former student, Marcos Chin, tells us, "There may be a 'bigger picture,' and I think, as you mature, you get more in touch with what makes you different from your teachers and peers. And that begins with drawing."
© Marcos Chin

of the line in relationship to the form. For example: lines nearer the light source tend to be thinner and lines farther away become thicker."

Stressing the Line

"And lines are weird," says Peter Arkle, who's frequently amused by the "strange things that happen" when drawing similar items at different scales—especially when drawing faces.

"Plus there's always a message," he continues. "It can be very rudimentary, but every drawing you make is meant to say something to someone. Would I continue to draw if no one could see my drawings? The answer is no."

"Ideally," Arkle goes on, "you try to make a funny (or smart) statement with a few, immediate lines. The idea is then much more important than the rendering. Thinking up clever ideas is much more stressful than just drawing. An afternoon lost in an illustration—including drawing thousands of hairs—is a much happier time, compared to a day spent trying to come up with ideas!"

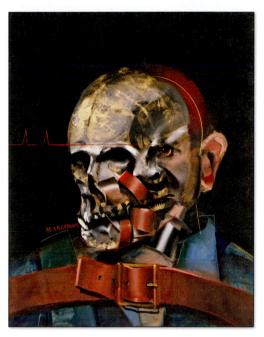

Figure 7-3: The work of Arisman.
© Marshall Arisman

✔ Check Point: One Wild Hair

For Arkle, "Drawing every single twig on a tumbleweed is lots of fun when you know that's exactly what someone wants." Here's this chapter's checkpoint, according to Mr. Arkle (who usually knows what *he* wants):

1. Consider lines that evolved from cartoons… speed lines off moving objects, for instance… this practice is exactly in the middle between drawing and writing.

2. Drawing a big portrait of a man with stubble, it's easy to use dots (very short lines, actually) to represent the hairs. If you draw a tiny version of this same guy, the same dots might be as big as the dots representing his eyes. Often, you can get away with this! We are used to perceiving what lines *mean* rather than what they look like.

3. I still rarely use tone in my drawings. Even when working in color, I start with a solid black and white line drawing and then add flat color.

4. And I use color in a very basic way: grass is green, the sky is blue, and tomatoes are red.

5. I always try to get it as simple as possible; this deliberately makes the drawing easier to read.

6. Color decisions can be daunting. I perpetually get to a point when I feel like I have run out of colors…

7. …which, of course, is ridiculous. Limiting colors and tones can be useful, and looking at the real world only helps.

8. I love to keep nearly everything monochromatic (or tones of one color) and have one unique element that can then pop out.

9. I also love to draw hair at a scale where one hair is nearly as thick as the line coming out of my pen. Up close I am making loads of wavy undulating abstract lines, but from a distance I am making a realistic drawing.

10. A similar thing happens when drawing food. Up close: loads of dots and weird little scribbles; from a distance: an accurate drawing of a salad leaf.

The work of Arkle.
© Peter Arkle

Balance

Based in Brooklyn, Paul Hoppe says, "There is no universal purpose of drawing. But it's really about communication and intention. Even a simple, sharp truth affords some room for nonsense, for experimentation, for play," he opines. "That balance varies from task to task."

Mechanically, Hoppe is always concerned with balance: the ratio of line weight to paper size. "Puny lines on a large piece of paper just don't create tension and can't divide the space for me." For Hoppe, thicker strokes focus his direction and set up primary shapes while thinner lines establish detail (as well as secondary directions and elements). Invariably, his lines have a degree of rough power. "I love the irregularity, the energy—the very way that brush (or pen) and ink behave," he smiles, "it's not a static thing."

Figure 7-4: "I use all sorts of tools and pens," Hoppe comments. "Variation—and play—add the element of surprise. I even use white correction pen within large, black shapes. This helps me create elements I just couldn't do if I were actually trying to draw these forms and lines in the negative (by leaving them out)."

© Paul Hoppe

What's (or Where's) My Line?

This might be an unusual way to discuss the topic of *line*, but I challenge you to think about line quality by considering the *absence* of line.

Huh?

Sure! It's all relative—and relevant. Line quality *is* important to Michael Cho, but line itself? Not *so* crucial these days. "I used to obsess about super-clean line quality when I did more outline-based illustration," Cho explains. But now he's not as concerned with *pristine* as he is with *precise*, whether it's a sterile line or a messy stroke. "I'm not seeking perfection," he says, "but I do want the exact line *I* require."

Keeping It Light

Cho stresses the quality of *light*, which conveys mood and atmosphere. Learned essentially by studying the work of the great Alex Toth, Cho follows a number of dictates governing that process:

1. Eliminate the redundant line.

2. Don't render the line; render the shading cast by the light.

3. Drop out lines to suggest light (the sun bouncing off a surface; imply a bright light by putting down a lot of black around it).

"This opened up my thinking tremendously," Cho informs us. "You don't draw both sides or all the edges; you figure out the lighting and draw the shadow. The viewer fills in the other line with their imagination."

In Cho's fine illustration, contour and mass—plus the aforementioned mood, atmosphere, and character—are implied with value. Some of his best work is in silhouette, and he often adds a half-tone that becomes a third color (beyond black and white). This third color allows Cho to flesh out form, fills in receding space, and bolsters visual interest.

7-5a © Michael Cho

7-5b © Michael Cho

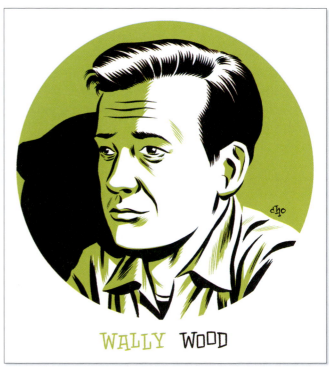

Figure 7-5a-d: The gods are with us tonight, as seen in these great portraits by Cho.

7-5c © Michael Cho

7-5d © Michael Cho

Value, according to Cho, is "really the most important element. Unless it's a full-color drawing, I work these two colors simultaneously, somewhat spontaneously, and it's just plain fun—far more than if I was doing two separate plates (or overlays) in a prescribed order."

Figure 7-6: Cho's work is greatly informed by shape and form, limited color, plus texture and pattern. "Texture and pattern can act as a separate color, add another value, and may even serve as problem solvers," Cho says. "For instance, texture can break foreground from background."
© Michael Cho

At the Core

The fundamental element of *line* deals with mass and form; it can establish and strengthen spatial (and shape) relationships through gesture or detail; by addressing the whole or partial form (inside or out); or by perceiving the edges of that subject matter.

Consider the *combination* of basics that enables visual organization—that facilitates a practical application to broaden your experience. "It's about the organic relationship of parts to the whole—value to color, color to line, line to shape, shape to form," says Jacqueline Kahane Freedman.

Freedman, a Cleveland-based freelance artist and teacher, advises you to seriously regard those relationships. "If you're talking about line, understand the directness of your strokes; that each mark has a life of its own," she says. "All the lines you make should relate to the growth of the drawing—down to up, inside out."

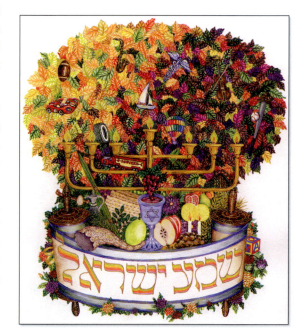

Figure 7-7: "My illustration and teaching is based on life experience," says Freedman. "Art. Life. It's all about the same stuff: Basics. Tradition. The relationship of parts to the whole."
© Jacqueline Kahane Freedman

Mythodology

Jack Tom grew up in San Francisco and presently lives and works in Connecticut. He's an accomplished illustrator, designer, and teacher of Graphic Design, Typography, and Illustration. "It's not easy to articulate in words what artists do and how we do it," says Tom. "But I truly believe drawing is thinking. And thinking and drawing is communication."

Figure 7-8: Tom's illustration is always about design.
© Jack Tom

When he considers visual communication, Tom starts with line, "the guideline to the drawing itself," he says. "I use color to enhance emotion, mood and meaning, and I adore the mythology behind certain colors from an historical standpoint."

"But good illustration boasts all the important elements of design. When I'm doing an illustration I am thinking design—always: color and value; line and shape; balance, composition, and point of interest; a main idea central to the composition. Definitely good craftsmanship."

On Line

You know *line*! As a toddler, you were already a veteran scribbler of the Crayola® wars. And once you learned how to write, you actually began your career as a professional mark maker.

A line can throw you a curve (or be your straight man). Great lines think alike. If one line is a hoot, repetition is the life of the party. A line is the meeting between two points, but lines can also divide (organize) or separate (clarify) those points.

The most interesting lines may seem to have no specific direction (or apparent association) and frequently are anything but straight, but that's the point—an ostensibly random or chaotic path leads the eye to a more interesting final destination. What looks like nervous energy—even disorderly conduct—is actually an active, visual interactive exercise for artist and audience.

Learn to love your lines in all their glory! Great lines don't have to be squeaky clean, razor-sharp, or (especially) ruled and straight. Smudge or stutter line quality, risk a speeding ticket or slow down to a sheer crawl.

Figure 7-9: "At the beginning, it will be representational," Douglas Goldsmith says. "As students progress, concepts and storytelling, craft and design, movement and a sense of visual hierarchy—all become more important."

"There's an emotional connection crucial to successful visual communication. A weak idea, no matter how well you draw, is still a weak idea. You must be confident. *Not arrogant*—understand that making a mark without hesitation, a line that carries emotion, requires assertiveness."

© Douglas Goldsmith

Fudge focus or smear the value range (even within the stroke itself). Follow your density and relish unexpected and interesting value changes.

Empower your lines with subtlety or brute force. Disregard the edge of the paper. Feather your edges. Never bother to color within the lines unless you want to. Embrace irregularity—every stop and start, all the delightful hop, skip, and jump of it. Reunite thick to thin, thick and thin (twin concerns perhaps separated at birth by your realistic drawing phase).

Splatter the joy of the line over your page with echoes and variations of the above—all in *one* line, or one with all lines.

Figure 7-10: Matt Kindt says that he *almost* feels subject matter dictates the quality of the line. "It depends on the character," he explains, "their personality, gender, etc. I'll adjust my line subtly, maybe unconsciously." Kindt talks about capturing the moment and not overworking the illustration. His pencils are usually very rough, allowing for a lot of wiggle room and space to improvise as he draws.

"Loose preliminaries keep my interest up when I begin with ink and brush," he says. "Static images mean that my line ends up somewhat stagnant. With action, I'm practically drawing in real-time—the faster the action, the quicker my brushstroke."
© Matt Kindt

Over the Edge

Paul Melia suggested we think, see, and draw geometrically; to push the squares and rectangles, circles and ovals, triangles, etc. within the structure of your illustration.

But another great way we understand mass and form is through gesture and contour line. Gesture and contour help you relate space and shape as an exercise connecting part to part, or a part to the whole. The study of figure drawing—regarded by many as *the* hardest artistic challenge—particularly benefits from the practice of gestural line or contour drawing.

A contour line is not simply some puffed up *outline*—an outline is only the *outside* of the shell. Contour lines seek to reveal a *complete shape* by defining the *edges* of the whole form (inside and out).

Gesture drawings also cover that edge thing, as well as addressing the whole form (as in 3-D). A gesture study is not about flat vertical planes or diagonal lines (although such angular line treatment would make for an interesting application of the basic idea). Like contour drawing, gestural line is not a glorified outline of your subject matter.

A good visual metaphor? In your mind's eye, wrap a piece of string, yarn, or wire (representing line weight and character) *around* the form you are drawing. You are now essentially packaging the shape with that length of line—no mere gesture at all.

No Mere Gesture

Shoffner teaches figure drawing by starting with a gestural approach. "You must get a jump on the action of a pose immediately," he states, "especially in illustration where we often re-draw or refine our drawing." Shoffner says that there's a natural tightening which can make finished art a bit stiff or artificial; if you don't capture the action early, you won't get it back later.

7-11a © Vivienne Flesher

7-11b © Ward Schumaker

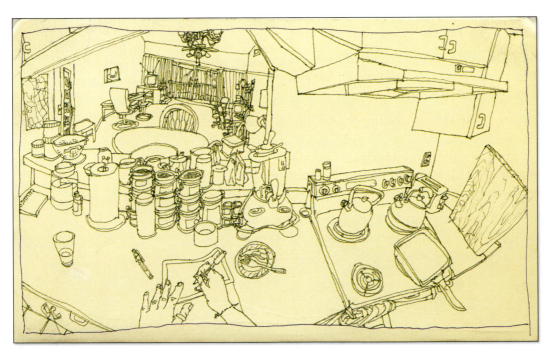

Figure 7-11a, b and c: We've met Tina Sweep previously. Ward Schumaker is married to Vivienne Flesher. They pursue their painting, illustration, and photography in San Francisco. "She's upstairs, I'm downstairs," Schumaker says, "and we meet for lunch in the kitchen."

All three artists offer fine perspectives on the power of purposeful, raw—even spare—line quality.

7-11c © Tina Sweep

A proponent of weight and mass drawing, Shoffner advises building up the bulk of the figure from the inside, although understanding structure is ultimately critical.

As Shoffner points out, targeting weight/mass is a good way to bulk up a gesture drawing. It also adds overall tone, crucial for composition. From here, you apply lighting and smart cropping—all of which zero in on expression.

At the Start

Glen Cebulash is an Associate Professor of Art and Art History at Wright State University, near Dayton, Ohio. "The most relevant starting point for most of my work is gesture," he says. "In that sense, it's fairly linear. It's about line quality; I throw a lot of lines up there and begin a process of erasing them and pulling back out of that."

Sometimes Cebulash does that with charcoal and erasers, but will also use that charcoal with ink or white acrylic (using the paint as the eraser). It's all very automatic, quick, spontaneous. And counter to what you'll hear frequently in these pages, he doesn't plan out the drawing (or painting for that matter) ahead of time. "I like the thing to evolve on the actual surface itself as opposed to doing preliminaries," he states. "The tendency is to improvise over days or weeks, drawing/redrawing, painting/repainting."

Figure 7-12: Beginners tend to faithfully define boundaries or overload on the small aspects of the figure or minor details of the drawing. It's the classic conundrum of not seeing the forest for the trees. In Shoffner's drawing class, figure studies aren't focused on anatomy, but *action* (what the model is doing, not what the model looks like).
© Terry Shoffner

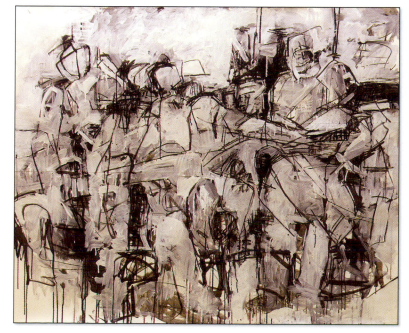

Figure 7-13: Cebulash works large. Scale is a consideration: a shoulder to elbow motion or full body response. It's not about small movements; not so delicate. He'll tape charcoal onto sticks (or switch to his left hand) to take the grace out of the act, and purposely leave pentimenti (ghosts of the under drawing or guide painting) in the work as residue of his process, his instinctive "rules of engagement."
© Glen Cebulash

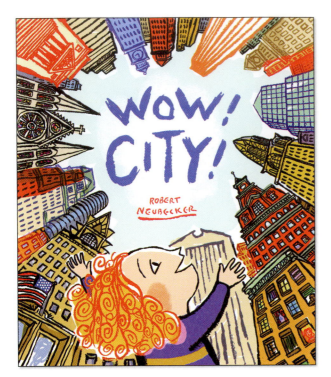

Figure 7-14: The exuberant, joyful work of Neubecker.
© Robert Neubecker

Joy

Robert Neubecker worked as a successful freelance illustrator for 20 years before doing his first children's picture book, *Wow! City.* Neubecker's illustration is really about joy and exuberance: the sheer fun of drawing, the passion of problem solving, the pleasure of an honest job well done. "And it's all about the *line*," he states. "Color is second. But line, for me, is like singing to a bird. I love to do it."

Prints Charming

"You can put so much emotion into a 'simple' black line," Neubecker tells us, and that rich, heavy black line is drawn with a brush and then colored on the computer. To keep it fresh, he'll often work without a pencil; just hit it straight with brush and ink.

Sometimes a drawing is actually done in pieces. Individual picture elements are redrawn by hand until Neubecker is satisfied with the result; each then scanned separately, and everything combined in the computer. And you might notice his, well, finger print—literally—all over his work. "The finger print thing?" he says reverently, "I got that from Saul Steinberg. He's a major influence."

The fingerprint motif introduces a little organic texture and breaks up flat, bright digital color. "Formerly, I'd stamp my finger prints from colored ink pads," Neubecker informs. "Now (after a period of not using finger prints at all) I use Photoshop. You can make a custom brush tool from any pattern, so I just use fingerprints."

Figure 7-15: "I'm an illustrator because it's a way to express my feelings, to communicate with people," Neubecker says. "I thought it the most relevant art form I could do—a thinking person's way to make a contribution to society. There's a wonderful service aspect to it. This is my niche; it's where I fit."

© Robert Neubecker

Speak to Me

Diane Fitch is a Professor of Art and Art History at Wright State University. "Technical issues are almost never to the point," she tells you when asked about *how* she teaches drawing. "Students often think that's what they want in terms of learning how to paint or draw; but to me that's really inconsequential."

Think Differently, Act Appropriately

Consider her point. Drawing is both thought and action. With a palette knife in your hand, you'll have to *think* differently than if you're wielding a pencil, brush, or fat piece of charcoal—the media just mentioned make decidedly different types of strokes.

"These are my eyes, my hands, my sensations," Fitch comments. "But how I translate that is mitigated by the tool. Don't smother your visual vocabulary by using an inappropriate tool for the job."

Team Effort

Teaching is a collaborative exercise. And it's not a *how to* approach when Fitch considers the demands of—and on—teachers and students. Technical proficiency becomes a direct result of making things happen (as in: "Dark edges flatten this shape out; let's discuss how to change that"). Keep your eye on the prize: the means of expression are through your *visual language*, first and foremost. This base gives student and teacher common ground to work from—the real vocabulary of shared visual experience.

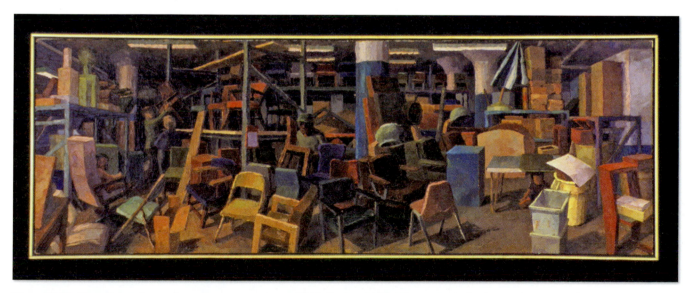

Figure 7-16: "I can't teach you how to express yourself," Fitch states. "But I can teach the language through which you can express yourself *visually*, by communicating *sensation*." She suggests that what you really want to ask is, "How does this drawing move me?"

© Diane Fitch

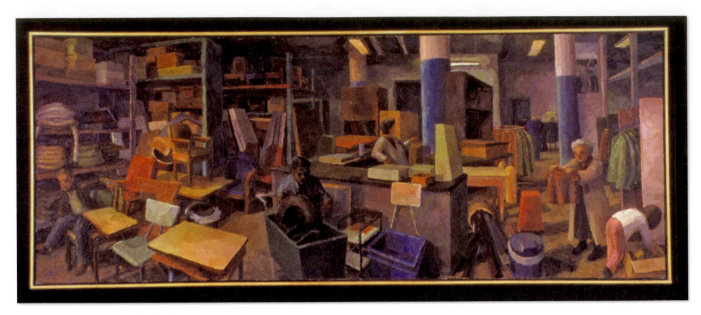

Figure 7-17: The work of Fitch.
© Diane Fitch

Show Me State

In our rapid-fire, hyperkinetic world, it behooves us to slow down, to look methodically at a drawing (or painting) and understand how the work reveals itself gradually. Fitch tells you that a drawing should be *constructed* deliberately, as well. This kind of patience is almost a lost art these days. "It's a lifetime commitment," she comments, "and there's a real need to teach that, too."

You must learn to sit with your art, to appreciate the patience (and rewards) of looking slowly. "Truly looking isn't passive," Fitch points out. "When you study a drawing or painting, you are an active participant. But that drawing or painting should *unfold*. I love when a piece reveals something new, even after repeated viewings."

Switch!

Mike Quon loves to switch from one medium to another: from markers to stick and bamboo reed pens; from brushes to fountain pens to felt tips. "When I was in fifth grade," he remembers, "I went to Chinese language school, where I learned how to use the traditional brushes to write."

"One Chinese brush is the equivalent of a half dozen western-type tools," he states. "I get my fine lines by using the point, and produce thicker lines by simply increasing the downward pressure. The whole brush can also be used for washes and broad areas."

Quon works quickly, so markers are another natural fit. He'll even dip a dried out marker brush pen into a bottle of ink—a smart idea that makes wonderful (and obvious) sense when you think about. "With markers I can really draw quickly, especially on location, and cut down my drawing time."

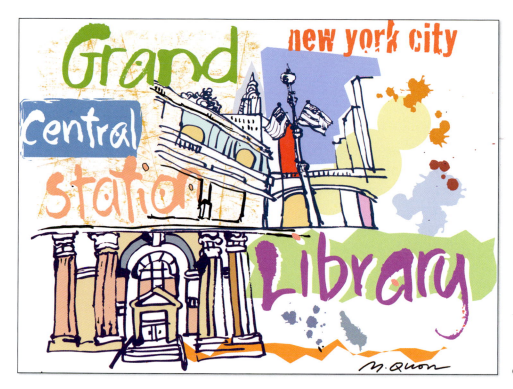

Figure 7-18: Quon often combines mixed media. With any of these combinations, he slings a lot of ink, blotting and not erasing much. "Since I like bold and juicy lines," he says, "I have fun loading my brushes up and experimenting with splatters, splashes, and drips. Brushes naturally create lines that obviously reflect a nuanced, human touch."
© Mike Quon

The Essence of Exquisite

"There is nothing more exquisite than a line drawing," says Melanie Reim. "It is the foundation of all else, simultaneously as important as it is revealing. Drawing is a triumph."

"Master and understand this foundation," Reim goes on, "capture the essence of the story with the point of a pen or pencil (or the swipe of a brush), and a great reward awaits you."

But we should point out, of course, that this payday is contingent on good composition and diverse spatial relationships; great shapes combining with a variation of line and tone. This establishes a solid structure that is the benchmark for successful picture-making. And that structure provides your point of departure.

"The value of line is all there in black and white," Reim says with a sly smile. She will tell you that a line drawing is like having a conversation with your viewer. Flow, length, weight, attitude—even the whimsy of lines—all contribute to the dialogue of the drawing. "No mark is too small or inconsequential," she says. "Never dismiss even the most casual of lines, for line is the starting place to tell your visual story."

Figure 7-19: "Recording from life tells the artist and the audience what is important to that picture, to that viewpoint," Reim says. "Line puts you present in that moment for more than a click of the lens, and what you deliver on the page elicits both the image and the sensation of the event."
© Melanie Reim

CHAPTER SUMMARY

A good art education targets the basics, and the basic line is both ancient and modern. Thinking about drawing as a language may be somewhat abstract. We examined the idea that drawing is about the balance of translation and abstraction, thus there's always a message or statement (even though there may be no universal purpose of drawing).

Drawing is really about communication and intention, so line is greatly informed by shape and form, value, texture, and pattern. We considered construction and subject matter as these concerns dictate the quality of the line.

We sought to understand mass and form through gesture, contour, and continuous line. We looked at the emotion of a "simple" black line and made the more complex statement that technical issues are almost never to the point. We concluded with the sentiment that there is nothing more exquisite and informative than a line drawing.

Working It Out

1. It's in the Details.

Over the next _____ [days or weeks] of class, we will draw something different every day. Your options follow. Choose a different challenge each day of the assignment.

- A complex mechanical item. Draw every part.

- Something organic. Draw every leaf, twig and branch.

- Hair on a head (yours or a model or imaginary). Draw every hair, draw the face as well (as a counterpoint to the complex lines of the hair).

- Fur. An animal: draw every hair.

- Stones in a stream/on a riverbank. Draw each stone individually.

- Sand on a beach. Stipple the sand.

- Something flat, shiny, and very smooth.

Size: Free choice. For an even greater challenge: work larger, keep the line thin or better yet, to scale (a hair is a true hairline, no matter what dimensions you are working at).

2. It's a Poor Workman who Blames His Tools.

Over the next _____ [days or weeks] of class, we will draw something different every day. Your options follow. Choose a different challenge each day of the assignment.

- Do a drawing with every pen in your art box.

- Do the same drawing repeatedly, each time with a different pen.

- Do a drawing with your opposite hand.

- Do a drawing with the wrong tool for the job.

- Draw a small (even microscopic) item very large.

- Draw a large (even huge) item very small. Keep the level of detail as accurate as possible in both scenarios.

- Do a drawing with your eyes closed.

3. No Line Zone

Think about line quality by considering the *absence* of line. Line quality can also be about what you're *not* doing with line. Do the still life set up in class. Don't render the line; render the *shading* cast by the light. Drop out lines to suggest that light (the sun bouncing off a surface; imply a bright light by putting down a lot of black around it). As Cho suggests: "You don't draw both sides or all the edges; you figure out the lighting and draw the shadow. The viewer fills in the other line with their imagination."

On Your Own

1. Field Report

Practice the art of reportage and build your repertoire as a storyteller by drawing on location. Go to the mall or a coffee shop and draw from life—no cameras! Be present in the moment with a heightened sense of observation and awareness; deliver on the page both the image and the sensation of the event.

2. Tread

Line is greatly informed by texture and pattern. Do an extended series of drawings (interiors, exteriors, industrial/organic, objects, florals, etc.) with lines that are made up of natural and/or mechanical textures and patterns.

3. No Visible Pantry Lines

Line is influenced by shape and form. Do an extended drawing series of your home (exterior and interior) *without* lines (or outlines): only shape and form. This is not an exercise in light and shading per se (or pure positive/ negative) as with in-class assignment # 3 above.

Chapter 8

Color

© Boris Kulikov

Experience Color

Color! Whole, weighty volumes are written on this subject. As we see the world in just this way, perhaps color makes an image that much more "real." Color certainly heightens emotion and enhances mood.

This chapter discusses color concept and practice; how color works, and how the viewer perceives that function. We'll examine color relationships, mixing, and blending; both the "hard book science" of color theory and more organic approach of color by *experience*: keen observation and everyday practice (which includes invaluable trial and error).

"Real world" color theory is *real time* color application (on sight, on site, on paper, on analysis): you analyze color relationships by appreciating a breathtaking sunset as well as the beautiful color wheel.

As I bring up many times in this book: it all comes down to *communication*. What are you trying to say—and do—with color?

All Things Being Equal

If I only had six words, I'd sum it up this way: *Hue, saturation, and value— enough said.*

Hue is about color choice (red as opposed to red-orange or red-violet). Saturation is intensity and purity (said another way: bright or dull). And value is, said simply, light and dark.

Separating color and value is problematic: a tactical mistake (as in concept), and technical disconnect (think process and procedure). So Chapters 8 and 9 are liberally cross-referenced (as are other chapters) to support our premise: that it's all about the connections of learning.

Collected are diverse views and statements from our many contributors. It's not our intent to confuse the issues via contradictory information (or to create a competition of design elements). Color and value are joined at the hip; we're not trying to divide and conquer or create sibling rivalry. Our goal is simply to offer an artist's color truth.

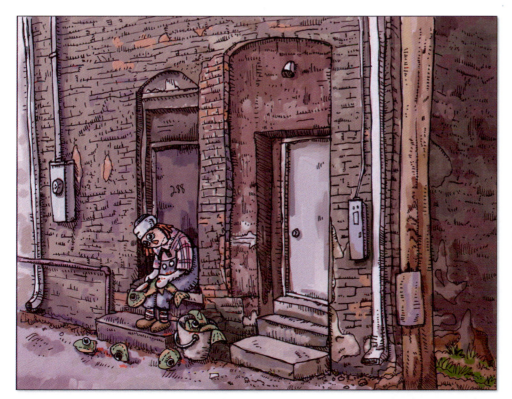

Figure 8-1a and b: Bryan Ballinger knows the theory. "But it helped me a great deal to start pairing that with my own observations," he says. This understanding of how colors work together (and how color works in the real world) has been invaluable to this artist. "So, if I'm trying to express the emotions inherent in a scene at sunset," Ballinger says, "it benefits me to appreciate how the sun, sky and atmosphere work together to create an evening palette of mixed warm and cool colors."

8-1a © Bryan Ballinger

8-1b © Bryan Ballinger

Smack Down

Do you ever think about the concept of *drawing* vs. *coloring*, that your art is more appropriately about color rather than line? Perhaps it's the other way around. Or maybe it's somewhere in between. It's not really an adversarial relationship; not so much a competition as it is a partnership of aggressive teammates: Charlie Hustle and Ms. Flow.

Whether color is indeed the "thing" of your drawings, or line is the root of that work, "coloring" complements "drawing," lines and colors are a mutual admiration society.

Natural Selection

Color is personal (for you and your viewer). Color is emotion and feeling. That's true to art, and in life. "She saw *red.*" "I'm kinda *blue* today." The world at large is actually one big Color Theory 101. Without it, you wouldn't know how to dress in the morning (and by that benchmark, some of us are indeed better colorists than others).

To repeat: color is actually about relationships. It's not a question of *red*, per se. It's really about the color that sits beside that red and the *relationship* established by that union. *Compare, observe,* and *be aware,* you'll see that book learning is super, but there's an amazing education right before your eyes.

✔ Check Point: Look … Up in the Sky!

Mike Maihack lives in Tampa, Florida. He's a full-time illustrator and graphic designer, and drawing comics is his primary passion. Maihack provides our check list for Chapter 8:

1. Red, the hot head that it is, tends to emote excitement or rage. It will make sure it is the most noticeable color in the room.

2. Blue gives off the feeling of melancholy, sadness, or even peacefulness. I like to think it has a cold yet welcoming personality.

3. Yellow is that happy hue that tends to brighten everything it touches—for better or worse.

4. But like alter egos, it's hard to ultimately separate color and emotion…

5. …Superman is depicted using a combination of red, blue, and yellow, but isn't necessarily associated with all of those feelings. But remove any two of those colors and you're left with a superhero emanating a different emotional state than what you know.

6. I don't necessarily think "good" color can fix a "bad" drawing. But it certainly can *enhance* a good one.

7. Even if the viewer doesn't realize it, color will provoke a certain mood—however so subtle.

8. Realize that red, blue, and yellow are just three hues in millions. Every various shade and saturation is going to mix differently on a page, and it's up to you to make sure all of those emotions get along (if not, you end up with a big mess).

9. But if you get it right, you can take a gray, emotionless drawing and enhance its personality to better communicate with the observer. What's so enjoyable is that everyone is going to have his or her own emotional response to these colors. So color becomes just one more way to attract multiple people to a singular idea.

10. Consider black and white as colors. They too are going to spark certain responses. Some illustrations just work better in pure black and white.

Maihack plays dominant hues off subordinate colors in these great illustrations.
© Mike Maihack

Trip to Mark It

Visualize how particular colors act together; explore, experiment, and enjoy the fieldwork. Go out into the natural world of color (and color combinations); see for yourself. Go to the woods, head into town; window shop, graze in the fields. Color concepts—as well as color sense—will come.

Boris Kulikov says that working with color is actually a combination of both the line and tone experience. Yes, color on its own certainly impacts the viewer, but color in combination with lines and tone is particularly potent. Kulikov ranks all the tools as equally important, but feels that color may be the most important tool for creating mood.

"There is an important difference between a color as paint and color as the hue itself," he goes on. "What we have in paint tubes is not quite a color yet. Anyone can paint and still never reach a desired intensity or saturation. There are color theories; but from my point of view, an artist must study and then, well, *forget* what you learn."

"Color sense only comes with knowledge plus education, skill with experience, as well as trial and error."

Heart, Guts, and Soul

Color drawing *feels*. It's a live-wire connection to the heart and soul of your audience. Rick Sealock knows this right in his gut, he has over 20 years of experience and expertise in conceptual and interpretive illustration.

"Interpretive" illustration puts it mildly. A Sealock drawing is really like no other.

"Everyone understands pain, grief, anger, happiness—and that's where I grab them," Sealock says. "Color in illustration helps to seduce and educate on a conceptual level. Color can manipulate, communicate ideas and passion, or visually solve a problem."

Figure 8-2: "Accept theory, but then make it your own," says Kulikov. "Red, yellow, and orange warm and excite you. Blues and greens are more relaxing. Violet can make you feel depressed. Color is contrast and nuance."

© Boris Kulikov

Figure 8-3: Strong color chops demand discipline, determination, and direction; this savvy is not accidental. Drawing is a way of seeing, then visually interpreting the world around us via the core elements—like color.
© Rick Sealock

To do all that you must exploit the extremes of both concept and technique. You mix media and mark-making to push design rudiments. You reinforce perception and affect by distorting line, lighting, and palette.

"But I like to think that there is an intelligence to the madness or maybe a genius to the silliness of my work," Sealock laughs, "and it all starts with learning the basics, the fundamentals of drawing—like color."

Color Me, I'm Going In!

Learning color fundamentals (and understanding color basics) should not be a scary proposition. And it doesn't have to be a dull and boring exercise either.

But knowing how color truly works doesn't make you some sort of art geek. Sure, there may be shortcuts to the proverbial pretty picture, but I'd suggest the straight path first. Learn your way, then figure out how to shave time off the trip.

For instance, as Jacqueline Kahane Freedman points out, "Color is not really topical. It's not just a 'red apple.' If you can see that 'redness' that means there's *light* present, and in light there's the full spectrum. So you must accommodate the complete range."

The Paint Whisperer

How do you integrate the full spectrum of light? Freedman taught her students that dark values (the shadows) are a great place to blend in that gamut of colors. "Here they won't look 'muddy' because of that dark mix,"

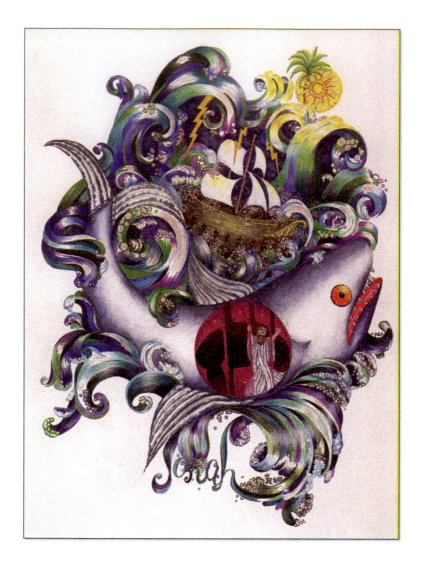

Figure 8-4: If you're seeing red when you think about color theory, then there must be *light* present, and accommodating that full spectrum of light will be your objective.

© Jacqueline Kahane Freedman

she explains. "In addition, the area of less light just between the highlight and the middle value is an excellent place to include very light 'whispers' of the pale reflections of adjacent colors (also the colors of light itself—especially sunlight)."

Light 101: How We Understand Color

There are rules, folks. However, we all inherently appreciate color theory because biologically, the eye is physically hard wired to process the right color information. Thus, as illustrator and educator Shanth Enjeti says, "One goal for a teacher presenting color theory is to make students realize we all have the same intuitive understanding of how color works. 'Masters of color' operate from an innate awareness of color theory."

Part of that understanding is becoming aware of how your eyes process *light*. Get this, and you can bend and push the regs, take big steps, and make bold moves. But it is also important to have a good handle on the core values (for instance, tonal range and the luminosity—brightness—of hue).

Wheel Meet Again

Get familiar with the color wheel. You'll most likely recognize all the common hues; you may even know the exact order of the wheel. And spinning around any color wheel will be color terminology you're at least aware of. The basic vocabulary ("warm and cool"; "temperature"; "value, hue, saturation"; etc.) is universal, but how do you then compose a painting or drawing with that?

Many artists firmly believe that color basics are learned through experience plus trial and error. Diane Fitch, for instance, says this builds color *sensitivity*, whether that's gained through a color class (and a variety of exercises) or working from observation.

The goal either way is to gain color *control* based on color *knowledge*, not luck or guesswork, not circumstance and unadulterated emotion. Your battle cry: color by plan, not by default.

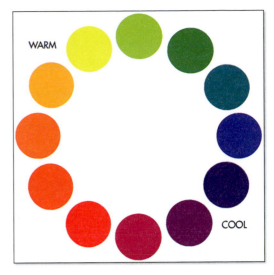

Figure 8-5: This simple color wheel has each hue equidistant from the other.

Where There's a Wheel, There's a Way

"Hey, I've heard of the color wheel," Sealock laughs, and probably every Freshman art student paints a color wheel (or creates a chart of gradated values) at some point. Here's an example of a basic color wheel.

Pick a color. Go directly across the wheel and move an equidistant step left and/or right. Stay within that basic "cone of reference" and you have the fundamental DNA of a pretty solid painting. You can go *much* deeper, of course, but the color wheel can be that elegantly simple. Try it. If you want to accentuate yellow (as an example), you'll be looking at purple, red, and blue (with the opposite one-two punch being the purple, of course). Conversely, you can flip the cone to tap into colors adjacent to the yellow.

"If you're starting with a palette based on every tube of paint in your art box you're heading for trouble," Enjeti states emphatically. "Using all 20 tubes of paint you have on hand just spells disaster. Work up to this (if you must), but a limited palette is the number one rule of thumb I stress to students."

The Whole Relationship

The thing about color relationships is that you must keep *the whole* right up front. Your first marks act as the gauge to subsequent color application. As the work develops, you modulate from this *color key*. It's figuring out how to develop the relationships by constantly keeping the *whole painting* in mind.

So: "I can't go as dark as my color key, otherwise all my low values will look the same." Or: "The white teacup goes a bit blue here … my light and shadows are reading warm against cool. Okay, that blue runs through all the shadows in the piece, unifying the entire painting." And it may just be that *every color is in every color*. Look to Cezanne for a classic role model here.

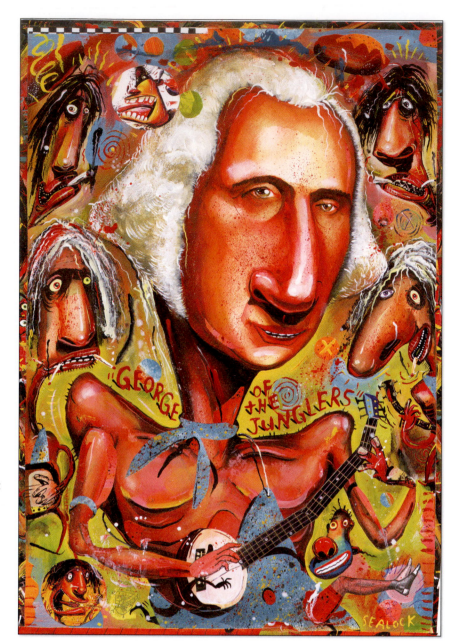

Figure 8-6: "I'm not a complex color theory kinda guy," says Sealock. "I'm totally about the basics. Cool against warm, bright against dull, light against dark, etc.—my images are based on contrast to create depth, lighting, believability."

And value? "Learn it, buy it, or steal it," Sealock suggests, "but you need to be able to see this within your work—it lets you understand your palette (a.k.a., color theory)."

© Rick Sealock

All this can come through *seeing* (and you can do that without an overtly intimate—or emotional—relationship with the color wheel).

I'm a Visual Person

I am definitely *not* advocating we scrap all the wonderful books on (and fascinating science of) color. Not at all. But may I suggest we simply keep our eyes wide open, as well? Be a keen observer of the world around you. Do that and you'll effectively take what you need to build a cohesive drawing or unified painting. Match this by studying art history. This is invaluable—the color sense and visual organization of past masters is one of the best ways to learn color. Back *that* up with sound color theory and you're going to be a color *monster*.

Training (Color) Wheels

Day to day color theory is a big factor in our everyday color sense (and application). Much of our color training is by osmosis. As artists out and about, you know more than a few things about practical color. Which should give you an appreciation of *continued* practice and the wisdom to recognize that you always need to know more.

Mix it Up

Most of us look for some sort of shortcut, the least painful method to get results fast. It's just that kind of world. Of course, I'm speaking in gross generalizations, but it's only through deliberate *examination* and actual *application* that we learn to truly finesse color. The eye becomes much more sensitive over time, and this only happens through patience, practice, and observation.

Color theory can be learned (and taught) in a variety of different ways, but for the most part, it's really all about color *mixing*— understanding the color we see and what pigments it takes to get that color onto our paper or canvas.

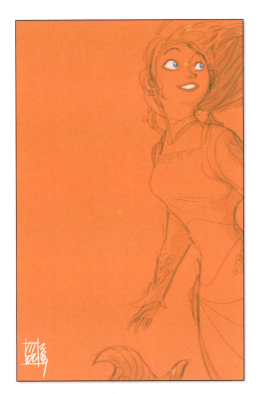

Figure 8-7: Visual sensation is, according to my dictionaries, "the perceptual experience of seeing; to gain insight into or an understanding of what we see." So you must find your visual sensation, then figure out how to mix that. Here's the visually sensational work of Louie del Carmen to emphasize our point.

© Louie del Carmen

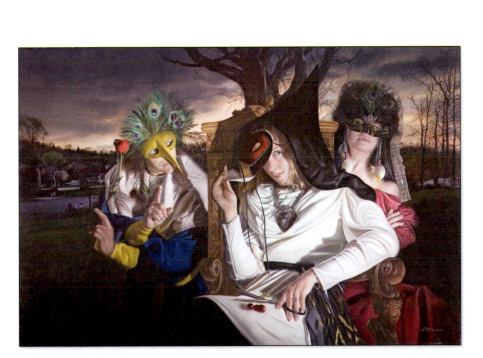

Figure 8-8: Shown here is a painting by our cover artist, David Bowers. You can get lost in the small, sometimes weird worlds Bowers creates. His paintings incorporate sly and very modern themes within a subtly classical framework. Symbolism is a main ingredient, as is the impeccable technique that enhances his message—and there is always a message in a Bowers piece.

And his message here today is that, "Color is not so much about science. Color is pervasive. Color should be intuitive. I don't do color studies because I don't believe in applying or teaching color theory out of a book; I think color is something you have to experience. I just let the color *work*. You start out simple and head from that foundation."

© David Bowers

Figure 8-9: Mrs. Albers' boy, Joe.
© Michael Fleishman

Is What You See Really What You Get?

The influential Bauhaus (1919-1933) was a pioneering German art school that changed the course of modern art education. Folks like Josef Albers (1888-1976), and Johannes Itten (1888-1967) initiated extensive studies that have profoundly affected the science and application of color right to the present day.

You may have heard of "Albers color theory." What *is* that?

Color: From A(lbers) To B(auhaus)

The one-minute answer is that you always keep color interaction (not isolation) in mind. Without going too deep into a premise that has spawned a library of texts and countless college courses, let's just say that in Albers color theory a color must be evaluated in conjunction to its neighbor(s)—in context with the surrounding color. And please remember, this brief explanation is just in the nuttiest of nutshells.

The Problem of Perception

Beyond Albers, the color of objects can also appear quite different when viewed under varied lighting conditions. And, although we see color similarly in the observed world, there are certainly individual variations. When we try to actually control color, most people have difficulties due to labeling (or our left-brain habit of identifying color by its color properties).

Shoffner relates a great example here. "Take a 'white' wall behind the model stand," he says. "As lighting is adjusted on the model, subtle colors and values usually appear on the white backdrop. However, many students will only see 'white' because they know it was painted with some bucket of paint that said *white* on the label."

So it is more important to analyze color from careful *observation* than it is from knowing the color properties of an object. "And understand that different colors are going to stand out differently on a page," says Maihack. "Red tends to pop and is actually the closet to pure black in drawing attention to itself."

"Blue is the direct opposite," he adds. "It recedes on a page (making it a wonderful hue to use for imagery that falls back in a painting). Knowing how colors relate to each other and how the eye recognizes them helps to determine where they belong on a given illustration."

Figure 8-10: Brightness and intensity of colors (or chroma) is another key to control color variation. Maihack points out that even a low chromatic red is going to recede next to a very intense blue. Thus, color possibilities are essentially limitless (as all great possibilities should be). But keep in mind that "anything goes" can easily overwhelm your process and decisions.

And as art becomes increasingly digitized, it has never been more important to understand how color works (and how we perceive it). In our era of millions of colors with one nudge of a mouse, color is more of an issue than ever.

© Mike Maihack

A Rose by any Other Name

"You can't divorce color from value," says Glen Cebulash, who tells you that every color has a value, and that colors interact *through* value. Thus, color has two functions: 1. to *decorate* value (to basically give color to an already established value structure) and 2. to generate light (and hence, *space*).

There are a few things to consider here: Color is not a separate function of—or secondary to—value. And maybe we aren't seeing color as something to respond *to*—it's more of an interaction *with*. But one could protest that we *do* respond to color; we always respond *to* color. What do you think?

Draw/Paint

To build a painting (or drawing) with color, you must always consider the evolving relationships playing out on your paper or canvas. "Line will break into color, reestablish gesture, and be subsequently painted out again," Cebulash tells you. "There's an interaction, a space, and rhythm. Drawing is not 'put into' the color or vice versa. You step back ... look ... and respond. More color; more drawing. You can draw with paint, you know ... is this not drawing anymore?" Reader, what do you say?

Figure 8-11: If Cebulash makes any a distinction between drawing and painting, it's more about emphasis. Is the finished thing about mark making and value? Is color the dominant expressive mode? "There's a back and forth between the two," he sums up, "but a drawing certainly doesn't have to be black and white. A painting doesn't have to be in color. The distinction is always a tricky one."
© Glen Cebulash

Is Paint Lighter than Air?

Melanie Reim points out that, "The power of negative space often goes unacknowledged in the planning of an illustration. I would argue that the ability to 'render the air' is as important as any foundation. Being a good editor of space (and information) is absolutely vital."

So how does one draw or paint air? Based on instruction from Cebulash and Fitch, Kathy Moore says the trick is to intellectually put a word to a particular color. In your mind's eye, break down and describe the color you see. "Ask yourself, 'What am I *thinking* when I'm painting this? What am I *seeing*? Is my painted response the same as my visual response?'"

"It all comes down to concentration and practice; continually tweaking the ingredients of an extended recipe—it's a pinch of this, a dab of that," says Moore. "This is laborious, but rewarding. It takes a long time to 'get good.' I'm not there—*yet*."

"And value sense goes hand in hand with color savvy," Moore says. "Dark and light actually have *color*—you may not have the intensity of direct lighting, but shadows still have color.

"Take a local color," Moore goes on, "let's say, something is green. But it's not *just* 'green,' of course. One side of this green shape borders a yellow object—that side will appear as a yellowish-green. That's the way light works; it reflects."

"Space, shadows, light source, even the color wheel come into the mix: what plays with green on the color wheel? Red is opposite green on the wheel; let's take this green down a few steps with red."

"There's that technical side of it," she tells you, "but while I'm *looking*, I'm simply responding visually. There's no plan. You *observe*, and you keep lighting in mind."

Figure 8-12: "In my work, I emphasize color," says Moore, "the color I see and the experience of mixing colors. It's a visual perception thing, and a slow process—like I can actually sense the space."
© Kathy Moore

As Serious as a Heart Attack

For many artists, color is purely instinctive. They simply respond joyfully to bright color and brave color combinations (or carefully considered but sparse color palettes). "I have *never* been one for color theory," Jill Calder remarks candidly.

According to Calder, color, in some circles, is not regarded as "seriously" as black and white. But she takes exception here. "Color just slaps you in the face if used smartly and boldly."

In that way, Calder feels color is really an extension of your personality. There are plenty of illustrators tapping into color combinations you'd never think of using yourself; but somehow, these artists make it work. Certain colors seem particularly suited to their palette; it's a part of them.

Calder encourages her illustration students to explore and experiment with color. And she wants her students to slowly build their knowledge of how different colors work together.

So for students addicted to black and white, she suggests using dark tones of blues, purples, browns, and greens instead. "By doing that, they begin to see that

Figure 8-13: Calder's work is smart and bold, as shown here.
© Jill Calder

8-14a © Mark Todd

Figure 8-14a and b: "Working digitally is so much quicker," Todd points out. "Plus I was forever disappointed with how my paintings reproduced. A painting's color was always a little bit off, muddy. Digitally, my work seems to reproduce closer to the original."

8-14b © Mark Todd

they can still create a powerful image with more 'ping' to it," she states. "Once down that route, they have the confidence to start experimenting with other colors, adding them into the mix."

The Fun of It

Mark Todd says he has a lot of fun with color. He'll often put unexpected color in places—a large block of a single color; perhaps he'll cover the entire painting with a vivid or concentrated color. "Color in my work tends to be what anchors the piece and gives it weight," he considers. "A solid color can often serve as the blank canvas for which the line can explore."

"Now, in terms of shading and/or turning a form, I use value sparingly," he states. "Sometimes I'll scumble to create a tone or soften edges and bring a little character to the work."

"Some of my gallery stuff tends to have more extreme lights and darks," he tells us. "Areas may be completely blackened in, while other spots are left untouched, creating a strong, expressive element in the piece."

Bang for the Buck

As far as color goes, less is definitely more for Todd, who tries not to throw every color of the rainbow at a piece. For this artist, a limited palette is far better. He will often desaturate colors by around 20 percent so the art sits back on the page. "I like that yellowed, aged look; those dusty greens and muted tones," he says.

"You may think you're getting more bang for the buck if the piece is screaming with major, primary colors," Todd continues, "but if you target your choice, color is more effective."

For certain imagery, Todd will go to the other extreme: vivid, fluorescent pinks, bright oranges; color that literally glows and jumps off the wall at you. It's a deliberate contradiction. "As I tell my students," he laughs, "we're always going to contradict ourselves, just be honest about it."

Cel It

"I could never quite capture the spontaneity of my sketches," says Todd. "I explored straight acrylic paints, ballpoint (and a variety of different) pens, pencil. It was really 'down to earth' kinda stuff. But I still wasn't satisfied with my line quality until I switched to ink and brush."

"And then, through friends in the Los Angeles animation industry, I discovered cel vinyl—a cartoonist's acrylic ink," Todd tells you. "This medium is flat, smooth, easy to work with—and fast." With cel vinyl Todd gets a lot of detail and bright color that really pops. This paint—combined with a mix of basic acrylic, house, and spray paints—is his medium of choice for gallery work. His advertising and editorial freelance assignments are initially done with brush and ink (straight India ink, not cel vinyl), scanned and colored digitally. "I try to keep it consistent with the other art; I don't want it to look overtly digital."

The Slow Reveal

Before she learned to paint in college, Jaime Zollars drew for hours a day, and always in black and white. She found converting to color work was difficult and slow-going. Zollars reasoned correctly that more (and perhaps brighter) colors can certainly make an impact, but found the opposite to be true for *her* work.

"Including every color or over-extending the saturation in my paintings turned off viewers, overwhelming them," she says. "There was too much color to absorb; content was often immediately dismissed along with the piece."

It took Zollars "a long time" to figure out how to use a limited palette and still achieve that feeling of full color. "I have much more fun using color to reveal an image to a viewer, instead of hitting them over the head with it," she says. "Working with just a handful of colors in a piece is plenty to tell the story."

"And because there are limitless combinations of color and value, maintaining a very limited palette (three or four colors) may just help you to maintain your sanity while bringing a complicated composition to life."

Solid Value

"Most of the feeling, emotion, and atmosphere in my work is created with color," says Zollars, "but starting with a solid value study is the best way to create a successful piece."

"Work that successfully uses value to communicate the message—for instance, those illustrations that can photocopied in black and white and still read appropriately— will not disappoint when reprinted in magazines, books, or postcards, no matter how wrong the color prints."

"Even though I instinctively rush towards color first," Zollars says, "I am always striving to make my values work before approaching color decisions."

Figure 8-15: "I mix it up," Zollars says. "The sky can be lime green and your mountains purple ... you don't have to be confined by established norms. I even collect wallpaper samples from the hardware store and play with random combinations of these swatches to find something surprising and new."

© Jaime Zollars

CHAPTER SUMMARY

This chapter dealt with the fundamental concepts of *color* and sought to focus on the relationship of theory, emotion, and content of color. A six-word summary: *Hue, saturation and value—that's it*. We said that understanding how colors work together (and how color works in the real world) will be key. We mentioned that color is personal and color is actually about relationships: as you grow as an artist, you'll explore and experiment; you'll *visualize* how particular colors act together.

One take on color theory is that you accept the theory, but then make it your own, so in this chapter we looked at color in concept, perception, and practice. We examined mixing and blending; the "book science" of color/value theory and more organic approaches of instinctive color/value through *experience* and observation (which includes trial and error). And we made the case that strong color chops demand discipline, determination, and direction; and that this savvy is not accidental.

Working It Out

1. Pushing the Envelope

Write the names of all the hues on a (12 step) color wheel on separate slips of paper. Place these names in an envelope. Fish in the envelope and pull out 3 random colors. Use these colors to create a painting. Black and white are optional.

2. Now You See It...

Here's a fun, challenging exercise presented by the *Color Theory* teachers at Edison Community College.

Do a full-color "white" painting. Here all colors are predominately white with only a bare hint of color. From a distance, this painting will appear as pure white; you should only catch the subtle tints when you inspect the work at extremely close range.

3. ... Now You Don't

Create a full-color "black" painting. In this one, all colors are overwhelmingly black with only a touch of color added. Further back, the painting will look to be all black; you'll only notice the delicate coloration when you approach the piece closer in.

Home and Away

1. Rainbow Connection

Do an extended series of paintings. In the first, throw "every color of the rainbow" at it. With each successive piece, eliminate one specific color until your final painting is monochromatic. Black and white are optional.

2. Put Your Shades On

Do an extended series of color pieces with the absolute brightest palette you can think up: vivid, fluorescent pinks, bright oranges; nuclear greens—high end, intense color that literally glows and jumps off the wall at you. While your high-end palette will be a constant, each work should be done in a different media.

3. Self-Publishing

Recreate an *entire* magazine: photographs, illustrations, typography, ads … and do it *freehand.* Color fidelity is important and design quality is paramount; but image, line, and type features are not, so the project can take on an abstract or surreal look at its finish. Media and size: free choice.

Chapter 9

Value

© Paul Hoppe

Of Equal Value

Often called tone or shade (and perhaps, simply "lights and darks"), value is powerful and expressive, even—and particularly so—when those values are "only" black and white. Regarded by many artists as *the* most important building block, value establishes form, sets weight, focuses the eye or moves you through the composition; value creates a sense of depth. Value can clarify the object itself, or define a thing solely through the spaces in between.

As mentioned in Chapter 8, when writing up the color/value material, I saw that you really can't (or shouldn't) separate the information, it's too intertwined. So to organize this wealth of material, I designated *color* and *value* as two different chapters (maybe "twin" chapters is a better metaphor); and under these general umbrellas, I cross-reference insights and observations to support the basic thesis of this book: connections.

And again, you'll hear different opinions (not to mention varied process) from the numerous correspondents in this chapter. I'll repeat: it's not our goal to befuddle issues or confuse you with contradictory info. We are not trying to drum up a contest between the design elements; our only mission was to offer that artist's take on the subject at hand.

Valued Content

"The key to a good composition is value structure," says Tina Sweep. "Values will define content for the viewer. Is it a dark shape on a light field? A light figure on a dark background? Value is the most important key to establishing the composition. The darkest dark next to the lightest light (or the object with the most value contrast) will draw the viewer's eye."

"Spatial distance can easily be established through a progression of values back into the picture plane (a full range of values from dark to light, while more visually pleasing also helps define each object)."

Figure 9-1: Let's connect two dots I bet you may not have considered before: Sweep reminds us that, "Pattern is a subset of value. Pattern, when used effectively, can act as tone to define objects and show a progression of spatial relationships."
© Tina Sweep

Figure 9-2: The work of Kulikov.
© Boris Kulikov

Figure 9-3: The work of Melia.
© Paul Melia

Game Plan

"Value—tone, shade, lights, and darks—are as important as any of the other tools," says Boris Kulikov. "Actually, I can't say what is more or less important, it all depends on each particular project."

It's a bit of a game, isn't it? If you want to "cheat" on a viewer and make him believe that the flat, two-dimensional surface of the paper is 3-D, then value is the essential thing.

" Value," Kulikov states, "is actually what you are addressing when you set out to work with color."

Value and You (Value and Hue)

If you know value, you have true picture *control*—in both concept and composition. "Value is more important than color. It comes first," Paul Melia states resolutely. "If you can learn about values (and use them well), color comes easy. In the old days—and especially in European schools—first year college students were not even allowed to *think* about color. These students had to draw in black and white and understand tone."

"Color skills were established by understanding the difference in value and intensity. It's a hands-on deal. If you don't 'see' the basics, you can't build on them."

Fear Factor

"I'd like to offer a color course called *Terrified of Color*," Shanth Enjeti smiles, "so you'd know exactly the type of student who should be taking this class." I see where he's going here. Maybe learning just a few of the basics is the best way to start building color confidence. In fact, Enjeti always tells his students to begin working monochromatically.

As a student, when people would bring up items such as "secondary" and "tertiary" colors, Enjeti would sit back and think, "Ommagosh . . . what are we talking about here?" But when somebody sat him down and said, "Do a black and white painting focused on *value*" or "Now do a red and green painting focused on *tone*," it changed the way the young artist looked at color theory.

"Your color sense begins to gel when/if you can just work simply and think about how you put combinations together," he says. "When I experienced the rudimentary principles in action, it became intuitive after a while."

Central Casting

Value solves compositional problems and resolves perspective. If you understand value, you can nudge (or shove) the viewer around the picture plane. Value plays center in the depth of field. It fills in spaces, adds drama (or clarifies and simplifies). Everybody has at least some color savvy. I won't qualify "good" or "bad," but we all possess an innate sense of *how we feel* about color. For this to be properly demonstrated in your work, you need to understand the value system.

Adjust the Contrast

Value . . . all relative—and all powerful. Mood is determined by the values: be it dramatic or dreamy, merry or melancholy. We say "I'm in a 'dark' mood" or "Let's keep it light, shall we?" And as you go round the blend you'll find at the heart of this perception is *gradation.*

Value also establishes weight and balance, focus and definition. To establish weight (and the rest), we need contrast and change. In other words— wait for it—*relationships.* Value relationships. There is no "value" or "tone" without change or contrast: dark *against* light.

Value *contrasts* sort out composition, heighten drama (in both design and concept), or add subtle visual impact. Value contrast also determines where an object is in space, building the illusion of depth. All good reasons why value contrast is another important component of strong visual design.

Break it Down

Dice Tsutsumi is an illustrator and an art director for Pixar Animation Studios. "Value is what I use to describe my artwork more than anything else," he says. "Value equals lighting. I guess I tend to see how objects *react* to light more than an object itself."

"Professionally, I'm often described as someone with a good color sense. But I actually think that I have a decent sense of value—I tend to see value structures well and that's what makes my color work."

"I keep value structure as simple as possible. I have this 3-value theory that tends to work best for me. The value structure must work no matter what color we use (it's harder than you think). So I also try to simplify colors as well as value. I normally break it down to warm and cool—and really playing with color relationships as I push warm and cool."

Figure 9-4: Illustrator Jay Montgomery is a part time professor at SCAD Atlanta (Georgia). "Initially, I create an illustration with values (plus line)," Montgomery says. "I get the concept down first; color enhances and adds to the concept. Color theory certainly plays a big part in my choice of colors and I try to not always go for the 'real colors' of a subject. Sometimes these colors are all the client wants, so that's what I give them. But when it's more open to my interpretation, I like to play around and experiment with color on the final. Working digitally I can do that much quicker."

"I like to work out a concept in pure monochromatic colors. The concept has to work without the introduction of color—the simplest concepts that can come across with pure values alone are the strongest. That's why it's important to work out your values ahead of time in a sketch or tight pencil."

© Jay Montgomery

Figure 9-6: The work of Tsutsumi.
© Dice Tsutsumi

Push It

Complete disclosure department: as compared to value (and color), line is probably not Tsutsumi's forte (according to the artist himself). However, he says he has just as much appreciation for line as everything else. But back in college (where he studied "old school traditional" oil painting), the artist forced himself to avoid lines in order to see only shapes of values and colors.

As he got into an illustration/animation career, Tsutsumi was exposed to many different kinds of talents, which, as he tells it, prompted him to expand his horizons. "Since then," he says, "I've been pushing myself to describe shapes with lines as well as values and colors."

Figure 9-5: Ed Charney is Art Department Chair at Wittenberg University, in Springfield, Ohio. "Students may tend to understate values and underplay value contrasts," he says, "but the realm of values—the whole range of gray tone between pure black and white—clarifies an image and allows you to understand the correlation between value and color."

© Edward Charney

Value: The Musical

"Lately I've been splashing color into every thing that I do," says Andrea Wicklund. " I start drawing. I'll pick out different colored pencils and pens. I then begin the filtering process, introducing color all at once. This is fun but I can get hung up on color exploration and exhaust my options right away. So by the time I get to the final, the results are stiff and not so fun; boring."

"Now I realize that as long as I have a very strong *value pattern* that's mapped out already, colors simply happen," says Andrea Wicklund. "You just go with the flow. I think about the mood and balance that with a little theory. 'How much of this painting do I want to be cool colors; how much warm? Where am I going to place all this?'"

"I see color as a musical of grays," she states. "Warm or cool, just pretty much pick any color that falls into a particular range and it will work; you then save saturated colors for focal points."

That's What I'm Talkin' About!

"For me, the whole deal is light and shadow," Nancy Stahl says. When Stahl made the decision that she wanted her work to showcase strong volume, she also realized that "you can't have volume without value. Working dark to light also allows the image to be simplified, as some information can be left in shadow."

Figure 9-7: The work of Wicklund.
© Andrea Wicklund

And while black and white can often be the strongest of combinations, color is very important to the New York-based artist, as well. "Color is where I feel most free," Stahl says. "I don't give clients a color sketch. I leave color to the last so I can change it in the end. And now on the computer, I can often change it at the *very* end."

But when people speak of color theory, Stahl candidly admits she "never took a course in it. My colors are intuitive. I think with my color and composition, I don't want to limit myself to formulaic solutions."

And how valuable is trial and error when dealing with value and color? "Now you're talking!" Stahl laughs. "Without trial and error we aren't growing. It's essential. If everything is nailed down before you do a drawing or painting, there are no surprises. The result may be very polished, but it won't have any *wonder* in it. If you were curious when you did the drawing, then others will sense that exploration and respond to it."

Figure 9-8: Stahl feels that students don't need to have their "quest for the new" hammered out of them with formulas of what is supposedly "classically right," and that error *must* come into any study or you're not truly venturing into unexplored territory. "I'm all for education," she tells us, "if only for the time that it allows students to intensively work on what it is they will do when starting out. It shouldn't be the end of the line, either. Every day, every observation is an education."

© Nancy Stahl

✔ Check Point: Illuminate Me

With these ten short essays, award-winning illustrator Matt Kindt sheds a little light on this chapter's hot list:

1. It's more interesting to lay in dark areas and shadow to suit the story and situation. And I usually apply blacks in a way that sets off the main character or visually establishes the pace for the reader.

2. Initially, I was pretty lax about filling in blacks and adding shadows and dark areas. Now my rule of thumb is that if I pause to question whether an area should be filled in and darkened, then I just do it—usually I'm pausing because I'm naturally lazy.

3. A careful use of spot blacks in every panel sets up the entire work. Saying that, remember that if a book is nothing but heavy blacks and pronounced line quality, it tends to lose its power.

4. I go as heavy as I can without losing the quality of the line. I revel in thick and thin brush strokes, the long sweeping lines that delineate a figure or face.

5. Dropping subtle shadows in or blocking out bits of the background or corners is what really works for me. I learned a lot by studying old comic strips like *Dick Tracy* and *Terry and the Pirates*—how Chester Gould and Milton Caniff tapped into big blacks with spare hatch and line work.

6. Story and content should dictate the look (and design) of the art. Artists who use strictly thin line and no solid blacks are completely different storytellers. The impact and feel is radically different.

7. The image (or sequence of images), paper choice, line weight, color—or lack of—it's all about content.

8. You don't bend the content of a story to fit your style, it should be the other way around.

9. In *Super Spy*, I used color to add mood plus a sense of place and time. Careful color choices were all based on geography and time …

10. … it's subtle and I wanted it to just work subconsciously. So when you see cold colors, it makes you feel a certain way (and maybe you're not even aware of why you feel it).

The Work of Kindt.
© Matt Kindt

The Work of Kindt.
© Matt Kindt

Figure 9-9a and b: "Color," Hoppe laughs, "is a painful thing. It can overwhelm a good drawing, especially in these digital times. It's a fine line between doing too little and doing too much. I am always concerned that the coloring does the drawing justice."
© Paul Hoppe

Toned

"Many times I establish the values first and then pick the actual colors I want to use," Paul Hoppe points out. It's been mentioned elsewhere in the text, but bears repeating: value establishes order and sorts out composition by adding focus and distributing weight. Group elements of the drawing by similar value and—boom, like that— the image gets organized.

If Hoppe is doing a drawing in "plain" black and white, he thinks a bit differently. Here definite value patterns need to be established. "I try to avoid linear drawings that have no depth," he tells you. "I add heavy blacks and variations in line weight to have a sufficient play of black and white instead of something that looks like a drawing from a coloring book."

A Light Experience

Marshall Arisman says that light creates form and form creates shadows. Shadows define space and delineate the surface where the shadow falls. "No one can teach you light," he brings up, "it has to be experienced."

When Arisman started painting and drawing, he only worked in black and white. Even today he'll start all his paintings by doing an underpainting in one color—usually burnt umber. "I work out all issues regarding form and light before I even think about color," he says. "For many years I saw colors in terms of their grey scale value, not their 'color.' I paint with my hands,

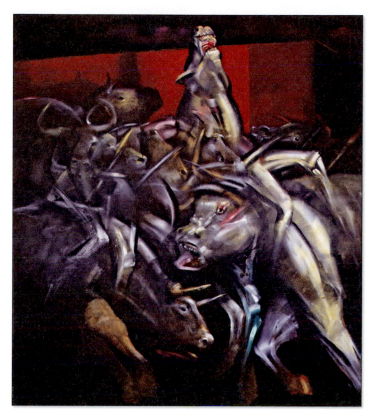

Figure 9-10a and b: Color helps define mood for Arisman, who goes on to say, "For me, mood is ultimately an issue of value, not color. 20 years ago I started seeing auras, the energy that comes from all living things. At first I saw only light, but now I see color. That colored light made color a much more interesting element in my work."
© Marshall Arisman

mixing color directly on the canvas. If you ask me to duplicate a color in my work, I can't remember how I did it."

The Value of Color

Digitally you can hick up—okay, click up—"gazillions" of hues. Okay, I exaggerate here: a hue is a family of color, that color's root (red, green, blue, orange, etc.), there aren't "gazillions." But my point is that just because you have access to this mad rush of color at the push of a button, doesn't mean you know how to put these colors to use. Same goes for actual paint (from bonafide tubes) on real canvas.

Peter Cusack recommends just using a simple value system. "Four clear value notes," he advises, "very light; light; dark; very dark." The way in which these simple value notes interact is "the art" of it. Sensitively observed, close value relationships can create a highly realized, still mood (think Jan Vermeer).

Direct Results

Don Kilpatrick teaches illustration at the College for Creative Studies in Detroit. "I employ a basic and simple approach that eliminates a lot of heartache early in the game," Kilpatrick informs. "I tone my surface so I

Figure 9-11: Like Wicklund above, Cusack talks about color and value in musical terms. "Build a color composition with one beautiful color voice," he says, "supported by an orchestration of subdued colored grays." Or he'll advise you to consider a duet of two color voices, each complementing the other from across the broad stage of the color wheel. There's also the choral possibilities of dark and light values—lyrical notes characterized by temperature (warm or cool) and color that fits mood and narrative.

Cusack begins every painting with—at very least—a simple sense of hue, tone, and design. "Do paint under a good balanced light," he advises. "And accept the sometimes baffling color discrepancies between a printed piece and the original."
© Peter Cusack

have a middle range of values to play with, working lighter to darker in tone until I have a full range of values."

"It is a principle that applies to any medium," he says. "I do this when I am creating color roughs as well. I try and do this even if I have a tight deadline. It saves me a lot of trouble, and gets me acquainted with what it is that I am striving to accomplish."

Key Change

Value and color are very important to Kilpatrick's work and, "enhance mood to any piece of art," he says. Kilpatrick tries to work within a given color key (see Chapter 8). This helps him create that mood, and leads the viewer through the illustration.

"I feel that you can make a 'cool' color 'warm' in temperature, and vice versa," Kilpatrick says. "If one works within a color key, you can do a lot. I have learned a lot by exhausting my color choices; by mixing and mixing paint, and keeping a set palette. Trial and error is, in my opinion, one of the best ways in learning color and value theory."

Figure 9-12a and b: Color is key for Kilpatrick.
© Don Kilpatrick III

9-12b © Don Kilpatrick III

A Contrast of Values

Accurate interpretation of value (tonal representation) is one of the most important aspects of understanding color. And it's crucial to understand the *contrast* created by value (as expressed in black & white or full color).

"I begin with pencil drawings," Terry Shoffner says, "where we analyze the lights and darks and work to get correct values. Then we do the same value study using painted complements to shade and gray colors. The harmony of color and value is hard for some folks to understand, so this is a way of bridging those two. I recommend that students begin with acrylics, as they are more forgiving. You can simply paint over until the observed color is achieved."

You're Hot . . . You're Cold; You're Warm . . . You're Cool

Shoffner's careful tonal assignments serve to analyze values and contrast before students ever proceed to color. "There is a point in the semester when I have students begin to identify color as cool or warm rather than by hue," he says. "We use the two extreme complements plus the addition of white to achieve variation in the color values."

"If you mix equal (visual) amounts of the two complements, you will end up with a dark value which can get to near black, in other words, an absence of either warm or cool," Shoffner informs.

An interesting experiment to check out, I think. Try mixing purple and yellow, red and green, blue and orange and see if the initial values of these color combinations will create that dark value (or resemble the black Shoffner mentions).

Figure 9-13: Think of the extreme sensation you get when Van Gogh lumps reds against greens in his paintings. Discover the power of simultaneous contrast and neutral grays. Complementary colors (mixed together or side by side) offer the most marked effect for either consideration.
© Terry Shoffner

"When two complementary colors are placed next to one another they create a visual vibration," Shoffner continues. "This vibration is called *simultaneous contrast*. You get that same effect when you mix these same colors to create neutral tones. Even when the values are narrow, simultaneous contrast gives them the appearance of greater contrast. It is really a bit of an optical illusion."

Gray Areas

If you think we're saying that color tends to be grayed down, you're reading right. For instance, getting shadows into a very bright red can be a challenge. But you generally will get much richer, vibrant color (certainly much richer, vibrant *neutral* colors) by adding a color complement to take it down, rather than adding black. And many teachers advocate banning black pigment from your palette altogether!

Find any reference material that shows strong complementary relationships. For example, in a photograph of a desert scene, a clear blue sky against brown sand would show the extremes between an orange and blue complementary color combination.

The blatant color relationships are obvious, but the subtle grays (of stones, and rocks, and trees) are still created in the same way—there's just a greater mix of the opposite color.

Black Paint Is from Mars, White Paint Is from Venus

"If you're a first year color student," Enjeti recommends, "I would avoid black paint like the plague. It sucks color right out." I agree. But in a pot vs. kettle moment, I'll confess I like black. And sometimes I can't help going for the black paint (and so does Enjeti). I'll hedge my bet to say that you will too. So, perhaps it's best to advise you to err on the side of caution.

Using black (and for that matter, white) paint is akin to seasoning with salt and pepper—good cooks apply with sense and discrimination. Too much salt or pepper, and that's all you taste. It's the same with black and white paint.

Try to mix from, say, six colors. So grab that dazzling yellow and vibrant purple. Pair an intense red with the mother of all greens. Pick the deepest blue to match your brightest orange. The high and low values are all there.

Clear as Mud

"Let's call all that pure color your *color thesis statement*," Enjeti says. "This statement may mean identifying your minority color as well as appreciating the full range of *mud* as created with your color opposite (a.k.a., color complement)."

To use hue, you must understand "mud." Mud gets a bad name, and it's usually because it's often misunderstood and frequently mishandled.

Opposites Attract

It's a simple, but beautiful, plan. So again, for example, if you're using yellow, you'll be mixing with purple (as its color opposite). But, you have to know *how* to use the mud you get from that combination of purple and yellow.

Enjeti points out that mud is in vogue, and currently a hot color trend. However, playing in the mud really starts with understanding color before you mute it down. The thing is to still have *enough* color in there; if your colors are out of proportion you won't make this palette work.

And always ask, what will serve the art best? Know your mud (keeping the play of opposites in mind) and you will certainly understand intense, vibrant color. And, as a direct result, your choices are now wide open.

"Do a monochromatic study with a wide value range," Enjeti proposes, "but view the color just in one place. Initially, don't sweat the whole color array." And Diane Fitch adds this technical aside here: "You put down a 'piece of paint' in each area of color . . . your first marks act as the gauge to subsequent color application. As the work develops, you can modulate from this key."

Being Green

Says Fitch: "Essentially do a black and white painting, but do it done with purple (as an example). Then strike a yellow note on it. Get two things working—your figure/ground and your color thesis—and fill in the values between."

This exercise sets up a simple, and excellent learning experience. Mix your yellow and purple and/or slowly introduce other local colors. Yes, you are working with physical pigment, but it's almost a no-brainer, if you keep thinking in terms of *light*.

So if you're in that purple lighting situation with an "oddball" color—say, a guy in a green shirt—*you must mix your purple into that green shirt*. Never take the local green straight into your painting. It doesn't belong (on your canvas, in your palette) unless *it's in that light*. So you tint by *mixing the light* into that green. This is smart color, and you must work it out of color confidence.

Figure 9-14: If you look at Norman Rockwell, you will see that he was quite the red/green aficionado. Parish was a blue/orange fanatic. Check out NC Wyeth and you'll see he embraced that whole reflection/complement thing, as well. "Complementary hues create a context for color as you want your audience to know it," Enjeti sums up. "It's using simple color theory as a doorway to then advance your exploration."

© Shanth Enjeti

Local Hero

"Value sense goes hand in hand with color savvy," artist (and teacher) Kathy Moore says. "Dark and light actually have *color*. You may not have the intensity of direct lighting, but shadows (and shading) still have color." Moore is saying that training one's eye to see what value (and color) commands is an intuitive decision on the part of the artist.

It could be argued that the biggest cause of "bad" art and "mediocre" color is the exploitation of the *local color* mentioned above. When you use color to represent an object (maybe to capture a realistic appearance), you are working in local color. So, the red of that apple literally means "red." Remember Shoffner's description of the "white" backdrop?

"Local color: the 'color of the actual thing' is how I use the expression," Enjeti explains. "A red apple can be easily mixed; I can efficiently recreate the 'red of an apple.' I can see the apple, I understand the properties of the pigment itself. I can match that red."

"But," Enjeti continues, "when painting that apple in the orchard at sunset, I must mix in the atmospheric color to represent how the color truly appears to the eye in that circumstance."

How Things Really Work

"Take a local color," Moore says, picking up the thread, "let's say, something is green. But it's not *just* 'green,' of course. If one side of this green shape borders a yellow object—that side will appear as a yellowish-green. That's the way light works; it reflects."

Thus, in the real world we are always seeing *tinted* light—sunlight is actually blue, after all. If you are painting realistically, it wouldn't be a stretch to mix blue into your entire palette. Think about the so-called "golden hour" at sunset, how the glow of those exquisite orange-reds gloriously effuses the light. It's no wonder filmmakers juggle entire schedules—and budgets—to shoot at these fleeting, but magical moments.

"Space, shadows, light source, even the color wheel comes into the mix," Moore will tell you. She knows that fixating on the local color—the red of the apple as the definitive red, without being sensitive to context and the color of light—often spells the death of a painting or illustration.

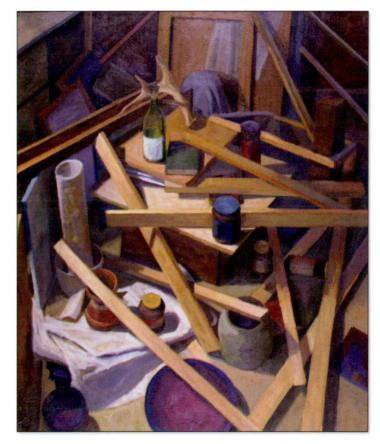

Figure 9-15: Hear, here; more Moore.
© Kathy Moore

CHAPTER SUMMARY

In this chapter we asked you to consider that value sense goes hand in hand with color savvy. We discussed some basic facts: that value, often called tone or shade (and perhaps, simply "lights and darks"), is powerful and expressive, even—and particularly so—when those values are "only" black and white. We said that value is regarded by many artists as *the* most important building block; we looked at how value establishes form, sets weight, focuses the eye, or moves you through the composition and creates a sense of depth.

We discussed the idea that the key to a good composition is value structure; that value is a key element for defining form, as well as suggesting weight. Value can direct the eye, establish focus, and promote depth. Value solves compositional problems and resolves perspective. Mood is determined by the values. Value also establishes weight and balance, focus and definition.

This chapter also suggests you discover the power of simultaneous contrast, neutral grays (as well as "mud"), and a color thesis statement.

Working It Out

1. Gray's Anatomy
Do a full-range (or for a different challenge, an extremely high- or rather low-valued), full-color drawing or painting in gray scale—all tints and shades of just gray (including white and black).

2. Am I Blue?
Do a full-range (or for a different challenge, an extremely high- or rather low-valued), full-color drawing or painting as a monochromatic study—all tints and shades of only one color (challenge: no pure white and/or black).

3. Pos/Neg
Do a full-range (or for a different challenge, an extremely high- or rather low-valued), full-color piece in pure black and white. Adapt, eliminate, or reduce your mid tones to black and white only.

Home And Away

1. Clear and Simple
Do a series of drawings or paintings using Peter Cusack's simple value system:

    a.   four clear value notes: very light; light; dark; very dark

    b.   only one clear value note: very light

    c.   only one clear value note: light

    d.   only one clear value note: dark

    e.   only one clear value note: very dark

2. Out from the Middle

Do two large (in the neighborhood of 36 in. x 48 in. or bigger) drawings or paintings using Don Kilpatrick's basic approach. Tone your surface so you have a middle range of values to play with:

a.   work lighter to darker in tone until you achieve a full range of values

b.   work darker to lighter in tone until you achieve a full range of values

Media is free choice; subject matter is free choice; one piece can be non-representational.

3. You're Golden

In the real world we are always seeing *tinted* light—sunlight is actually blue, after all. If you are painting realistically, it wouldn't be a stretch to mix blue into your entire palette.

Working from observation, do a series of drawings or paintings on the same spot, but at different times of the day: 6:00 a.m. (or just before the dawn); at dawn; 9:00 a.m.; noon; 3:00 p.m.; 7:00 p.m. to 8:30 p.m (sunset). Make it a point to work at the "golden hour" of sunset, when the glow of those exquisite orange-reds gloriously effuses the light.

Chapter 10

Texture and Pattern

© Ray-Mel Cornelius

Onomatopoeia

Dots and dashes, dabs and scrubs. Drip or dribble, flick and splatter. Squirt and spray, skim and comb, smear or wipe. Sponge and scumble, cluster and repeat; group, repeat—and do it again. Did I miss anything?

Texture and pattern occurs naturally all around us—for instance, wood bark and spider webs. Mechanical, man-made patterns (like tire treads, gears, and circuits) abound. Texture and pattern mark up our world.

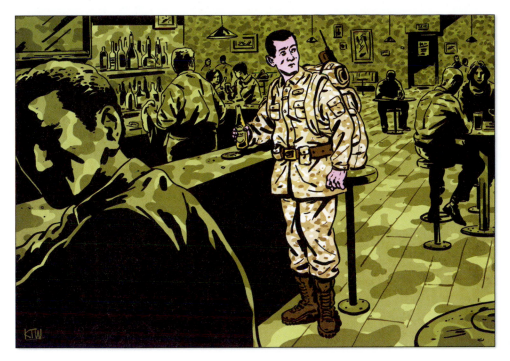

Figure 10-1: Kyle T. Webster did this illustration for the New York Times, and it was hardly business as usual—it's more conceptual than his norm. "It's a piece about how soldiers feel out of place in NYC," Webster elaborates. "Because city-dwellers in general are uncomfortable with the realities of combat and the military, they have their own camouflage, so to speak. The example given in the story was a soldier (in uniform) walking into a bar prior to leaving for Iraq and feeling immediately like he had crashed the party."
© Kyle T. Webster

Real world or rendered whirls, texture and pattern are important for providing visual interest. Texture in drawings may be truly tactile (a heavily built-up layer of oil pastel; the mottled tooth of cold press paper under a coat of colored pencil) or implied (thick to thin ink strokes suggesting heavy wood grain). In actuality, texture can be about the tools as well as the outcome of those tools.

Speaking of Which

Repeat shapes, colors, and just marks in general produce a pattern. Patterns and textures are often lumped in the same conversation. You can apply pattern and texture simultaneously (by building up a pattern of thick, heavy brush strokes, for instance).

Random, aligned, or clustered patterns often contain subsets of *more* patterns, and are usually determined by the organization of pattern elements. Frequency and number, sizing and spacing, contrast, similarity, and irregularity all add to the mix.

Tempo

Digital illustrator Petra Stefankova employs real textures— high-resolution photos of actual stone, marble, paper, wood—as if they were actual brushes. This produces a textural rhythm and pattern that can't be planned in advance. "It's a real challenge to mix different textures and make them work together," she tells us. "The tempo of such patterns is crucial," the artist says, "and you must keep this in mind."

Figure 10-2: "Without pattern (and texture), a drawing can become very flat," Mike Maihack says. "Sometimes that's what I want, but other times it does a disservice to the subject matter."
© Mike Maihack

Figure 10-3a and b: These studies by Avram Dumitrescu illustrate the above point about patterns and subsets of patterns.
© Avram Dumitrescu

As Stefankova points out, one recurring problem with digital art is that rhythm. Illustrators used to working with traditional tools may not appreciate that digital brushes can limit a desired effect. The outcome looks all too bland and uniform.

"Artists usually enjoy the advantage of consistency while using traditional media," Stefankova states, "and actually *some* uniformity is a good thing. In a traditional artwork—pencils or watercolors or whatever—the under painting is applied first; after that you layer the heavier pigments. Every touch the artist makes naturally blends with previous marks, depending on the physical characteristics of the materials and pigments."

Figure 10-4a and b: Stefankova embraces technology. But she also understands analog ground rules and taps into those basics, using the mix to stunning effect.
© Petra Stefankova

But the digital artist just may have too many options. It's a "be careful what you wish for" scenario: if you don't follow some principles driven by traditional media (like choosing proper tools, relevant textures, etc.), it can result in a piece that is way "over the top." As Stefankova considers, "A computer may offer you hundreds of different tools, but this is dangerous if you don't use that mix properly."

Out on a Limb

As Melanie Reim points out, "Texture in mark making must follow the form or direction of the shapes in your drawing in order to maintain the integrity of the underlying structure. Otherwise there is the potential for flattening the form."

Reim drew up a little figure drawing for us to illustrate her point (Figure 10-5). Notice that the left leg has marks going horizontally *across* a reasonably designed limb. But the leg on the right has the marks following the structure/shape of the leg and its muscles, and so reinforces the strong design of the limb. "When line (or texture or pattern, for that matter) merely transverses the plane," Reim says, "it has the potential of flattening what is there."

Don't necessarily fear a "flat" drawing—this format certainly presents distinct creative opportunities and challenges—but texture and pattern can neatly add that other dimension to the work. It's not simply about marks, but the way in which texture (and pattern) can create dimension (not to mention color and value) in a piece.

Figure 10-5: The work of Reim.
© Melanie Reim

✔ Check Point: Order and Chaos

Randy Wollenmann has been developing illustrations and designs for a broad range of markets, from tabletop giftware to children's learning materials. He provides our hot list for this chapter.

1. M. C. Escher put it best when he said, "We adore chaos because we love to produce order."

2. Pattern supplies a sense of harmony. Pattern provides a resting place for both eye and mind.

3. Texture in an illustration gives the viewer something tangible to relate to. Your visceral, subconscious response kicks in.

4. Texture and pattern—real and simulated; natural or mechanical—add a slice of interaction both familiar and understandable.

5. Texture and pattern cut across traditional technique, decorative pursuits, and conceptual (as well as narrative) concerns.

6. Bear in mind that pattern can help to organize and simplify. Texture can work to change things up.

7. Texture and pattern—like a visual surprise, even a treat—make the art come off less stiff, not as formal; a design can appear a little more organic.

8. You *might* see the two almost being interchangeable: texture is pattern; pattern is texture. But, honestly, I'm not sure that's true. This just might make it that much more confusing, but there *is* a link.

9. When I think of pattern, I envision a clear repetition of design elements and their repetition within an illustration. To create a less rigid design, I usually try and add other elements that are not a part of the basic pattern structure.

10. When I consider "pattern" I think of it as a design tool. When I consider "texture," it's more embellishment: icing on the cake, like a skin.

Wollenmann has a pattern of doing fine (and finely textured) illustration, as seen here.

© Olympia Sales

© Sunrise Greetings

© Randy Wollenmann

Bend, Break, Bust

When working texture and pattern, all the foundations are important. You have to understand the fundamentals. "Picasso would not be *Picasso* without him learning those guidelines at age 12," Andy DuCett smiles. "He was able to bend or break the basic precepts because he had an incredible mastery of those principles."

Pattern helps on both a formal level and conceptually. "The thing about it is," DuCett continues, "you must trust that you're moving in the right direction. I like the idea of pattern. Strong repetition of pattern speaks to a mechanical sense of applied energy and time. Through pattern, a drawing can be revealed as almost an *object* rather then 'just a drawing' on a piece of paper."

DuCett consciously works in pen and—at least initially—begins without an under drawing (but see his comments below). He rarely does roughs and has no idea where the piece is going to end up. Pencil complements his pen line and meshes with the general concept and visual direction.

Value—the density of tone, or the way that tone reads on a flat surface—also comes into play. He plugs a little incidental color here and there to pop select areas of his tableaux forward.

Big

"Pencil on paper adds a warmer element," DuCett says. "Think of old master drawings. Leonardo cartoons. I like how [when working in pencil] value fluctuates as you modulate line quality, which affects space and offers the eye a little variety, more to digest.

"There's something really human—*warm* concept versus *cool* modern technology—about the nuances that don't look planned. Drips and dribbles, dots and dashes, flicks and splatters are spontaneous opportunities to lose control and take some chances."

The drawings shown here began with the little gift of a huge sheet of paper (36 in. x 48 in.). "I had a piece of masonite that was just a bit bigger than the piece of paper," he remembers, "so I clipped the paper down to the board and said: I'm going to do a *really big* drawing."

Don't Blow It

"You see the studio door opening up to the world at large in that bottom left corner," DuCett says. "I skipped around from there. It wasn't *hard* to connect the parts, but I was somewhat nervous to do it."

"From a certain distance and time investment," he continues, "the notion of 'I don't want to ruin this' starts creeping into your head—which is completely contrary to the process." DuCett says firmly that purposeful under drawing alleviated the sinking sensation that he might ruin an established drawing. "At this juncture, you do a quick sketch on the side: practice; see how a specific object looks in your head, and *then* transfer it to paper."

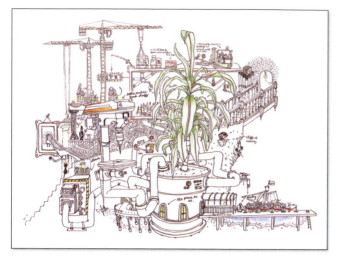

Figure 10-6a and b: Yes, DuCett uses reference. But he also studies and seeks to understand his resources: "I recognize that corner...and that's a Doric column...okay, this is three-wide...now we have to go five deep." Here, DuCett smiles a bit as he says, "I can get sucked into the patterning. 'Damn, there's an extra two columns there. Oops, this is 30 feet longer than the building!' I get lost between looking at the thing and actually drawing."

© Andy DuCett

But more often than not, he preferred to just dive in, right on the sheet. "There's something about everything taking place and coming out on that paper," DuCett remarks. "That's where it starts becoming representational of the endeavor itself."

Talk the Talk

Nate Walker is an instructor of illustration at Montserrat College of Art (in addition to being an alum of this great school, and Fred Lynch's former student). From both sides of the desk, Walker is well aware that texture can help an illustration stand out, as well as give insight into an illustrator's technique and decision making process.

But for Walker, texture was something he came to consider late in his artistic development. "My early style was purposefully devoid of all texture," Walker says. "I felt it was important to hide all evidence of mark making. I equated a clean, smooth, and uniform surface with skill."

Proud of this skill, it still wasn't long before he realized that those little surface marks of pencil and brush were what breathed life into the work, and showcased a deeper level of process within the picture.

"It's why I now focus on—and fully consider—all the marks on the page," he says. "I make them part of my process instead of choosing to hide them. It gives me an opening to begin the coveted 'conversation' an artist has with his art; where we respond to the work (and vise versa)."

Exploration and Discovery

"Texture and pattern are always important, and are elements I enjoy very much," states Ray-Mel Cornelius. Cornelius has explored texture (with pattern)

Figure 10-7a, b and c: "Pattern?" Walker considers. "I really don't have much of a conscious relationship with this. I am generally more interested in the random and chaotic parts of my work. This is where I find the most inspiration."
© Nathan Walker

in different ways. Back in the day, he stippled over flat color. Here, the stipple sometimes defined the form; sometimes it functioned as decorative pattern. "The process always created its own visual (if not tactile) texture," he says.

He's used color and value as a modeling device, with the texture provided by the paint method—a sort of scumbled dry brush mixed with brush stippling, on either canvas or watercolor paper. Again, the texture was more visual than tactile.

Eventually, Cornelius began using underlying materials (such as modeling paste, matte gels, and medium) to create textures that could be experienced

Figure 10-8a and b: The work of Cornelius.
© Ray-Mel Cornelius

both visually and tactually. "Recently, as my painting technique develops," he says, "I've discovered a style that refers to my earlier work, using color as a decorative element rather than one that defines form. This employs a rougher, digitally produced version of the stipple motif, more pure pattern than modeling technique."

Every Little Thing

"In school," Jaime Zollars remembers, "I rendered out every little thing in every piece to a fault. I would paint patterns on dresses, and textures on the tiniest of details. Often this would become tedious for me as the artist, and tedious for viewers overwhelmed with information when the piece was done."

Zollars would like to tell you that she had a brilliant revelation resolving her obsession, but the solution was not so sublime, and more a matter of necessity. "I had an illustration to start and finish overnight," she says, "and there was no way for me to complete the task. The piece had a pine tree with thousands of little needles to paint. This illusion of texture was an important element to the piece."

"I experimented with a paper punch and a stack of magazine pages. I collaged these pieces on my drawing with gloss medium to form the shape of the tree. The sharp edges of the paper collage pieces made a nice tactile physical texture on the page, and the patterns in the source material created a rich illusion. I had created a tree without painting a thing."

"All that was left was to unify the elements into a convincing tree," Zollars says. "I had saved myself hours, came up with something better and more intriguing, and a real joy to create."

Figure 10-9a, b and c: "I feel compelled to fill every area of my paintings," Zollars admits. "But a piece with blank space takes more courage to put out there. It illustrates a certain level of confidence in the work. It took me some time to develop the courage to simplify my compositions."

"I prefer working with a textured negative space to parallel the grain in my collage elements, instead of using flat color or leaving the canvas untouched," she says.

Teaching herself *not* to fill all the blank areas with more "stuff" became easier once Zollars started incorporating textures into those flat areas (even background space will almost always have a texture to it). White space is never left white, but is painted white, with hints of grey noise, light purple splatter, or yellow dots. "This suggestion of texture—while creating more uniformity in my illustrations and satisfying my compulsion to fill the piece—still feels like blank space to the viewer."

© Jaime Zollars

CHAPTER SUMMARY

This chapter looked at *texture* and *pattern*. We considered that texture and pattern occur naturally and mechanically all around us; that without texture and pattern, a drawing can become very flat. We said that texture (and pattern) help an illustration to stand out, while providing a sense of harmony (and giving the viewer something tangible to relate to). However, we clarified that one shouldn't necessarily fear a "flat" drawing—there are creative opportunities here as well.

We discussed how repeat shapes, colors, and lines (or marks in general) produce a pattern; that patterns and textures are often discussed/applied simultaneously; that random, aligned, or clustered patterns often contain subsets of *more* patterns (usually determined by the organization of pattern elements: frequency, tempo, and number; sizing and spacing; contrast, similarity, and irregularity).

Working It Out

1. Valued Customer

Create a portrait or self-portrait that offers a full range of values. The kicker: *all values must be expressed as a different texture or pattern*, no gradation or continuous tone.

2. With and Without

Do a realistic scene that boasts multiple (and varied) textures and/or patterns. Do another illustration, but this time keep it completely devoid of all texture and pattern: just flat color and tone.

3. Sequential Stories

On a large sheet (minimum 18 in. x 24 in.), draw 10-20 panels. Create an ordered sequential design of repeated simple shapes in each panel. The repeat pattern should "tell a story," and must go from "Point A" to "Point B" (for instance, small to large, left to right, light to dark; even something a bit more conceptual, like calm to frantic, or sleepy to wide awake).

Home and Away

1. Open Up

Create a series of illustrations that are all about open, wide expanses: the desert, outer space, the ocean, the sky, etc. No pure, flat color fields! Nuance white or negative areas with texture and pattern.

2. Touching

Create a series of illustrations that use color and value as a modeling device, that use actual tactile textures and underlying materials (such as modeling paste, matte gels and medium) to create textures that could be experienced both visually and tactually.

3. Sequential Stories

Do a *really big* drawing (36 in. x 48 in. minimum). Texture and pattern will be crucial to facilitate your space as well as maintain visual interest. Full color or grayscale. Media: free choice.

11

Shape and Form

© Mary Thelen

Work Out to Get a Better Shape

Your gym coach bellowed it out all the time: it's not so hard to get in shape (and it's never too late). What's the big deal about shape and form? Concentrating on shapes (and patterns of same) develops negative space—which works to manipulate form and visually entice the viewer. And that may help you sell the message or give the concept some breathing room.

"It's an easier and quicker solution to a problem than any written or verbal explanation," Steve Simpson states, "far faster (and clearer) to draw the form of a box than to try to explain

Figure 11-1a and b: "Focusing on shape rather than detail creates a clearer message," Simpson follows up. "Because of this, objects and characters that read well as silhouettes help get concepts across quicker and cleaner."
© Steve Simpson

what it looks like." And with a nod to Chapter 10, Simpson says you may even find that emphasizing pattern through shape is relatively basic.

Simpson, from Glenageary, County Dublin, Ireland, feels that rethinking shapes is a kind of whittling and re-molding that brings out the strongest visual forms. "I'm looking to find a natural balance," he tells us. "You can be easily drawn into aesthetics, but that's not terribly productive. Get the shapes right first."

Sum of All Parts

Continued definitions: shape has more to do with the *overall* visual perception of the parts of an image. Form, then, is the rendering of that organization. Chris Spollen can sum it up in ten words or less: "A student must be able to think and tinker." For Spollen, this means wide-open doors and new vistas of opportunity. Thus, the illustrator is developing a current set of *sculptures* by cutting and cobbling actual aluminum cans.

Working in three dimensions demands that Spollen look at his art on many different planes. He equates his initial sketches to "thinking with the mind's eye," and labels the sculpture that evolves through these thumbnails as "True 'Ameri–Can' Art."

The Shape I'm In

"A composition is a design of shapes," says Tina Sweep. Sweep will tell you that the viewer (visually) reads the shape of an object to (intellectually) identify it. The *form* of that object is expressed through rendering, which establishes the object in the picture plane and creates the illusion of depth.

Figure 11-2: Check out Spollen's cool sketch-based rocket gun, fabricated with cans. Because, as we all know—and even though some Jedi consider them to be a bit clumsy or random—hokey religions and ancient weapons are no match for a good blaster at your side, kid.

© Chris Spollen

"The *shape* of an object is like a flat silhouette," Sweep continues, "defining for the viewer what the object visually represents to the design as a whole. The *form* of that object has dimensionality through multiple sides, which also define differences within the object or between other objects.

A Weighty Subject

Out of Denver, Colorado, Mary Thelen says that drawing is all about weight. Initially reducing natural forms to simple, abstracted, 2-dimensional statements, Thelen's art focused on shape (and color). "Eventually," she tells us, "I worked back to representational art, retaining the simplified flat shapes and bold colors, keeping line as a secondary element to create texture and depth or movement."

Using shape and color to establish mass and emotional impact (rather than to contrast values), Thelen juggles size and positive/negative space, playing off smaller, busier shapes or placing shapes "off register" with the background to give a feeling of motion. "Tonal values don't interest me so much," Thelen admits, "but if they interest you, you can do a lot with them to add dimension and depth to your composition."

Interaction is key: typography breaks up large areas to create pattern and texture; black against white squares off with strong color; big chunks of composition bounce against a neighbor. "It is important to create an illustration where color and shapes are balanced," she considers. "But being able to do that means you recognize when to abdicate certain design principles (like placing things *askew*) to achieve a particular effect."

The Job Takes Shape

"My work has always been about drawing," says John Hendrix. "It is important that the images I make announce that they are drawn—that they come from a hand putting pen to paper." For Hendrix, a line on the page is more powerful than a sculpted form, if only because of its efficiency.

Figure 11-3: "At its most basic," Sweep states, "illustration is a means of visual problem solving." And when you're talking shape and form, positive/negative—a.k.a., figure/ground—is a big part of the solution. As Sweep says, "Negative shapes are just as important as their positive counterparts in a piece, and must be analyzed with the same design approach."
© Tina Sweep

Figures 11-4, 11-5, 11-6 and 11-7: As demonstrated here in these illustrations, you manipulate shape to promote visual organization and perception.
© Mary Thelen

Figure 11-5
© Ray-Mel Cornelius

Figure 11-6
© Gwenda Kaczor

Figure 11-7
© Susan Loeb

Line functions in many ways, and Hendrix says his strokes are more about shape (and less about movement). "My lines have a diverse job description," he'll tell you. "I often use line to create value *shapes* by using parallel marks in sequence to build a field of tone."

And speaking of that tone, Hendrix asks you to fully appreciate these value *structures*. "If you're not considering how a figure and its environment separate in space," he says, "the final result will create a noticeable lack of visual variety, misleading the viewer."

Color, Value, and Shape

What about color? "Value and color both work to build shape recognition," Hendrix continues, tying the thread. "Shape recognition is when your color, value, and line create a hierarchical organization that allows a viewer to clearly understand the space placed before you.

"And you work the entire surface at the same time," says Hendrix of a basic rule to follow when addressing color ideas. But as he'll remind you, his colors, first and foremost, work as values. "I can't underscore how important this is to create convincing figure/field relationships," he states. "Look at the work of Philip Burke. His portraits, full of violent and seemingly random colors shifts, still communicate clear, convincing likenesses. Burke is a master of using color as value structures. It doesn't matter what hues you use as long as your value structure is sound."

Figure 11-8a and b: "Clarity is *not* the same as simplicity," says Hendrix. "What an illustrator should strive for is clarity. Clarity is about managing your visual hierarchy, color palette, value range, and composition to create a unified whole. The magic happens when unconnected pieces come together to serve one goal. The viewer does not see a value structure. The viewer does not see an analogous color palette. The viewer does not see an asymmetrical composition. The viewer sees an idea."
© John Hendrix

Enough Rope

Sterling Hundley tells us that contour is a visual symbol used to infer the shape of an object. Thus, he thinks of contour—and line, for that matter—in terms of lassoing shapes. "Line," he says, "is a manufactured icon that is used to describe content. It is subject to follow rules, if the intent is communication.

"As a general rule, if a piece of artwork requires the use of line for clarification, then the shapes, as defined by value, are not working properly. "But line that is used out of choice," he continues, "and not out of necessity, points to a successful understanding of how value and shape work together."

Off the Bat

"It's always about shape first," says Hundley. "People fall in love with line— it's very seductive. I think about value right off the bat, and shape-oriented value at that," he states. "The only way to make images clear is to make sure your shape and value are working properly. Color conveys mood, but currently, it's the least important aspect of my work—an afterthought to shape, value, and ideation."

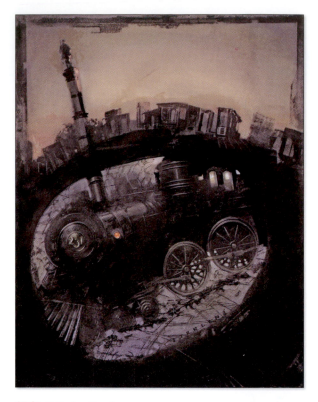

11-9a © Sterling Hundley

11-9b © Sterling Hundley

11-9c © Sterling Hundley

Figure 11-9a, b and c: Shape dominates Hundley's work. *Engine231* (Figure 11-9a) is the reverential tale of an entombed locomotive. *Sleeping Prophet* (Figure 11-9b) is about the clairvoyant, Edgar Cayce. Yes, pattern is key to this piece. But Hundley will tell you that such pattern is informed by shape. "The pattern here is not just pattern for decoration's sake," he points out. "The pattern is integral to the story and the idea of the piece. The strong shapes (plus high values) of Cayce's face and hands play against the dark tones and simple mass of the sofa, compelling the viewer to look here first."

William Henry Harrison (Figure 11-9c) is meant to be viewed both vertically and horizontally. Looked at from one direction, the crowd listens to the new chief of state. Flip it and you have a front row seat at the wake. Notice how the podium slyly and seamlessly becomes a coffin: smart art doesn't get any better than this, folks.

The Million-Dollar Question

Hundley points out that the general assumption is that artists are referring to subject matter—a figure, a building, a tree, for instance—when discussing value/shape. "But if an artist can remove themselves from content when designing their composition with abstract shapes," he says, "they can begin to understand how both positive and negative shapes interlock, and work with each other in the picture plane.

"In regards to drawing, the single most insightful question that a student can ever ask is, 'When you draw, are you drawing the positive or negative shapes?' My answer is always 'Both!'"

Figure 11-10: *Shipwreck* evokes Gustav Klimt in the way the figures are contained by the shape of the doorway, and the decorative flowers in the woman's hair. Conceptually, the entire image is built around that vertical wine glass and the offset liquid highlighting how the boat truly lies. What you think to be sky is actually water and sand. It's a clever second read: The couple is on the ship's deck, coming into the Captain's quarters, but the ship is actually wrecked on the beach, not afloat at sea.
© Sterling Hundley

Auto Pilot

Petra Stefankova does surrealist work she labels as "automatic drawings." She wanted to take these works a step further. Take them, in fact, into another *dimension*, as she exuberantly puts it. Stefankova's practice refers to an old surrealist technique of the early 20th century. "Automatic drawing" was touted as a method of expressing the subconscious where the hand was allowed to "randomly" meander around the drawing.

"The artist knows and feels what she draws," says Stefankova. "You understand the subject, but respond in your unique way … you have an opinion on the matter. It will require a lot of research, thinking; and like an actor who must study his role, you learn specific skills to interpret character properly and believably."

Must We?

Clear communication is especially pertinent when considering experimental and conceptual art—and often forgotten by fine artists who have great ideas on their mind, but don't realize that need (or relevance).

Stefankova seeks to motivate and inspire—and move with her audience. "I often draw when I feel that it's a physical and mental *must*," she says, "in that particular *moment*." So she plays with tools (mainly ball pens, pencils, and markers) and engages different surfaces (newspapers, bus or train tickets, even calendar sheets), ultimately manipulating her shapes in the computer. "Often, I'll select (or eliminate) details," she says, "simplify, break the pattern and rhythm. Even digitally, I find color control is much more fun when I allow it to flow freely and almost randomly.

"Concept is major, but it's the *principle* and the *process* which are crucial. Really, as important as the final."

Figure 11-11: A dash of cubism and a splash of the fauves is sprinkled in with simmering surrealism. Toss in stylized forms and a lot of color freedom, and all these three historical sources mix up a unique contemporary result for Stefankova.
© Petra Stefankova

French Lessons

California-born illustrator Martin French is an educator and lecturer, as well as an artist. He feels his ultimate artistic goal is to push a series of diverse contrasts: flat graphic areas to textural, organic rhythms; distinct light and dark patterns; elegant curved lines against straight hard strokes; the simplification of form vs. fine detail.

French says these contrasts add to the aesthetics of the drawing, but also create a very energetic sense of form and structure. "The variation of weight and value echo natural subtleties & nuances found in nature and the human figure," French comments. "There's no need to over-render the drawing."

"I'm looking to create a sense of energy and emotion in my images. A personal expression of the form, not simply accurate representation. I suppose I am always in search of that balance of raw expression and focused observation."

Figure 11-12a and b: "I learned design from figure drawing classes—more so than design or composition classes," French says. "I was taught to observe the flat shapes and angles created by the stationary figure."

"As I am drawing, the relationship of these shapes informs my initial observations. A distinctive line energizes those graphic shapes and creates the next layer of dimension and depth. I then take this as far as I want, building value, contrast, and detail."

© Martin French

Thumbs Up

For Jaime Zollars, dealing with shape and form is the first step to a successful piece. While some artists work very instinctively, she is (in her words) an analytical personality. "I always start with a drawing," she tells you, "then a color study, followed by a final piece."

While she's methodical, Zollars says she's found a process that allows her to be fairly free in creating that work. "My pieces start out as tiny thumbnail drawings, where I am most comfortable," she says. "Here I am less inhibited by gross exaggerations and bold gestures. I try to do at least 11 thumbnail drawings for any new piece until one really speaks to me."

"The reason a thumbnail will grab my attention is usually because of a specific shape or form that really jumps off the page. Maybe it's a sweeping river, or a bold hunched figure in a stylized arch. If my image is boring as a thumbnail, I'm learning that it will probably be a boring final piece."

Zollars says she's found that the shapes and forms of people, landscapes, and objects can be exaggerated in startling ways before the viewer gets confused by the imagery, and these shapes and forms can bring great interest and meaning to an illustration.

Figure 11-13: "To maintain the initial energy of that first drawing, I blow up my favorite thumbnail on the computer, and print it out larger," Zollars tells us. "I use vellum paper on top of this, upon which I develop a refined version of the initial sketch. That way I can add details to tighten the drawing while staying true to the movement and spirit of my first loose interpretation. My images maintain more life and are less likely to get bogged down, flattened, or 'corrected' for accuracy by my analytical side," she says.

"Maintaining some of the quirks in my first thumbnails really keeps me interested in the final piece, and for me, the result displays more artistic instinct and integrity."

© Jaime Zollars

✔ Check Point: The Angle

Jon Reinfurt graduated from, and now teaches for, The University of the Arts in Philadelphia, PA. He's formed conversations about shape—and more—from both sides of the teacher's desk. Here's his input for this chapter's hot list:

1. You know, if you just stay awake during your classes, you *will* learn. I stayed awake at least *half* the time. But seriously …

2. … School really changed the way I thought about art in general. Everything took on more meaning.

3. I had a painting teacher—James Dupree—who was another teacher who expected you to articulate—to verbalize—about your art. He exposed me to methods and materials that truly revolutionized my process, concepts (and ultimately my portfolio).

4. I'm a visual kind of guy. I'm into texture, simple shapes, and tightly designed compositions. I like very angular, awkward looking characters and juxtaposing elements to suggest spatial relationships that trick the eye.

5. I want to bend the image, distorting toward the surreal. I want to get away from painting what you might see in life.

6. I can fill you in on crash and burn assignments, oddball projects and deadbeat clients (or should we say, oddball clients and deadbeat projects).

7. There's a zen to cash flow and all those facts of the illustrator's life you only really experience after your school daze.

8. The learning curve sets in. Whether it's during lean spots or when it's fast and furious, you start realizing just how much you can handle …

9. … the stress, the workload; it's a balancing act. You have to pay attention to everything—including your own life apart from the assignment.

10. You should push yourself to your limits. For me it was, "Wow, I can handle a lot more than I originally thought I could!" It's all good preparation for whatever's around the corner.

Reinfurt's angular characters always look slightly out of their depth. This bit of tension (both visual and conceptual) plays nicely against the textured, simple shapes of his collage work. It all dovetails into Reinfurt's tight designs, the elements of which juxtapose wily spatial relationships that trick the eye.
© Jon Reinfurt

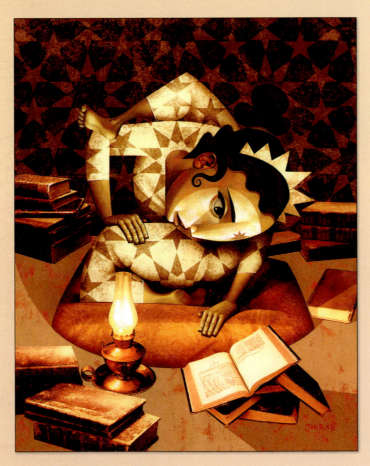

CHAPTER SUMMARY

This chapter was about shape and form: shape as the *overall* visual perception of the parts of an image; form, then, as the rendering of that organization. For many illustrators it's always about shape first; dealing with shape and form is the first step to a successful piece. The relationship of shapes informs the viewer's observations—it is far faster (and clearer) to draw the form of a box than to try to explain what it looks like.

At its roots, a composition is a design of shapes. Focusing on shape brings out stronger design. Illustration is a means of visual problem solving. And if you're talking shape and form, positive/negative—a.k.a., figure/ground—is a big part of that solution. Concentrating on shapes—and patterns of shapes—while developing negative space to manipulate form visually entices the viewer. Remember: negative shapes are just as important as their positive counterparts, and must be analyzed with the same design approach.

Working It Out

1. Geometry

Paul Melia suggests we think, see, and draw geometrically; to look for picture components that create squares and rectangles, circles and ovals, triangles (and other geometric shapes) within the structure of your illustration.

Create a portrait or figure study that includes nothing but squares and rectangles, circles and ovals, triangles (and other geometric shapes). The kicker: no tone work; don't shade your shapes or go for 3-D.

2. Blockheads

Again, create a portrait or figure study out squares and rectangles, circles and ovals, triangles (and other geometric shapes). This time, think dimensionally: shade your shapes. Go for a deliberate 3-D look by showing facets and gradations of light to dark/light and dark.

3. Shape and Nothing but the Shape

"A composition is a design of shapes," says Sweep. Do an abstract or non-representational design composed of nothing but shapes. Flat color. No lines on this one!

Home and Away

1. Shapes with Benefits

You will be doing five different designs. Create an over-sized abstract or non-representational piece composed of nothing but a *particular* shape: circles, squares, rectangles, ovals, triangles.

Lines are good for this one. Tone and shading are fine, too (but you don't have to go three dimensional), as is an impasto or textured paint quality, if you are so inclined.

2. What Was I Thinking?

Do a series of "automatic drawings." These type of drawings were meant to express the subconscious, where the hand was allowed to "randomly" meander around the drawing. Do one a day; 10 over a period of time, 10 days. Draw for a set duration: 10 to 30 minutes. Use a fluid media; go with the flow.

3. Yin/Yang

Do a series of illustrations where the subject matter or composition may be viewed (physically or conceptually) from two different perspectives. For example: vertically and horizontally; left or right; inside/outside; organic and mechanical; good and evil; Democratic or Republican; black and white. See handout for further clarification and specs.

Clarity and Struggle

For the inquisitive mind—always exploring, forever questioning—mysteries abound. Douglas Klauba could never quite answer this question: what would you be if you weren't an illustrator? "I felt that the solution—and the next level on my path—was to 'find' the artist in me instead of the studio technician that took over," Klauba considers.

Paul Balmer chimes in, "Going into a painting is like taking a mysterious journey. Some of it you have to know and other things you leave up to chance. Each painting becomes a battle between conscious decisions and letting go—those things that accidentally show up on the canvas; you either run with it or cover them over. The more 'accidents' the better the painting in my opinion," he smiles.

Brave Heart

"You know," Britt Spencer ponders, "I'm not sure you can really teach someone how to draw, but intense practice makes you better at your trade, and it then becomes natural."

"And there is that blend of technical prowess but never taking yourself too seriously that dives you deeper into finding the creativity of the moment," adds Robert "Buddy" Hill. This is one springboard that can help get your work to that next level Klauba mentions above.

Throw perseverance into your action plan, too. "If a drawing's looking good," illustrator Matt Hammill says, "I'll want to see it through to the end—as long as I can get over the fear of messing up."

And that's when Hill talks to you about taking risks. "The laughs may stop and you might fall from a great height," he says, "but this is an exciting part of the creative process—stepping over that line in the sand reaps amazing rewards."

© Paul Balmer

Chapter 12

Drawing in Character

© Rama Hughes

What to Call It

As I sought to title this particular chapter, I went through a list of synonyms to address the context and content within. Some givens: this book is predominately about figurative illustration, and by design this chapter indeed cross-references other parts of the book. It was a pretty good list; and most of the words do apply to the art and artists introduced in within. The original title, *Portraiture, Caricature, and Cartoons*, would have been appropriate only to a certain extent.

Figure 12-1:
© Dan Krall

Figure 12-2:
© Kyle T Webster

Figure 12-3:
© Rick Tulka

Figure 12-4:
© Stan Shaw

Figures 12-1, 12-2, 12-3, and 12-4: You've met Dan Krall (Fig. 12-1) and Kyle T. Webster (Fig. 12-2) previously. Rick Tulka (Fig. 12-3) is an American illustrator, living and working in Paris, France. Stan Shaw (Fig. 12-4) is an Illustrator/educator based in Tacoma, WA.

Caricature? Portraiture? Illustration? Cartoon? Who cares about the tag? All these guys offer wonderful drawings that simply *nail* the quirks of persona—and the vital essence—of likeness.

Then it hit me. Caricature? Portraiture? Illustration? Cartoon? Why worry about a label? Who cares about the tag? I ask those rhetorical questions knowing full well that there are folks who do. But I'll go down fighting asking this question, too: why is it that important?

The chapter doesn't fuss about straight (or traditional) portraiture, although there are remarkable likenesses rendered within, and not all are photographic in nature. It's not about classical or modern cartooning or caricature (while there are some spot on, state of the art examples of just that).

So whether it's old school or experimental, this chapter is not so much an exposé of the warts and all. It doesn't portray—or betray—in that sense, even though there are some weapons-grade samples of that to be found here. I say this section is more about rendering and description: character (internal interpretation) and characters (external representation). But let's see what you think.

Figure 12-6:
© Adrian Gottlieb

Figure 12-7:
© Adrian Gottlieb

Figure 12-5:
© Adrian Gottlieb

Figures 12-5, 12-6, and 12-7: Here's the work of Adrian Gottlieb. Gottlieb is a naturalist painter and portraitist based in Los Angeles. His striking art also represents exactly what this chapter seeks to address: that character development (external and internal) runs deep, regardless of style or technique.

Gotta Be Me

"Drawing only *seems* easy," says Guillaume Decaux from his studio in Strasbourg, France. Many illustrators feel that the *next* drawing will always be better than the previous one. Even if you're just sketching with a nub of a pencil on a scrap of napkin, you must rise to that challenge (or perhaps I should say rise to your particular challenge). You figure out *your* technique. *You* develop your own characters. While many illustrators may influence your graphic style, the point is to convey a piece that is drawn by *you*.

Good Vibrations

A line can have its own life. It's not just an edge for colors...line can be something provocative or intellectual, fragile or explosive; able to tell a story with sheer strength or subtle grace. I admire artists who are true draftsmen—regardless of technique—first and foremost.

So the vibrancy of Mark Todd's line work spins a high-energy tale for me. Artistic perception dictates certain decisions, and technique plus tools serve that vision. Todd's design sense and structure, the balance of shapes, accentuates his point (and unique point of view). His individual grasp of the fundamentals: concept and composition, color and value, visual focus and intellectual direction—all the foundations in general—make for a great drawing.

Figure 12-8: The work of Todd.
© Mark Todd

Loving It

"I just love to draw," Rama Hughes says. "Even when I am not physically drawing, I'm drawing in my mind: drawing people—studying people—and faces especially. My motivation? To put what I see onto paper."

He flirts with conceptual work, but has always preferred to draw narratives: real people and real stories; the telling expressions; what he calls "those true and pregnant moments (or, at least, the moments that feel true)."

Hughes feels deeply that his artwork is just a reflection of his mind: what he notices, feels, and thinks about. His mind is a reflection of the world—his world. "It's a box of mirrors!" he smiles.

Comic books are an enormous inspiration for Hughes. A good comic book (or the absence of this beloved resource) sparks a powerful need to make his art.

"But I am really influenced by *everything*," he says. "I even feel a kind of guilty urge to draw," he considers. "Like when I'm not drawing, I really *should* be drawing. If that desire to draw isn't there, my feeling that I *ought* to draw takes over."

Figure 12-9: An image really doesn't feel complete to Hughes unless there's a person in there somewhere. Why is that? "I am devoted to and fascinated by humanity—this eensy-beensy sliver of existence. . .that's *me*. Despite all the suffering, the world is a beautiful place and we are fortunate to be here. That is what my work is about; that's what I'm trying to say."

This is the illustrator's take on the Mona Lisa, and that's Hughes' wife, Christine, by the way.
© Rama Hughes

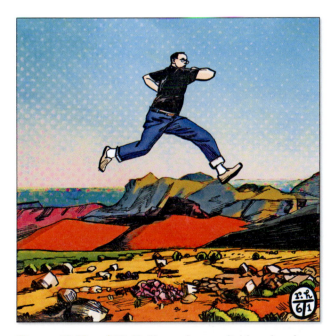

Figures 12-10 and 12-11: "I am always pitching drawing as an *activity*," Hughes says. "In my opinion, the number one reason to draw is the act of drawing. It slows you down and forces you to study what you may never really consider. In that way, drawing is a form of meditation. And because of that, the act itself is worthwhile—even if the pictures are lousy."

"And I like the idea that drawing is a democratic art form," he states. "A person doesn't need a big budget or a dozen collaborators. To create another world, he only needs a pencil and paper."
© Rama Hughes

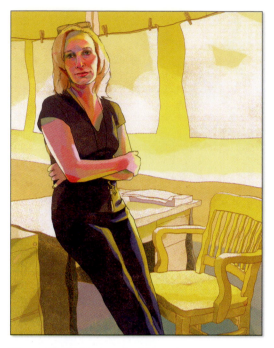

Figure 12-12: The work of Saunders.
© Zina Saunders

Getting Ahead

There is a poignant quality to Zina Saunders' portraits, which she attributes to the emotions she experiences while painting. "It's my affection for these people," she smiles, "and a true thrill for me to develop these portraits."

Her portraits for her series, *Overlooked New York*, have developed as the artist has grown herself. "When I started this, I was still working traditionally. The project proved to be a rich learning ground for me in developing as a digital artist (in addition to developing as a reportage artist). Many of the first portraits were half traditional and half digital, and I was working on a single layer!"

"You never know what will turn out to play an important role in the development of your style or focus; in the case of *Overlooked New York*, it proved to be both—another reason why it's a good thing to follow your passion and see where it might lead. The same can be said about my political work, as far as content and concept goes."

Stretch

Saunders does pencil sketches before painting the portraits digitally in Photoshop. She has created her own library of brushes. At 300 dpi, and usually about 10 x 14 inches. RGB. No filters. As with her gouache, she'll lay in an underpainting. First, pencils; put down a wash, then paint the picture. Sometimes she'll begin the painting traditionally and scan that, then paint to completion in Photoshop. "It all depends on how to best convey what's in my mind's eye," she comments.

"I paint on a traditional support—an Arches hot press watercolor block—and my computer in exactly the same way. It even feels the same: the brushes I've created have particular textures to mimic the texture of certain kinds of paper. It's been a long technical process, developed over the years."

Saunders herself is often a favorite model; her characters reflecting her self-reference. "The whole time I'm painting," she says, "I imagine what the character is feeling in that moment. This process is a direct emotional connection with my subject—even if that person is made up. Even if that person is me."

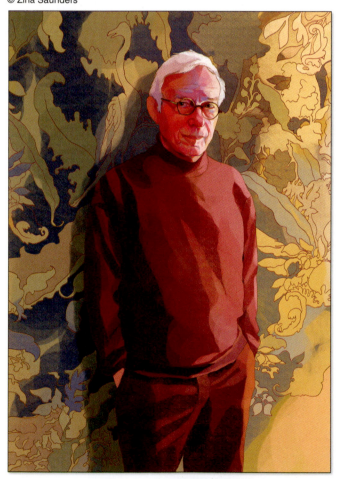

Figure 12-13: "What I'm doing here is *stretching* the studio concept," Saunders says, "getting out, meeting my subjects, talking to them about their passions. *Then* I go back home and paint. It's a much more interactive way of doing illustration."
© Zina Saunders

Ashcan Cool

One of Peter Cusack's heroes is legendary painter and teacher, Robert Henri, who referred to students as "sketch hunters." Henri pushed his pupils to be more interested in *what* they painted rather than *how*. He urged them to go out into the streets and paint the reality of New York's underside.

"His brilliance," says Cusack, "was the ability to separate method and technique from the search for the authentic. Henri set his students free and their imaginations afire. In return, his students painted fast and furious, with unbridled creative energy."

"The visceral quality found in the work of the Ashcan school is something I strive for in my own work," Cusack considers. "For so long I've been a student of light and form, a student of a life that is *still*, well lit, ready for a measured solution."

Here's Looking at Hue, Kid

A young Rick Tulka picks up his first crayon, and knows instantly he's going to be an artist. Flash forward. While a student at Pratt Institute, Tulka picks up his first illustration job.

At school, he's given the freedom to develop his own projects. He lands his first part-time job in the industry—which ultimately leads to more freelance illustration work and eventually his full-time freelance career. Jump to the present.

"You can't learn how to draw; it is already a part of you," Tulka comments, when discussing his roots. "My parents were very supportive. I had excellent art teachers in college." At school, Tulka worked in an academic program called *University Without Walls*, where his mentor was David Levine, a major influence on the illustrator (as well as a great teacher).

"Levine would often say, 'it isn't always fun,' and he was right," Tulka remembers. Even though people think it's really cool to be an illustrator, *it is still a job*. And it's never easy.

"But, on the other hand," Tulka considers, "some jobs are dream gigs and you love every moment. Every year is different, which makes it exciting."

We'll Always Have Paris (Part 2)

After 19 years of working freelance in New York City, Tulka decided he'd had enough. The illustration business and competition had changed dramatically.

So, in 1995, after 2 years of planning (including a '94 trial run where he tested the waters by meeting with art directors and showing his portfolio), Tulka and his wife moved to Paris. *France*.

Figure 12-14: The drawings Cusack creates from subway reference seem linked to Robert Henri's challenge. He's enthralled by the *fast* experience of working on the train and the endless variety of portraiture and character: the hats, the headphones, the hairdos, the hoodies.
© Peter Cusack

Figure 12-15a and b: Relocating anywhere is a big thing. Relocating your life, let alone your business, to another country is a *very* big thing. For Tulka, the move to France was well worth it, mon ami: the stimulation of a fresh start in a different locale; the excitement and unpredictability of new creative opportunities (and challenges). And let's face it— after all, it *is* Paris!

© Rick Tulka

"The illustration business is different here," Tulka says. "Art directors still meet with the illustrators by appointment. Finding work here is as hard as New York, but I'm doing things I'd never have a chance to do in the States. For example: reportage."

"I've also been able to get jobs in other countries besides France," Tulka tells you. "As an artist, I feel my work has improved here. The move was worth it."

Home Base

Tim O'Brien lives and works out of Prospect Park South in Brooklyn, New York. Drawing is O'Brien's primary passion. "It's where ideas take form and sink or swim," he says. "It is how I translate the world I see (or imagine). Painting is how I color that world and how things sit in that atmosphere."

For O'Brien, drawing is the base. "I draw by thinking," he says. "First I design general shapes and then add a value structure to indicate space. Minute marks and texture soon follow. I am accurate with my pencil or pen, so I don't do wild gesture drawings in preparation. I get right to the way I want it to look." It is actually *value* that O'Brien is getting to when he draws. Color—for him, at least—is a secondary concern.

"I care little about making things bright and chromatic," he states. "I love the earthy tones of minimal color and usually paint most pieces in a certain color key. I sometimes try to achieve an antique look to my work, so gold or brown are favorite keys."

"Value is something that was pounded into my head in college as a primary element in creating form," O'Brien states. "I am constantly examining and re-examining a sketch in Photoshop to alter the value arrangement. I want to see how the organization of values might change the mood, attitude, or visual impact."

As in a one-frame movie, a figure may be the heart of a scene, but value structure provides the tracking shot, directing the eye to places O'Brien wants his audience to see. He calls this the *hierarchy*. And concept? Exploring concepts on his own has broadened O'Brien's visual vocabulary, and he always develops ideas within those parameters. It's what he calls the *filter*. "Illustrators take assignments and filter them through their taste and aesthetic," he says. "The outcome is style."

Figure 12-16a and b: As a realist, an O'Brien illustration is dictated by a hard set of rules. Anatomy, architectural integrity, logical lighting situations, and accurate likeness are some of the guidelines he must follow carefully. Freedoms the illustrator enjoys come through directing the eye via value shifts and overall design.

"I work hard to side step 'awkward' areas in a painting," O'Brien comments. "Tangents that confuse space, flat values; textures that are too similar—all things I try to avoid. There are no textbooks that cover this kind of careful image analysis. Looking at paintings and photographs and movies all self-educate the eye to see and consider new possibilities."

© Tim O'Brien

Buffalo Strips

Mike Maihack culls inspiration from all over. He's always quick to pull out that sketchbook. But he rarely draws something without a story in mind. Even if it's a story that's all of one sentence. Creating characters ends up being a large part of his doodling (as is using those characters in some sort of sequence).

"My drawings grow organically, as in nature itself," he says. "If I have to take out a ruler I get bored very quickly. And to me, it's much more interesting to form concepts 'out of thin air,' so I'll make stuff up (as opposed to representing something in the real world). That's why you'll find a lot of faeries and pixies in my work. I've also been drawing a comic strip about a cow and a buffalo for four years now, so you never know."

"But what I see in my head is pretty much never what shows up on paper," Maihack admits. "Frustrating! So most of the time I just start scribbling and let the drawing develop spontaneously. However, it's safe to say that if I have absolutely no idea of what I'm drawing, nothing interesting is going to show up on paper. I can get pretty stubborn in making sure the drawing is what I want. Sometimes I win. Sometimes I don't."

Figure 12-17: "*Cow & Buffalo* uses a light, airy line style because the simple shapes and humor of those characters evoke that kind of line quality," Maihack says. "If I had gone with a bolder stroke or rougher shapes, the strip might have a more serious mood than what I'm after."

© Mike Maihack

Ideas = Art

"Sometimes, certain stories influence content, sometimes not," Maihack says. If the story has a particular voice, Maihack styles the drawing appropriately, so you'll find he doesn't have one set approach as a result. Other times the drawing dictates storyline and the look of the thing. "So ideas and art are essentially the same," he comments. "The drawing is just the part people see.

"Shape and form probably present the most difficult aspects for me in a drawing," Maihack considers. "Because of that it can also be the most fun." And even though he's drawing two-dimensional characters, it's important to recognize that such characters react to (and in) a three-dimensional environment. "I'm always picturing my characters as a physical form and shape, and looking for new ways to spin those folks in the spaces they inhabit," he says.

"That might involve drawing from a different perspective," Maihack says. "Yes, even animated, exaggerated, cartooned forms. In fact, exaggerating the shapes is very important—otherwise characters are stiff, or the environment becomes static."

"The fun part is playing with that level and seeing how far you can stretch it before it becomes unbelievable." Maihack sums up, "and my drawings are meant to entertain. A drawing that relates to the subject matter the way it's supposed to will likely find an audience. And it's that audience that's going to keep pushing me to find new and better ways to keep them entertained."

Figure 12-18: Even the most realistic representations need a certain level of exaggeration if our minds are going to read them as *alive*. Think about it by reverse engineering that thought: ever label someone as "becoming very animated"? Or describe certain folks as "colorful" or "real characters"? Why is the expression "painted in broad strokes" a good short hand for a gross generalization?

© Mike Maihack

Windows to the Soul

Philip Burke's professional career began in 1977. "When I started, it was all drawing," he says. "My first paintings were kind of like drawing in color. Then it took on more of a painterly quality. However, there's still a real connection between the quality of line and the quality of the brush strokes."

"Drawing is like walking, and painting is like running," he considers. "When I paint I have to use a lot more of my mind and body. I'm standing—in front of a big canvas—and technically your mind has to deal with so much more."

"I think about value in terms of color. To create a 3-D image, what colors and values you use speak volumes. But you know what's more important," Burke puts out here, "are the eyes. Color is descriptive of a personality, but you go deepest with what you catch in the eyes."

The Spirit of the Thing

"I have no formal training," Burke tells us, "it's all intuitive." Plus Burke's portraits are not always concept-driven—it's more instinctual, his impression of the person. It is also interesting that Burke does these caricatures in the hope that the viewer may see something of himself in the piece.

But what's really fascinating about Burke's work is what's different about the man himself. Burke spends a lot of time doing art, it's a big part of his life; but it's not his primary focus. "What's most important to me," he says humbly, "is my relationship to the people in my life—and that has matured unbelievably in the last 30 years because of my practice of True Buddhism. I am becoming more aware of my connection to people (indeed, of all life) and the many different aspects of being human. Over the years, my work has started to reflect that richness."

Figure 12-19: Burke's work.

© Philip Burke

✔ Checkpoint: Pound for Pound

Based in Wyoming, Zak Pullen's frequently honored, character-oriented illustrations are seen in publications like *The New York Times Book Review*, *Sports Illustrated*, *Esquire*, and *The Wall Street Journal*. Pullen shares some pertinent notes for this chapter's hot list:

1. Line is *the* basis of form. Simple or complex, line drives you toward the end goal.

2. Gesture drawing is the best way to nail your first instinct. All the details are just stuff added onto your first impression.

3. "Dark against light and light against dark" was something pounded into my head all the way through school. Now I find myself pounding it into my own and others' heads as well.

4. Value draws your eye through the composition like a pinball machine. It can surprise you, or solidify your initial thoughts. What is important in my painting? It's here. . .it's there. . .it's light against dark and the dark against the light.

5. Painting with mood is another fundamental concept I've taken with me in life.

6. I enjoy the *wow* factor of color.

7. The hardest part about doing this for a living is not being able to see your own work with fresh eyes.

8. Know the rules before you break them. It's easy to get caught up in technique and make something look pretty. . ."Oh wow, everyone!" Problem is: a good painting on a bad drawing is—and will always be—a bad drawing. You can't hide it.

9. Composition skills: you either have it or you don't. Invite the viewer into your art; direct them, turn them around, and then march them out.

10. Never apologize for being able to communicate an idea through visual means. You're not asking the viewer to read 4000 words on the subject, your picture should fill their heads with 4000 words of their own.

A bit of a character himself, Pullen's visual storytelling hits that nail right on the head.
© Zachary Pullen

CHAPTER SUMMARY

Figurative illustration cross-references this chapter with the book at large. This chapter addresses the context and content of representation, description, and interpretation. We discussed caricature and portraiture, illustration and cartoons, and didn't care much about labels. We examined straight (or traditional) portraiture, and the art of the likeness. We looked at classical and modern caricature and cartooning.

Working It Out

1. I Fought the Law

Pick a fundamental principle (for instance, "when considering design, a center of interest that is indeed dead center in a composition is static and boring") and build your illustration by going against that grain. In other words, bust the rule and see what happens. Visually, can you break the law and get away with it?

2. Mashed

Do your version of a famous work. Adapt, distort, alter, morph this classic—whatever it takes to remake your own masterpiece in your unique voice, with your special vision.

3. Goin' on a Line Hunt

In class this week we're going to be "sketch hunters." We'll do a daily "draw crawl" in and around the art building or school grounds. You will be asked to do multiple drawings, and to the best of your ability, hit the quota. This pushes you to be more interested in *what* you draw rather than *how*.

During the last 20 minutes of each class we'll look at that day's results and product. Ultimately you will be asked to pick some of these roughs and develop the images into full-blown, full-color illustrations.

Home and Away

1. Character Study

Do one caricature—or portrait—a day (or more) for one month. One challenge is to do a different caricature each day. A related—but slightly different—task is to do the same subject (but in a different manner) every day. Yet another variation here is to do a self-caricature (or self-portrait) in a different style or technique every day.

2. A Month of Sundays

Do a daily comic strip for 30 days, including Sundays. For more of a challenge, do 30 full-length (and full-color) Sunday comics. Develop a cast of characters (and storyline), and, of course, continuity of those characters and storyline. The panels should be ruled (as appropriate), inked, and colored.

3. My World

Do a daily *editorial* cartoon about one month of your life. The time frame is open-ended, so for instance, the cartoons could target that memorable summer you spent at camp when you were 12. We'll discuss editorial and political cartoons and look at the genre in class first.

Chapter 13

Drawing Is Provocative

© Ric Stultz

Sums It Up

Can we agree that illustration by definition is tied to copy? If so (or if not), I'll direct you to our chapter, "Words and Pictures," to read more on the idea. And from that vantage point, Maggie Suisman says she connects personal political concerns to her art by illustrating texts.

Suisman is a painter/illustrator based in Brooklyn who tends to gravitate towards topics that are important to her. When not working in line, Suisman explores collage primarily, employing her materials expressively, to reflect a sense of immediacy, emotional honesty, and to maintain her childlike sense of play.

She brainstorms ideas visually. "Sometimes I'll sketch dozens of ideas that make no sense," she comments, "before hitting on one that sums up just what I'm trying to say." Wanting to make a strong statement—often with type—Suisman's images need to be audacious and clear (both conceptually and visually). So, for work done as part of her graduate thesis, she chose a poster format that evoked old Russian propaganda art.

Hard Boiled

Peter Kuper was Suisman's advisor on this project. "We talked a lot about what message I was trying to get across," Suisman comments, "and how to really engage people to read the text on posters (called the *Factory Farm* series)." Kuper encouraged Suisman to boil the text down to as little as possible. And he would ask her, "Do you need this image—what is it doing for you?"

Message

Suisman specifically teaches comics because sequential art is a narrative form offering an accessible opportunity to address issues with social and political content. On a conceptual level, she cares about the message, using her political and social agenda to fuel creativity. But as a teacher, she focuses on getting her students to reflect on *their* culture and their environment. "I want them to approach making art as an analytical exercise," she says, "so I ask about *their* opinions and concerns."

Here is where Suisman's own work and teaching intersect, beyond the mere mechanical aspects of making comics and illustrations. There's a clear crossover between her personal art (and any interests the artist has about illustration) and what she asks her students to address in their assignments. "Hopefully I inspire others to think critically or even to have hope," she'll tell you. "I want my students to bring the same approach to making art, so it's not just about being technically proficient."

Figure 13-1: "Likeness and good drawing do matter," Suisman comments, "but rather than rendering perfectly, I want my love of color to come through. What's great about collage is that I can use watercolor, cut paper, colored pencil, whatever I can get my hands on."
© Maggie Suisman

In the Moment

Kuper was an influential and inspirational instructor for Suisman. Based in Manhattan, he has written and illustrated many books, and he's taught at SVA and Parsons in New York City. Kuper's narrative format elegantly translates to what the illustrator calls "visually picking a moment."

"It is not always that way," Kuper says, "but there's a crossover—that 'comics' influence comes through in just about everything I am doing. I like for the opportunity to go beyond what one illustration can do, plus I simply enjoy telling a story," he states.

Even a casual glance at Kuper's scratchboard or stencil and collage illustration reveals he obviously revels in this practice. "Putting together writing and drawing like this is ideally suited for all the areas I want to cover," he says.

Figure 13-2a, b and c: Suisman's visual manner goes directly to the heart of the matter.
© Maggie Suisman

"When I do a piece," he explains, "I think about the flow of the illustration—how your eye enters and moves through the picture." Kuper is conscious of the fact that you are usually going to enter an illustration from the left. Which, of course, is exactly the way one *reads* a story. It's the same mindset he applies to drawing a comic page, where he deliberately directs your eye from panel to panel.

The Writing Is on the Wall

"Drawing *feels*," says veteran illustrator (and illustration instructor) Rick Sealock. "Emotion, mood, and personality. . .this is where I work and play, it establishes my connection with the audience." According to Sealock, the psychology of the cave wall is still deep within us all, and emotion in imagery is like a conduit straight into the heart and soul of the viewer. Everyone understands pain, grief, anger, happiness—and that's where Sealock pulls you in. This is his psychology of illustration. "*That's* my cave wall," he laughs. "Seduce and educate on a conceptual level. Manipulate to communicate ideas, passion, and emotion as I visually solve a problem."

Figure 13-3: Kuper's comics are often dictated by either personal experience or a subject that deeply concerns the illustrator. He recently returned to New York from a two-year stay in Oaxaca, Mexico. Here, amongst other events, he documented that city's tumultuous teachers' strikes.
© Peter Kuper

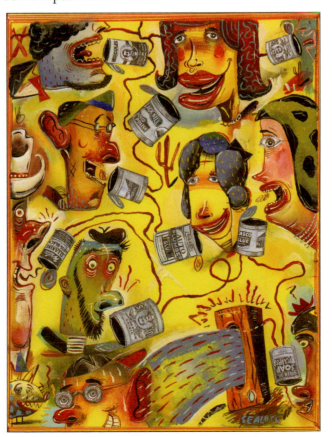

Figure 13-4: Manic? Edge? Sealock *lives there*! He employs extremes in both concept and technique, but, as he says with a smile, "I like to think that there is an intelligence to the madness or maybe a genius to the silliness of the work."
© Rick Sealock

Merged

At school, Ric Stultz determined that somewhere between graphic design (marketability) and drawing (hand-created imagery) was illustration. "Illustration merges the technical application and commercial acceptability of graphic design with drawing," he tells you, "and drawing is what I primarily love to do. People find interest in my illustration because there's that hand crafted element."

Being Direct

Stultz's work is a direct product of his urban environment; the spontaneous imagery often depicting the commonplace or everyday—innate objects given a little bit of life. For example, he'll use a cassette tape as a corollary for the way children of the 80s are aging. His *Drawing on Violence* series is about turning a bad blow around and coming to grips with it.

Figure 13-7: "Push, pull, and play," says Stultz, "balance murkiness and definition. How do I characterize the space: how can I make elements pop forward; how do I pull out the highlights of the painting?"

© Ric Stultz

Articulate Matter

"An image 'coming through the gloom' promotes a sense of texture and creates depth," explains Stultz. "I take the image to the brink of destruction," smiles Stultz, "paint out; fill it back; redefine. Clean it up. Dirty it up again. There's a harmony I'm looking for—I love that. It's like the work has really been *through* something, as if the painting sat in sweat, or everything kind of bled out. The more I paint, the more I can control the gap between concept, process, and end product."

"I really love paint spatter because it resembles particulate matter," says Stultz. "When you are in your house and catch a strong stream of sunlight coming in the window, you see all the stuff suspended in the air. When you are outside, a lot of what you see floating by is not all air." he explains. "That's particulate matter. So the splatters are like the particulate matter in the background of the painting."

Back. Back Further.

In Anthony Freda's mind, everything starts with drawing. When not working on an assignment, Freda feels that subject matter is not as important as the *act* of drawing itself. And the more you draw, the less intimidating that bright, white, perfectly blank page will be.

"My aim is to capture a line that travels clean and directly from my soul to the page," Freda says, and he'll ask you to think back; to consider how the drawings of small children are pure and completely self-confident. "I want to create that same line," he states, "a line that displays no desire to impress or please the viewer but has some element of *truth* in it—that's my goal."

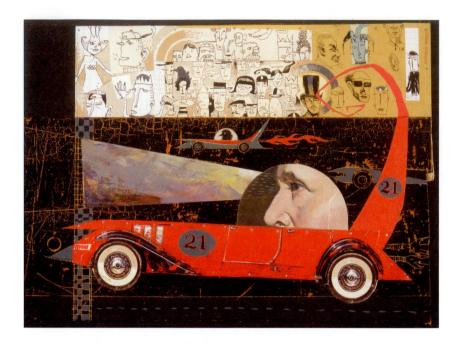

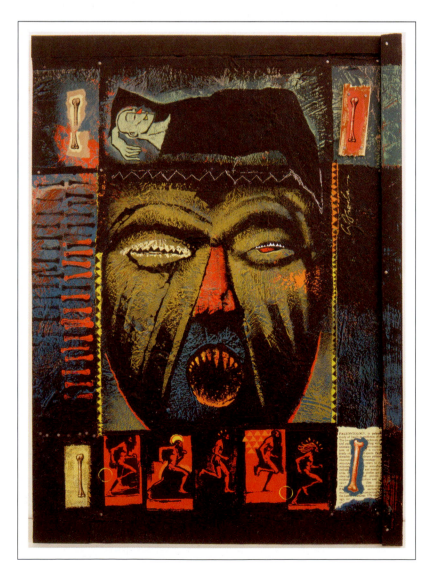

Figure 13-8a and b: To Freda, the pen is mightier than the pencil. He can't start a drawing without his favorite pen gripped in his mitt. "The friction of pencil dragging against the tooth of the page fights against me," he'll tell you. "The smooth flow of the pen gives no resistance and somehow even drags ideas out of me that I hadn't consciously thought of yet!" This is not to say he never uses pencil. Freda loves the artistic tension created when colored pencil fills in areas delineated by his pen; but he feels the texture of waxy pencil riding on top of paper grain is better suited to shading rather than actual drawing.

© Anthony Freda

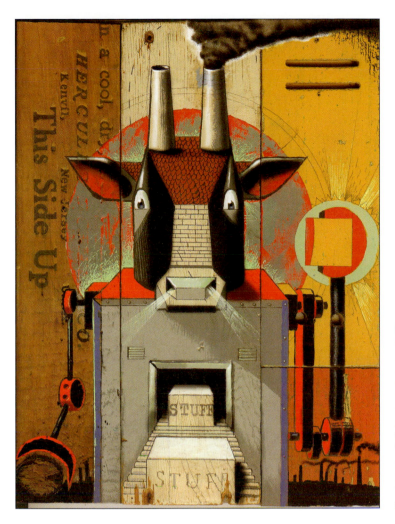

Figure 13-9: A story for *Wealth Manager Magazine* promoted investments in manufacturing stocks. Freda used the cliché of the bull to represent the positive outlook of the piece and combined it with a factory, creating what the illustrator tags, "a literal bull factory. The fact that this was also a subversive commentary on the article was probably known only to me." Until now!
© Anthony Freda

Sans Salvador

"Now, the *idea* for a drawing is mysteriously created," Freda tells you. "Dali hoped to achieve a state of mind where his sub-conscious and conscious minds were in play simultaneously." For his part, Freda will jot down every visual metaphor a story presents, and then start scrambling concepts. "I know this is obvious," he smiles, "but writing ideas down on a big piece of paper and 'connecting the dots' helps me come up with a hopefully interesting juxtaposition."

Line It Up

Jannes Hendrikz, Nina Pfeiffer, and Ree Treweek are Shy The Sun, a dream-spinning creative troupe based in Cape Town, South Africa. Hendrikz and Treweek are the directors, Pfeiffer is the producer. Treweek illustrates and Hendrikz is the film compositor.

"Line is inevitably observed in the flow of animation," Pfeiffer says. "Within such a moving artwork, it's essential to draw a line for the eye to follow, especially if a story is being told. Without these linear indications, composition becomes messy and story telling is rather a challenge."

Tone in/Tone On

First shown on a commercial break during the telecast of the 2008 Beijing Olympics, "Sea Orchestra" is a knockout showcase of bravura animation.

Line work here is noteworthy not only as it pertains to actual shapes, but for how that line impacts the overall visual flow of the piece. Value—and value *between* tones—became essential to distinguish shapes and create depth. "Value is a most important building block for us in the scheme of things," Pfeiffer says. "We craft the illusion of depth through value. We bring order to the chaos of detail through lights and darks."

Figure 13-10a and b: "In 'Sea Orchestra', we wanted to create as much detail as feasible," Pfeiffer tells you. "Every time the viewer looks at a frame of animation, he should notice something new."

© Shy The Sun and United Airlines

Go Deep

Think of it this way: Line establishes flow. Tone defines intensity. Color contributes to sensation (and reader, you know this already: color communicates with the viewer on an emotional level). "Color does not necessarily make our work more real," Pfeiffer states, "but definitely places it within a realm: be it fantastical, surreal, or odd.

"Color is a very critical part of our process, a lot of thought goes into every inch of color. If it does not work, we'll change it again (and again) until we are entirely satisfied. Color provides us a means to go deep into every facet of detail, contributing to the notion of space and the impression of distance."

Figure 13-11a and b: Even while considering color and tone, Pfeiffer reminds you that one fundamental concept of a line is as an actual stroke. "However," she quickly points out, "line is also created by the juxtaposition of colors, composition itself, or the sheer sense of motion—lines can be formed without actually using a *drawn* line.

"Using line to 'cheat' space is a hallmark of our style," says Pfeiffer. "Placed next to each other, it's obvious that all edge widths are the same, but if you pull back or forth into space, that edge becomes thick or thin, contributing to the viewer's sense of 3-D form and depth. Line provides the base of objective experience."

© Shy The Sun and United Airlines

Figure 13-12: Initially, Montgomery creates an illustration with values and line. He gets the concept down first. Color and value enhance and add to the concept; tone and hue pop the subject off the page and bring it to your attention. "And my general rule is rather classical," Montgomery points out. "Place the darkest dark and the lightest light where the *source* of concept is."

A dark image on a light background (or vice versa) is a power statement. "This draws the eye to the heart of the image," Montgomery says, "and creates that legendary '3 second read' you need."

© Jay Montgomery

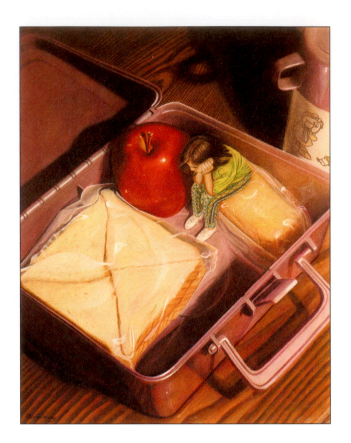

The Media Is the Message

Like most artists, Jay Montgomery starts with thumbnails. If a piece is "pure line" he is very keen to contour line *weight*. Where there is more contrast (of tone or edge), he leans toward a stronger stroke. In fully rendered, realistic images, line work at the final stages may be non-existent. "I transfer a line drawing for speed," he says, "and spend the rest of the time hiding the lines. I was always taught that realistic form should not be defined by line but instead by value (and then color)."

As a student, Montgomery's illustrations could wow you with detail and photo-like qualities, but the work could read too flat (and too literal to its resource). "I wasn't thinking about how values can actually enhance the idea of the art," Montgomery considers. "Bill Mayer opened my eyes to looking at value as it relates to the *message*. This changed the way I worked out my concept."

Alphabet Soup

In his fine book, *Creative Illustration*, Andrew Loomis discusses the five P's: Proportion, Placement, Perspective, Planes, and Patterns. Montgomery advocates a studious regard for these elements and suggests another professional checklist as well. "In terms of image development, consider the Five C's," he suggests, "Conception, Construction, Contour, Character, and Consistency—in that order. If you have seriously thought out all these P's and C's—consciously or subconsciously—you are well on your way to creating an illustration that will get you called back by the client."

✔ Checkpoint: Seize the Day

Providing our hot list for this chapter is Matt Klos, who lives and works in Baltimore, Maryland. Klos earned his BFA at the Columbus College of Art and Design and an MFA from the University of Maryland, College Park. He teaches full-time at Anne Arundel Community College.

1. My work is really about piecing together moments; about capturing an instant in time and then capturing another—to seize a fluttering moment that was there and was tangible.

2. This moment can be relived in a more concrete way than through mere memory. It's about *truth*: a truth better than a photograph because, unlike the single dimension of a momentary snapshot, the end result is the sediment of thousands of moments.

3. Line is shape construction. A rapid application of painted line plots the composition. I constantly draw back into the wet paint .The line gives voice to the colored shapes and helps arrange them—connect them—in a meaningful way.

4. I love the juggle between paint and illusion. I want my paintings to look *painted*. The marks should be seen and enjoyed. The human hand should be present.

5. If I am able to balance space and light—two opposing forces, one flat and graphic, the other transient and illusory—something magical can take place.

6. I had a wise teacher tell me, "You paint like a lot of people in your life, but you end up painting how *you* paint." All your choices speak to the viewer. The work becomes a biographical visual novel.

7. I used to paint these "theatrical" paintings with expressive figures in them. But after a while the overt emotion seemed false. I realized that the things I was really interested in could be found in an empty interior instead. So, I let go of the figures—they interfered with the concept.

8. If you nail the value of your composition—if the shapes of positive and negative space have harmonious value relationships in pictorial terms—then you will most likely have a successful image. . .

9. If the value is right, the artist is free to use expressive color. Color has two fingers on the pulse of emotion. . .

10. . . .and of course, color is where the real difficulty begins!

The work of Klos.
© Matthew Klos

The work of Klos.
© Matthew Klos

CHAPTER SUMMARY

This chapter was about making strong statements and addressing important topics of personal concerns or emotional honesty through an artist's expressive use of materials. We talked about engaging viewers by offering accessible opportunities to tackle issues of social opinion and political content. This chapter asked you to care about the *message,* be it a political, social, cultural, or environmental agenda. It was about art as an analytical exercise: of perception and affect, critical thinking that goes directly to the heart of the matter.

Working It Out

1. Have a Pulse

How can value relate to *message?* Do an illustration where a dark image on a light background (or vice versa) makes an instantaneous power statement. The goal is to draw the eye to the heart of the image, which should also be main line to the message of the piece. Pulling this off may be harder than you think, but it's well worth it.

2. Snap Shot

Create a drawing or painting that captures a moment in time (or a sequence of instants). Here's the rub: eliminate the face and figure from the equation; utilize only inanimate objects, exteriors, and interiors. This work should be about a current space, the *now,* this moment—a timely instant of recognition, not nostalgia.

3. To the Point

Illustrate a profound concept (for instance, world peace) with a simple visual—and conceptual—statement.

Home and Away

1. 30 Days and Nights

Design and illustrate a calendar (one to two months) of stimulating locales, provocative events, and interesting personalities. Do your research and gather factoids and info about people, places, and things. Full color. Mixed media. *No* photographs.

2. Pluck It Up

Write and illustrate a 32-page book called *A Month of Mondays: Famous Personal Comebacks from Disasters, Pitfalls, and Hard Knocks.* While we do not wish to capitalize on adversity, this book about hardships and hard times should really be a provocative graphic novel on perseverance and pluck.

3. To the Point

Illustrate and upgrade a series of clichés, old jokes, or sentiments. Do this by way of funny or smart, profound or elegant visual metaphors that somehow improve the concept (for example: abstinence makes the heart grow fonder).

Chapter 14

Old School/New School

© Geneviéve Kote

Baseline

You probably deal with teachers (and diverse teaching methodology) every day. And chances are good you just might teach this stuff after *you* get out of school. So I thought it necessary to examine art education and educators in a dedicated chapter.

Some no-brainers: teaching methods are very different (no kidding). Some instructors regard the demo process as they do breathing and eating. Some simply don't. Many schools establish programs according to particular methods of working (as in, "here's the illustration department"), but other places think across the curriculum—often offering projects that allow for a variety of cross-referenced approaches. Usually, a comparison and contrast of freshman to senior work is quite striking. Technical quality? Sure, but it's probably more a celebration of growth and development (with technique just one criteria).

Outcomes

Work—and resulting skill sets—done from observation and fundamentals are invariably first year to second year (and typically attended by first- and second-year students); more conceptually based "synthetic imagery" (and sharper skill sets) comes in the third to fourth year.

For the art teacher, the secret weapon of evaluation—personal and/or professional, your stuff *and* your students' work—is to look at the thread of such work *over time*. It's vitally important that a body of work grows organically, as do teaching methods and experience.

Morsels

Old school/new school: in a conversation with illustrator Sterling Hundley (whom we met in Chapter 11), the idea of reverse engineering came up. Normally, illustrators start with the bigger picture—a story or headline, the general concept, some inspirational phrase—and drill the details of an illustration *down* from there.

Hundley suggested we begin with snippets of information—a certain color passage you literally "see" in your mind's eye; on that abstract you're indifferent to is a single brush stroke that absolutely resonates with your artistic sensibilities; the one section in the far right corner of that otherwise failed assignment you shelved last month—and build *up* from there?

Chunk

Something clicked. And I went on a treasure hunt and unearthed some old disks of long forgotten art files. There I found a scan of a color rough for a project I literally scrapped over 10 years ago. It's a remnant, actually: the only chunk of this work I thought was any good. I tossed the real thing when the piece tanked; I just have this scan of one *part* of the painting.

I took the sketch into Photoshop and adjusted the size and resolution. I color corrected it and tweaked brightness and contrast. I then exported that revamped file into a nifty program called Synthetik Studio Artist 3.0, and used this new art as my template.

Working with Studio Artist's "Impressionist Clone" patch, straight out of their default Paint Synthesizer preset, I painted this little study that resurrects a long dead idea (and aborted product).

Figure 14-1: Is it real paint? Nope; and without apologies (or filters, by the way).
© Michael Fleishman

Home School

Zina Saunder's father was pulp cover icon Norman Saunders, painter of the original—and legendary—*Mars Attacks* trading cards. When I was 11 years old, it was a badge of honor if your appalled mother chucked these cards in the bin, so I was pleased to hear Saunders' recollections of growing up (and drawing) with this revered and influential illustrator.

"I grew up in a house with my father being an artist," Saunders says. "He always gave me a lot of encouragement."

"When I was a little kid, I'd wait for dad to leave his drawing table, and I'd sneak up to add long, lush eyelashes to the girls in his paintings. Then I would skulk away, thinking I'd really improved them."

"Years later, in my twenties, I asked him, 'Dad, did you know I used to touch up your paintings behind your back?' He said, 'Oh, yeah, I knew that. I just fixed 'em up.' That was so *nice*, that he didn't yell at me for it. He would just go back and paint out my handiwork," she says.

Above and beyond their wonderful father/daughter relationship, Norman Saunders was a profound inspiration and influence on the young artist (as well as for scores of fans and other budding illustrators).

"I think a lot of what I'm doing with my artwork today is me trying to impress my dad," she smiles wistfully. "I want him to think I'm a good artist."

From Father to Daughter

"I love the idea of millions of people seeing my paintings," Saunders says. "Even though that magazine or book is eventually tossed away, my work has been seen by tons of readers. My father had no pretensions of being a gallery artist at all, and neither do I.

"I think he helped in a big way to develop my eye, but frankly, I think the main thing is you have to have that heart. And you really have to know how to draw. Work ethic and responsibility, talent and sincerity are not mutually exclusive at all. They go hand in hand to establish what an illustrator is."

Figure 14-2a, b and c: Here's a mini-gallery of some great work with the name Saunders attached.

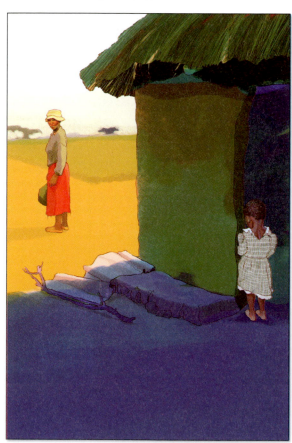

East Meets West

"Both American and Japanese education systems have pros and cons, " Yuko Shimizu tells us. Shimizu is a product of both schools, and says neither is perfect.

"The U.S. system encourages students to express themselves and cultivate a personal voice. But it's weak in teaching basic skills that allow artists to change and grow in the long run," she considers. "The Japanese education system does a superb job teaching basics skills, but is not the environment to cultivate that individual voice.

"I've experienced a 'happy medium' and benefited from both education systems (and living in each country). I'm trying to provide advantages of both to my students, if possible."

Figure 14-3: "You do what you need to do," Shimizu says. "If you feel something is 'too hard,' maybe you don't really want it. Hurdles are life's little 'tests' to see how committed we are."

"In your four years at school try to ascertain who you are and—as a direct result—what you want to create. That is the most valuable lesson I learned from my instructors at SVA. I try to get that across to my students, too. It's every bit as important as learning how to develop concepts (or how to draw and paint)."

© Yuko Shimizu

✔ Check Point: The Grayscale of Things

Marcos Chin graduated from the Ontario College of Art and Design, in Toronto, Canada, and teaches Fashion Illustration at the School of Visual Arts. Chin provides this chapter's hot list:

1. Remember that it's not really about the material or media you use; it's actually about your way of seeing and how it's visually presented on the page.

2. At the beginning of my academic career, my color sense wasn't as developed, but the *potential* was there. I *learned* how to use color.

3. You go through school, you learn different stuff, and you're exposed to new things. Somewhere along the way you let the old influences go …

4. … but it takes time to mature and focus (or refocus), to find who *you* are. I certainly wasn't aware of my strengths and my weaknesses—that's something I took away through school.

5. Have an open mind. Be willing to learn anything new if it will help you grow and become better at your craft.

6. My instructors made drawing *important* for me. Their critique, encouragement, and support strengthen my work to this day.

7. The sheer act of drawing over and again made me become better. Idea-making forced my focus off of sheer mechanics and took me to that next level.

8. Learn to grab the essence; to paraphrase *visually*; to communicate the main *idea* rather than getting all caught up in the details.

9. Visually communicate the message without blatantly giving away too much; nor put extraneous information in there, cluttering up the space.

10. The instants of exploration are the truly critical moments of growth. You're at school to make mistakes. It doesn't matter how crappy (you think) your art is. You have that time to learn; *use it.*

The work of Chin.
© Marcos Chin

The work of Chin.
© Marcos Chin

Get Some Rest

Geneviève Kote considers the life of a busy art student (who at some point will become an even busier professional). "Physically you need to get enough sleep," she cautions. "If you are tired you can't draw; you can't think well; every idea will seem too complicated, too difficult. Personally, I find maintaining a healthy routine to be a challenging motivation."

That challenge of incentive—getting a move on, then keeping it going—makes life in the studio an interesting test. "Are you a self starter?" Kote asks out loud, as she considers this arguable prerequisite. "I must have an assignment to start working," she says. " I was one who needed art school: to be surrounded by creative people who challenged and helped me improve faster and stay motivated."

Figure 14-4: "Graduation doesn't mean that you are *good* at this," Kote correctly assesses. "Wherever—however—one learns, if you don't work very hard … if you don't take it seriously … nothing will come out of your training."
© Geneviève Kote

Call and Response

As a student you are well aware of due dates. As a professional, with your very livelihood riding on making that deadline, the stakes are higher; the pressure just intensifies. Tina Sweep smiles when considering that prime motivator of all illustrators, the deadline.

"The most effective encouragement to make a drawing is a deadline," she says. She points out that it is easy to become consumed by the *possibilities* of a drawing—concept, mood, subject matter, media, etc.—without making any final decisions. "A deadline is the best way to assure a drawing will not only begin, but be finished as well," she states.

Do It Real

Teaching makes Stan Shaw quantify what he is doing in his own work. Shaw spent much of the first part of his career working on gut instinct, but you can only go so far with that. "Maybe you go back and forth between intellectualizing and working from your gut," Shaw considers. "Teaching, however, helps me understand what I'm doing, and understanding illustration is always an interesting test (for teacher and student). So I try to keep my teaching (and assignments) rooted in reality."

Figure 14-5: The work of Sweep.
© Tina Sweep

Figure 14-6: "I tell my students not to worry about style at all," says Shaw. "We'll discuss theory and technique (not just what and how, but *why*), symbol and subtlety, subject matter and reference, communication and the audience: the visual vocabulary as well as the actual act of making a picture."
© Stan Shaw

Challenging

Shaw requires his people to keep an illustration scrapbook that's reviewed and scored periodically. It's not a sketchbook. Putting a scrapbook together gives students an idea of the illustration out there, what kind of illustration they like (or don't). "I want to open their eyes," Shaw explains, "to promote an understanding of illustration, to observe and express an opinion on paper."

Shaw is continually refining his grading rubric: distilling it down, working toward understandable, mutually agreeable explanations of how students can view a problem and possibly improve their scores. He actually tells students to argue for a grade (or to make a valid point), but announces this only once in the term. "I want those students who are truly paying attention to pick up on it—I'm open to that. On the job, an illustrator may do something that is beyond the client—you have to then defend or argue for it."

Figure 14-7: "The Flitcraft Parable," starring Dashiel Hammet's Sam Spade (think *Maltese Falcon*), is set in Shaw's hometown of Tacoma, Washington.
© Stan Shaw

Figure 14-8: Badgers? We don't need no stinkin' Badgers! Done in airbrush, Shaw's "Out in the West" is described as a Western Fairy Tale. Boasting every cliché from all the old horse operas, this piece is a particular favorite for the illustrator.

© Stan Shaw

Giving and Getting

Lizzy Rockwell and her former student, Susanna Pitzer, shared some thoughts on the nature (and nurture) of students, teachers, and a life gravitating around both drawing table and chalkboard.

"In the context of teaching and outreaching through art," Rockwell says, "every situation is a completely new gig. My professional work filters into my academics quite a bit. I need to tap into all those parts of my brain."

On any assignment, Rockwell thinks: "This would be a great thing to teach." She is about that 100%. Teaching is something she consciously seeks out, or as she says, "It seeks me out. I knew from the beginning that I liked the role of teacher."

Figure 14-9: Rockwell loves doing demonstrations because her students get to see their teacher *taking a risk* (and making a mistake). "Watercolor—like certain life lessons—can't be undone," says Rockwell, "but it can be responded to. For kids on a difficult life path the *real* tutorial is 'Well, that happens. But you can react to it in a positive way.' You say that through the metaphor of painting. And I don't want students frustrated by an expectation of end results," she adds. "It can be a revelation to realize where you end up only when you get there."

© Lizzy Rockwell

"If I'm having an issue in my own illustration, I'll often find answers in what my students are doing," says Pitzer. "Tight art often translates into almost dullness. It's a good lesson for me, to watch my students get tighter and work with them to loosen up. Mainly because I need to remind *myself* to just go to town.

"You want to retain that *alive* quality, the newness," she considers. "It's about getting to the comfort zone and then letting go. Being *vital*; being invigorated. Facilitating that process really helps me get back to that place as well."

Keeping On, Inside and Out

Pitzer had a drawing teacher in college who made students *destroy* their work: pick your favorite thing in any drawing—now, erase it. The point being that if one element is too precious, it's going to get in the way of the whole.

"You must keep the door wide open to ideas," she tells you. "Honor ideas. Make sure they are noticed. Don't shut the door on potential—say yes! If it doesn't work, it's part of the process. If you skip those 100 terrible drawings, you'll never get to the masterpiece. It's all part of your path."

From the Other Side of the Desk

At least in art school, the onus of becoming a successful professional depends on what that student first brings to the classroom. One of Julia Minamata's instructors at Sheridan College was Head Supreme Illustrator *Provocateur*, Rick Sealock. "Some students believe there's a 'magic bullet' answer to illustrating," Sealock comments. "They expect the instructor to just give them the 'inside scoop' on how to get fame and fortune."

"These students want you to enable them to do a bare bones approach: to pass or slide by on what talent they have. It might be, 'Hey, I painted it three times already, (or) I spent over four hours on this, so it must be great.'"

But when students walk into Sealock's class he already expects them to be hard working and intelligent; creative thinkers as well as problem solvers. Which should be the norm for any student/teacher relationship anywhere. In a perfect world, all students would possess an imagination bursting at the seams, an enthusiasm (even a *hunger*) to learn, and a passion to draw.

Figure 14-10: The work of Pitzer.
© Susanna Pitzer

Figure 14-11: Sealock asks his students, "Shall we get onto the *good* work, now? I'll be objective with your images, but I'm going to constantly challenge your concepts and skill."
© Rick Sealock

Above and Beyond

Sealock observes that Minamata went beyond being a creative thinker and talented drawer. She also owned what he considers one of the most important prerequisites needed in becoming an successful illustrator: she had an excellent work ethic.

"She had the ability to leap headlong (and fearlessly) into the project," he remembers, "to go where angels fear to tread. Julia was *committed* to visual problem solving, and wasn't afraid of jumping in and getting her fingers messy."

Due to Its Graphic Nature

The graphic nature of the poster form combined with an ambiguous viewpoint was a perfect vehicle to challenge Minamata's creative abilities. A poster offers a layered challenge: create an image that sparks interest through a visual approach, prompts the viewer to interact with the design, and makes that reader question content.

"Everything comes into play to seduce said audience on a conceptual, technical, physical, and psychological level," Sealock comments. "And with any poster assignment, the student has to consider consistency within the visual theme. A poster in a series must be both different and original enough to compete *and* complement its sisters."

Figure 14-12a and b: "This work is challenging," Minamata says, "something a bit different. It was rewarding because it was challenging—and challenging *because* it was a bit different."

© Julia Minamata

Chaos and Control

Minamata works in silkscreen, and (perhaps in total synch with her intensive hands-on process) fully embraces Chaos Theory. "I like being a little out of control," she laughs, "although I might curse and stamp my feet while I'm doing it. I'm usually happier with that slightly off, screen-printed finish than the ultra-slick digital final on my computer."

For Minamata, "style" is an ever constant, continually evolving combination of "what you like, what you are influenced by, and who you are. I don't know that illustration style is about conscious choice," she says, "at least, it shouldn't be.

"Silkscreen printing seemed to be a natural progression," she says. "I used to work strictly digitally, but I got bored with it. Silkscreen process adds just a touch of surprise to my work that's exciting for me."

Second Time Around

Ken Meyer, Jr. was a seasoned illustrator with over 20 years of experience who did a brave thing: he actually went back to school (at SCAD, Savannah College of Art and Design) to look at his career and goals from a fresh perspective. "I am only now starting to scratch the surface," Meyer remarks. "After being in the workforce for decades, I am learning and clarifying anew, all of which is making me more aware of my skills and my challenges.

"I don't have much trouble keeping interested, but lately, the main challenges are time and ego. From where I stand, being an illustrator has been 'on the job training,' but there is so much more to learn out there," he says, with acquired wisdom.

Opportunity Knocks

"Education *is* key," his fellow student Vincent Zawada adds. "However, art education means different things for different folks. School is what you make of it. Some people are in art school simply to get that degree. But going to class doesn't do much if you are not willing to learn and push yourself (and your artwork) to the next level.

"School is an *opportunity* to learn and better yourself and your art," Zawada tells you. "But you must *act* on the opportunity. Hard work. Determination. Drive. The pursuit of being better. All play a big role in your growth as a student and professional—you have to want it."

Figure 14-13: Minamata's illustration is well-suited for the visual drama and visceral hook of theatre posters, as this illustration for the poster for *The Grapes Of Wrath* demonstrates. "Theatre is all about emotion," she says. "I want to capture /sensation/." To get to the root of that, she asks some core questions: "What do I respond to in these plays? How do I feel about the productions—and how is that conveyed to an audience?"
© Julia Minamata

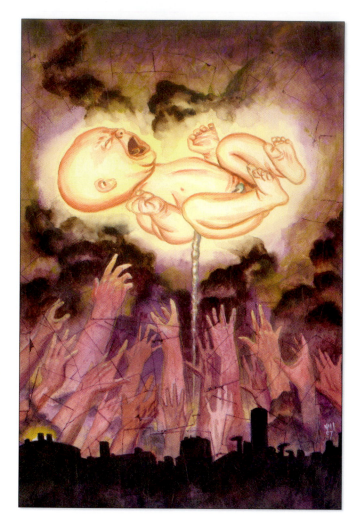

Figure 14-14: "When I went to college the first time out, I was a terrible student," Meyer confesses. "The results were largely my fault. School the second time around was a very good thing for me.

"In general, I am always learning. And I think most artists will tell you the same. Plus I do believe you learn from your mistakes … if only by attaining a sense of humility."

© Ken Meyer, Jr.

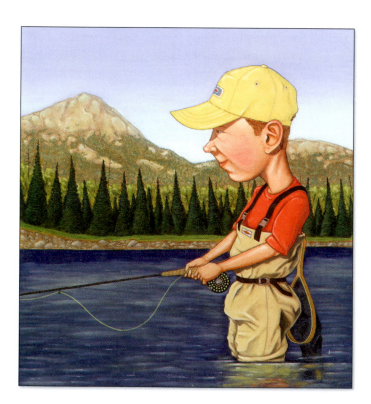

Figure 14-15: While a student at SCAD, Zawada says he learned first hand that, "It's the combination of good drawing skills with strong concepts that add up to success. But if your viewer does not understand the intended message, you haven't succeeded in the crucial task of communicating the idea. Concept *sells*— at school or in the field. Communication is the initial job of any artist."

© Vincent Zawada

What a Trip!

At SCAD, Britt Spencer felt "immersed in all that talent. Everyone was so *involved* in art. The talk, shared ideas; the classes, the professors were great. All year, all the time; every hour you were awake, you were around artists."

Fact is, Spencer hadn't yet graduated when he got his first book deal. As he tells it (in a masterpiece of understatement): "I simply took my portfolio to New York, went to a couple places and got the job . . . how about that?

"The trip really wasn't that successful," Spencer contends. "I went home with no job and a lot of generic (albeit diplomatic) rejection letters—it was kind of a waste of time. But three months later one of these art directors gave me a call and offered me a book. I jumped right on it." We should add that, ultimately, his good work was the channel to a great client, and a second book job.

Figure 14-16: After SCAD, Spencer stayed put in the community he built around the Savannah art scene. "I can't wait 'til I'm ten years into this process," Spencer smiles, "because the learning curve never stops. You just keep learning new things and perfecting your stuff a little at a time."

© Britt Spencer

Drawing on Experience

For their part, SCAD instructors Don Rogers and Kurt Vargo feel that the classroom must echo life in an actual studio. Both Vargo and Rogers emphasize illustration *process*. "Some of this stuff you don't show clients or art directors," Rogers says, "but as a teacher, you certainly do it. I cross-reference between technical and commercial art; kind of a straightforward commercial art approach."

"We work from a classical template," Rogers continues. "Show an idea. Here's the layout. Now, work from that. You allow for some creativity to get going, and this is where the students kick in."

"And in my classes, students can dictate their approach, but it's all about *consistency*," says Rogers. "It's okay if you draw in a very simplistic, stylistic manner. But then I expect you to refer to subject matter in the same way."

"From here," Rogers comments, "we deviate a bit from 'real-life.' Clients want it quick and easy. In the classroom, we take more time to develop personal insight and concepts."

Raw Talent

"For people coming out of such a foundation program," says Vargo, picking up the thread, "drawing skills are the most important thing to bring to the table. If you can conceptualize but cannot draw, you're only standing on one

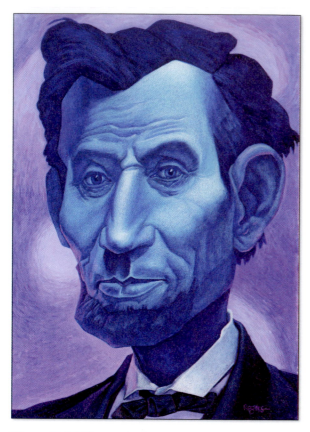

Figure 14-17: The work of Rogers.
© Don Rogers

foot—you may fall in any direction. But if you *can* draw, you can just about do anything, go just about anywhere."

Rogers agrees. "It doesn't matter how good your technique is," he sums up. "If you can't draw, raw talent won't carry you."

Take Off

"The classes we offer are hands-on and forward thinking," Vargo continues. "I teach classes that deal with techniques, content, and ideas, plus sections geared towards self-promotion and portfolio development. It's important to me that my students get good information, as I'm getting the same from them.

"I act like an art director *and* as a collaborator. I'll nurse ideas along, coach media and technique, and—hopefully—help them enjoy the design process. I act as a barometer of the current marketplace (and that real world Don mentions).

"I can't predict how student work will look, nor do I dictate what that should say," Vargo goes on. "They're playing on a big runway. They can take off when and if they choose to. My job is to wind them up and watch them go."

Figure 14-18: The work of Vargo.
© Kurt Vargo

CHAPTER SUMMARY

This chapter was about education and teaching methods. Education is the key. However, we also acknowledged that art education means different things for different folks. We looked at the art instructor as mentor, art director, and collaborator. We discussed student skill sets—first-year to fourth-year—in terms of technical quality, growth and development (technique being just one criteria), and evaluation.

We said that the doing and the teaching of art are "joined at the hip." We mentioned various education systems, a student's unique way of seeing and visual presentation; how to grab the essence visually. We explored the basic concept of art school; how quality art education should be rooted in reality (and nurturing); that schooling (not simply "school") is an opportunity to learn and better yourself and the art of the human spirit.

Working It Out

1. Self-Eval

   a.   Name 5 things you learned from a previous project.

   b.   State 3 things you did right on that project.

   c.   State 3 things you'd do differently.

   d.   What grade did you earn? Why? What do you think you should have earned … why? *Sell it* … why do you believe your work merits that score?

2. There's the Rub

Do a large (at least 18 x 24 inches) full-color or toned drawing; now erase any and all elements to create a new work. Drawing back in is optional.

3. By Example

Do a demonstration for your classmates of a technique you just learned (or don't know all that well). Get out of your comfort zone and take a risk. Handle the challenge and deal with mistakes in your demo without fear.

Home and Away

1. Scrap It

Put together an ongoing scrapbook. This collection should really encompass what kind of illustration you like (or don't). Critique and assessment; observations, bias and opinion; editorializing—all welcome!

2. Super Hero

Write/illustrate a graphic novel about a person you know very well. Grab the essence; concentrate on an aspect of your subject's character (or personality) or target *one* particular story.

3. Educate Me Please

Volunteer to teach classes at an elementary or secondary school, or at the local senior center. Arrange multiple sessions where you can offer an ongoing experience that can build on previous lessons.

Chapter 15

Drawing Imagines

© Mike Slattery

Takes the Cake

"Use your imagination!" How many times have you heard that one? Back in Chapter 1, I mentioned a box of crayons and a blank sheet of paper as the only prerequisite for you to use that imagination when you were a kid. And yes, 14 chapters later, maybe it's still that way for you, now. (I prefer the box of 64 with the built-in sharpener, myself.)

What's cool about using your "imagination" is to be both challenged at the outset and challenging at the end result. Perhaps imagination is really about spontaneity and improvisation, the rhythm of a concept from the flash of inspiration to the spark of the final.

As Nathan Walker put it in Chapter 4: "I paint the way I want to see the world." Reader, I bet you do, too. And be it conscious or subconscious, whether you're a cake decorator or visual communicator, the expression of your imagination shapes your visual language to express your reality on a gut level (or how your head and heart perceive it).

"I know a designer who, after many years, was discovered to be color blind!" Nina Pfeiffer proclaims. "What he saw was completely different to what the viewers had seen. He was still recognized as an exceptional designer—especially in his use of color. I always wondered if it was his 'handicap' that actually made his designs so brilliant." So here's a question for you, then: what kind of incredible imagination does it take to pull *that* off?

Turn Around

Douglas Klauba's technique evolved during his tenure at an illustration studio. Originally starting in watercolor and gouache, the frustration of doing revisions led him to working in acrylics, a medium easily altered for those clients wanting fast changes.

It was a learning process for the artist, and over the years Klauba realized he could enjoy this medium physically as well as experiment technically. Acrylics are now a comfortable outlet for both his creative and conceptual sensibilities, for as he says, "I am most valuable to a client when I can both conceptualize and perform."

Figure 15-1: A successful illustration invites you to get involved emotionally and/or connect intellectually. Early on, drawing skills were the most important aspect of Klauba's process. But he later understood that sharp conceptual skills went hand-in-hand with technique (as well as giving the art more depth and a personal stamp).

"I love when art communicates in a personal way," he says. "It brings the experience to another level far beyond the printed page or computer screen."

© Douglas Klauba

Getting to Know You

Klauba feels that self-knowledge is so very important and rarely stressed in art school. Self-realization is knowing your personality and understanding your tastes; pursuing your interests and being aware of your power as a draftsman and a thinker. It means playing to these strengths in your concepts and technique, and then applying all that to your vision.

"You recognize how much you can offer the art world," Klauba tells you, "and you will continuously work and strive to do your best—even if the job tests you, or takes longer than expected. I don't know who first told me that 'No one does it as well as you,' but this old adage is absolutely on the money."

Klauba considers the practice of illustration on-the-job training. This means constant study (and learning) for the artist, who says that you can never get enough education. But he wants you to bear in mind that it's important to actually practice what you learn, to truly understand it in physical terms.

"You'll learn to improvise when chasing deadlines," he says, "to understand your limits per project. You'll appreciate what you actually can do in the assigned time frame. All those moments that school can never prepare you for—but are just as important as a formal academic training in drawing and painting."

Reaching Out

Although he has a degree and attended art school, Klauba proclaims that he is essentially self-taught. "*Self-directed* may be a better term," he smiles. "Self-taught because I reached out for what I wanted to learn. I studied oil, watercolor, and pastel painting in school but I then taught myself to paint in acrylics and airbrush."

Klauba considers himself a life-long learner. He thoroughly enjoys this growth process—the continual challenges of an artistic life; the creative pursuit of both personal and professional goals. And he loves chatting with other artists, listening to illustrators talk about their craft, watching others paint and draw.

Figure 15-2: "Art is all around me," Klauba says. "It's the way I look at the world and it's part of the way I communicate. Art is my life form—an ongoing growth experience. Which in itself is pretty exciting if you think about it."

© Douglas Klauba

As Klauba will tell you, "It comes down to who *I* am. Art is imbedded into my heart. I don't think I can physically describe that feeling. I would be lost without that part of me."

Seriously, Clever

"You know, Illustration should be *clever*," Justin DeGarmo says, "whether it's humorous or serious subject matter." But the words "efficient," "expressive," and "pleasing" (at least, in a visual context) resonate for this illustrator, too.

DeGarmo believes illustration ought to display a breadth of style, and depth of process. He points out that you should strive for a level of sophistication in design, concept, and technique. "An artist must offer a steady composition and a balanced color palette," he says, "a mix of mood, lighting, and textures (visually and conceptually)."

Don't Rush It

DeGarmo says that "style" is "identity"; it separates one artist from the rest. Now, style develops over time. Some artists find their style earlier than others. Some force it; some rush into a style.

"I'm not sure why this happens," DeGarmo contemplates. "Maybe there's an urgency to stand out, and to gain recognition. But really, if something is just superficially manufactured for the sake of attention, the end result will most likely look contrived. How long can you keep that up and still be passionate about what you're doing?"

Is recognition all that's important? Shouldn't style grow and change along with its creator? Style comes from life experience, artistic taste, and inspiration; it must represent how an artist communicates.

"If you're lazy enough to steal a style (and worse yet, claim it as your own)," DeGarmo admonishes, "or you just have 'a style' for the sake of having style—well, that says a lot about your character. Not just as an artist, but as a human being. What does your style say about *you*?

"To a certain extent, we are all thieves," DeGarmo decrees. "We are all influenced by the art of ... well, *someone*, at least. But as long as you tell *your* story with your work ... as long as you tap into who *you* are as a person ... and take the time to think about what it is you really want to say—then you'll probably be all right."

DeGarmo says trying to create art that caters to the taste of others is like hitting an invisible, moving target. Good analogy. And sure, it may take a while to find your identity. But getting to the good stuff requires patience and hard work (oh so trite, but oh so true). If your work (no matter how well done) is a carbon copy of what's already out there, then what are you contributing? "Why are you an artist?" DeGarmo asks. "What are you trying to say with your work?"

Figure 15-3: Art education was enormously important for DeGarmo. And he's not just saying that to rationalize his monthly student loan bill.

"I suppose learning can be a form of art," he considers. "And learning can certainly be a life form /style. I plan to spend my whole life absorbing information, processing it, and using my art to communicate the things that matter to me.

"I definitely treat my illustration jobs as an extended education," he says. "I realize that art school isn't for everyone ... and it's obnoxiously expensive ... but I can't imagine where I'd be without it; there's no way I'd be doing what I'm doing today."

© Justin DeGarmo

Figure 15-4: DeGarmo often conjures images in his head without recording them. "That's fine," he says, "as long as I don't forget these images. I have to remind myself to record these things as soon as they come to mind. I could literally spend all day imagining a great piece, but if it never gets to paper, then how much time have I wasted?

"Often an idea does start from an inner monologue or daydream," the illustrator continues. "Once I begin sketching though, I can start to see what makes sense (and what's just ridiculous), because it's right there in front of me."

"The more I sketch, the more fine-tuned the idea becomes, and further opportunities for new ideas open up. So what started as a monologue is now a dialogue between my brain and my sketchbook—or hand, I suppose."

© Justin DeGarmo

Fulfillment

Former teacher and illustrator David Bowers tells us he was an illustrator for 15 years. Around 2004, he decided to limit his illustration assignments and began to focus solely on fine art.

Seeing his work in the mass market (for example, a painting on the cover of *Time*) was fulfilling, but fine art has been very rewarding. "Knowing that my paintings are showcased in a collector's home," he says, "the interactions I have with those patrons, and the fact that they are spending their own hard earned money, has been gratifying."

Inspirations

According to Bowers, his ideas just come "out of the blue," and he understands why some artists repeat themselves: it's difficult to come up with new ideas and constantly reinvent yourself.

Bowers likes to work in a variety of genres, from realism to fantasy and surrealism. Often working on a series of paintings on one theme, he'll then start two or three paintings in another direction. "I guess you could say that I am too easily bored to work in just one area. I've actually turned down children's books in the past because I couldn't imagine doing the same thing for a whole year.

"I'll fill sketchbooks with ideas and maybe pick one or two of them. It's hard not to be trite. A lot of competent artists out there are plagued by what I call the 'hokey factor.' They have ability—they can draw, they can paint. But they just do really banal subjects."

Perfect as Is

Bowers can look at a "loose" painting in a museum and appreciate it, but he personally couldn't abide with such a choppy-looking style. He's glad *other* people are painting in that manner, but he interjects with a laugh, "I have to be more precise. Working in oils facilitates the OCD in me."

"I can't get it perfect, but I can get it close," Bowers says. "I do the best I can with my ability right now," he says humbly. "My paintings are fairly small, but actually very painterly when enlarged mechanically."

Figures 15-5, 15-6, and 15-7: "I remember what it was like being a student," Bowers says. "It was quite difficult for me because I had my own ideas and some very strong opinions of what I wanted to do. Looking back, Bowers now realizes that he had a lot to learn. From both sides of the drawing board, this is all part of an age-old dance. Teachers must get their people to pay attention to certain facts of (the artistic) life. Students may not need this information *now*, but they just might need it in the future.

"As a teacher," Bowers recalls, "I always told my students to do their art because they love it, not for any recognition or the money. If money and fame are the only motivating factors, they will most likely not be successful."

And in his opinion, drawing is the foundation to successful artwork. "Be disciplined to draw every single day!" Bowers exclaims. "When drawing, it is hard to see the proportion of line; a chunk of color makes it easier to see proportion and form. That is why I sometimes see obvious mistakes in the underdrawing while painting.

"You have to be really *conscious* of what you're drawing." Bowers advises. "Sometimes it's easier to go right to the painting; but I usually figure my paintings out on paper first, before I transfer it to a panel or linen."

© David Bowers

Figure 15-6
© David Bowers

Figure 15-7
© David Bowers

 Check Point: World View

This chapter's hot list comes courtesy of Charlie Immer, an artist and illustrator based in Brooklyn. He holds a BFA in Illustration from the Rhode Island School of Design.

1. On the figure, line can be used to represent more— or less—tension in the skin. Like a thicker line when the skin is loose and a thinner line where it is tight (example: thin line at the elbow; thick line at the waist).

2. But I don't use much line in my work outside of the underdrawings of my paintings. I tend to rely mostly on lights and darks. I use value to create form.

3. Form is established through an understanding of light. However, it's hard to remember all the rules.

4. Reflected light, direct (and indirect) light, different colored light sources, more than one light source; placing dark against light to create emphasis or to pop objects out … value to me is easily the most important building block, but it was also the toughest thing for me to learn to use effectively.

5. I constantly squint at the work, so as to see only the values. This helps me establish the visual path through which the viewer will hopefully travel. I try to create sharp and soft edges to help clarify an object (as well as direct the eye). This is achieved directly through value.

6. As objects recede into space, they can be rendered with thinner lines (or a thicker line when they are closer to the viewer). For distant elements in the

picture plane, a thin, broken line may be used. This can also create atmospheric perspective as well.

7. I'll use complementary colors to pop and separate objects. Warm colors are usually somewhat inviting, so I'll use these tones in an opposite context.

8. Regarding this context: I like to create a cheery, candy coated mood in my work, but I like to play with color and go with hues that don't necessarily reflect the subject matter (like a rather violent scene expressed through a very pastel palette).

9. I toy with over-the-top cartoon violence. It's a lot of fun to bring characters to life and give my figures their own anatomy. I think that I am painting these bizarre worlds and characters with such care is the real statement.

10. A big part of my work is world building (as in creating my own unique world vision). And I like to think all of my art exists in that same world vision.

The world building art of Immer.
© Charles Immer

Shelf Life

After dabbling with acrylics and watercolors for some time in college, Martin Wittfooth settled on oils as his medium of choice. He was drawn to (and inspired by) the richness and velvety quality of oil paintings, and he wanted to achieve that same look in his work. He also likes having a hand-made original at the end of his process. "The great thing about a tangible original," Wittfooth points out, "is that its shelf life can continue past a mere publication date."

And despite it being a fairly lengthy process that frequently demands a great deal of patience, Wittfooth finds oil painting extremely rewarding. "This medium usually lets me pull off something close to what I envision at the start of a job," he comments, "even if the oil process doesn't always agree with reproduction techniques or fast turnarounds."

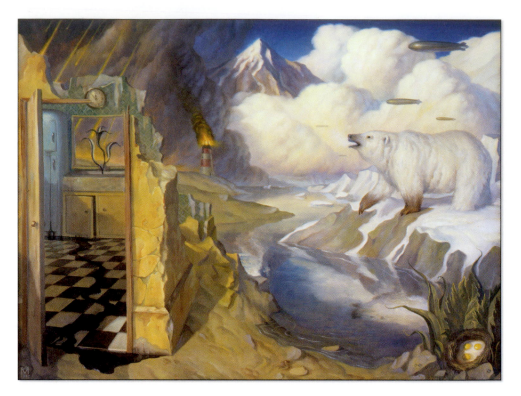

Figure 15-8: Much of Wittfooth's work deals with the rather broad issue of industry and nature: the "price of human progress." But he narrows concepts down to more specific themes in each painting, tending to include symbolism and other imagery that ties in or supports the main idea. "Perhaps the illustration at hand involves subject matter granting a new insight," Wittfooth says. "Even if it's subtle enough to be purely subconscious, I personally try to learn something new every time I sit down to paint."
© Martin Wittfooth

Learning

Wittfooth will tell you that illustration carries the beautiful potential of a life-long learning process. The vocabulary may only be limited by available mediums or specific methods of applying them.

Some artists are meticulous, their limited output produced at a practically glacial pace. Perhaps they only employ one approach throughout their careers. Others are as wildly prolific as they are eclectic. In any scenario, what may be said with the tools is practically limitless.

"The doors of possible exploration are wide open," Wittfooth comments. "In this sense, every new project—whether it's an editorial gig, a series of drawings for an art show, or a self-directed painting experiment—has promise."

Practiced, Practical Education

"I think practice is not only important for any artist—it's essential," says Wittfooth. An excellent point (and hopefully, old news for the readers of this book). And isn't doing a job in itself practice? So if one is lucky enough to be a full-time "successful" artist, isn't he theoretically practicing all the time? Well, yes—and with a bit of luck and energy, getting paid for it, too.

Mistakes are what make that success possible, says Wittfooth. He tells you, with field wisdom and confidence: "If you can learn what you *don't* want as an outcome, then working to correct that means we can ultimately arrive at something we want to achieve.

"I'm always inventing new mistakes … and on it goes," Wittfooth grins. He'll even "joyfully screw up" a color somewhere in a painting and actually decide that it's *preferable* to its intended alternative. "On the other hand,

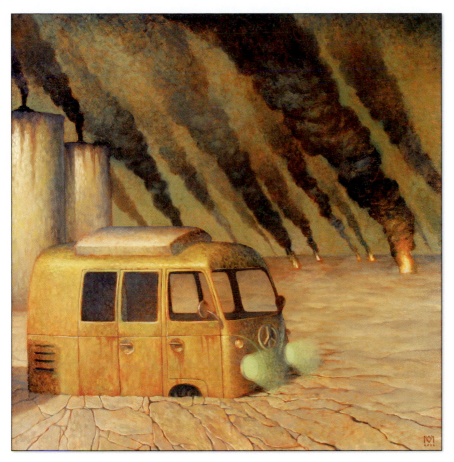

Figure 15-9: Wittfooth finds that practicing certain skills—in his case, drawing and painting from life—can greatly contribute to and enhance his professional and personal work. "Open-studios with a live model are very beneficial," he tells us. "I try to fit these in weekly as often as I can. And I believe that practicing observation skills and hand-to-eye co-ordination are crucial," he continues, "whether you paint in the realistic vein of Norman Rockwell or draw with the naiveté of a five-year-old."
© Martin Wittfooth

acknowledging success is just as important as noticing and correcting a glitch," Wittfooth comments. "Once I discover something that 'works,' that same effect (or texture, color, etc.) will most likely turn up in another piece at some point."

Captured

Mike Slattery will insist that, on the most elemental level, almost all artwork consists of making marks of some kind. "My work," he says, "consists of the tiniest fraction of a line spread over the whole image in order to create space and form. These dots are clustered or scattered in order to create the sense of mass on a two-dimensional surface."

When he considers an image as raw material, Slattery is thinking primarily of value and contrast. Texture is his next concern, but color is incidental and often added as a background element in the last stages of the preliminary process.

Overall concept is one of the keys. "I do very few standalone works," he explains. "They are all intended to work together in some way. I don't do landscapes or wildlife. I am most interested in cities and how people go about their daily lives. I am drawn to images that have the feel of the accidental and unplanned. I want the individuals that populate my works to be unaware that they are being transformed into a commentary on life itself."

Figures 15-10, 15-11, 15-12, and 15-13: After deciding on subject, value relationships, and how an image fits into the overall plan, Slattery feels that the arrangement of elements must now work in order for the image to succeed as a work of art. So in Figure 15-10, the thing that first interested the artist was the play of dark and the textures created by the video signal. "I want it to seem that if you watch it long enough, the image itself will update to a new image, " says Slattery. Figure 15-11 arranges lines and dots to create a tension that contrasts the flat space of the wall with the dramatic depth of the oblique crosswalk lines. "For me," Slattery comments, "the kind of composition that draws me most is one that has that tension between flat space and dynamic depth" (as also seen in Figure 15-12).

Finally, in Figure 15-13, you find people trapped within their vehicles, but we understand the human presence nonetheless. Says Slattery: "That they are immortalized in this moment in time forever, completely unaware, simply fascinates me."

© Mike Slattery

Figure 15-11
© Mike Slattery

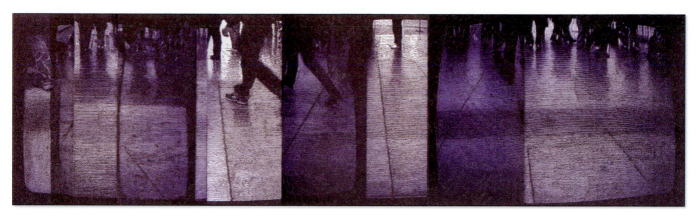

Figure 15-12
© Mike Slattery

Figure 15-13
© Mike Slattery

Duct Up

I have a thing for robots, ductwork, and rusty old machines. This piece covers all of that and also addresses another passion: utilizing—recycling, if you will—found or cast-off so-called *junk* as design elements. In a chapter about imagination, I trust you see the synchronicity of that.

And in this spirit of creative vision (and expression) I hope you are tuned in to the marvelously free and spontaneous mini-masterpieces your paint palettes become by the end of the day.

Case in point: I couldn't bear to lose four particular one-inch squares of paint scumble and splatter on a throwaway palette I was fixing to, well, throw away. This included what became the face of the head of the machine, already there, ready to go, as is. So I found another scrap piece of similar card stock, glued these loose ends down and built the entire painting around those four leftovers.

Figure 15-14: A paint palette destined for the garbage was the springboard for my imagination on this painting. The piece played to my love of robots, pipes, and rusted-out apparatus (as well my inclination to recycle and reuse stuff).

© Michael Fleishman

CHAPTER SUMMARY

This chapter was about tapping into one's imagination to (1) challenge yourself as an artist and (2) challenge your viewer at the end product. We explored the idea that imagination may really be about spontaneity and improvisation, as well as the follow-through of inspiration to concept to final. We considered that the expression of your imagination shapes your visual language as you express your individual reality (on many levels).

Working It Out

1. Spot Color

Create a painting from a palette. Don't just crop and/or frame your palette (although that is also a fun exercise), but actually go back into a palette and coax the work of art, literally, out of the mix.

2. I Once Made a Mistake but I Was Dead Wrong About That

Mistakes are what make success possible. Find a piece where (in your mind?) there is an obvious mistake. Think for a moment: what it is that you *didn't* want as an outcome, how the current "failed" state of affairs went down; how you might work to correct that. Now also consider that maybe this is actually a cool-looking passage. Use it to your advantage: do a painting or drawing based on this supposed mistake.

3. Attach/Detach

In class we will attempt to do an illustration that involves you emotionally (and/or connects you intellectually). The next session, we will try to do an illustration that does not engage you intellectually and/or emotionally. We'll compare/discuss outcomes (both product and process).

Home and Away

1. Dream Job

Create an illustration based on a dream. Don't fabricate a fantasy from your waking imagination, use an actual dream or nightmare.

2. Talking to Yourself

Create an illustration based on a recent conversation *with yourself*. Pep talks as well as self-evaluations are fair game on this one.

3. Alert!

Create an illustration based on a daydream. Recording where your mind wandered during that lecture in Art History class is quite okay here.

Chapter 16

Drawing Observes

© Charlene Smith

Look—Drawing!

When you do an illustration, you go through your process, but odds are, you are not consciously thinking through the steps. Art is nothing if it isn't about observation and perception and then recording. I'm not saying you hit the power button, tap the switch, and the drawing scans and does itself on autopilot. But in a real sense, we all have become—or are becoming—what we see.

People perceive in many ways, based first I think (and physically, at least) on where and how they live. Culture, society, and experience (including the influence of family and

peers) temper all that, of course. And there's this, too: we *see*, but
are we really *looking* at what we see? By that token, we *hear*, but are
we actually *listening* to that input? The stuff's coming at us, but are
we really taking it all in?

Maybe I could've called this chapter *Drawing Visualizes.* Or cutting
right to the chase: *Look—Drawing!* Well, that makes for an interesting
dynamic. As I say in my book, *Exploring Illustration* (Cengage): how
do you want your illustration looked at (in a physical sense)? How
you want your illustration seen (in an intellectual sense)?

Small World Department

Jenny Kostecki-Shaw is a veteran world traveler and people watcher.
She says she is now using more collage and found materials
(especially stuff she collects when she travels). "And I *prefer* painting
on cardboard boxes, drawing on scrap ledger paper, and collaging
with material others throw in the trash cans," she smiles. "For me,
what works is whatever materials inspire me in the moment, for
that particular piece."

And like Kostecki-Shaw, Dan Krall is another globe trotting
observer of the human condition. He posts some hilarious visual
commentary about those sightings (both here and abroad) on his
Web site and blog (dankrall.com). "Everywhere we go," Krall
reports, "99% of the people we meet couldn't be nicer—sweet,
friendly, helpful. However … *they are no fun to draw.*

"But we do run into a few folks who live up to the stereotypes—so, for
instance, in Austria, Bavaria—or even at a taco stand in California—you
may find some people who are very harsh and severe … *and they are fun
to draw.*"

Figure 16-3: Hammill says he drew *awesome* dinosaurs when he was a kid. Lately, though, he's been drawing more as a means to tell a story, rather than drawing as an end in itself.
© Matt Hammill

What's the Story Here?

For Matt Hammill it's all about communicating concept. Ideally, the composition and aesthetics of the piece just flow from the demands of the content—whatever tells the story best. "I draw little characters in little situations," he laughs. "I can't help it! I'm a narrative kind of guy."

Telling the Tale

Hammill often goes for quirky, humorous scenarios in his drawings, so he opts for media that won't weigh down content. "I generally try to make the story clear," he says, "and not have anything be too distracting." Value and composition work hand in hand. "I lay out everything in terms of light and dark before I even begin to worry about color," he says. "And I work much more with shape than with form."

For Hammill, a bit of extra detail works only as long as it doesn't overwhelm the main concept; you won't see him doing a twelve-hour oil painting for a three-second joke. But of course, the illustrator will tell you that, in the end, even working quickly takes far longer than you think it will.

Just Do It

Robert Brinkerhoff thinks that people tend to separate the cognitive (the thinking, planning part) from the actual construction of something. So, "doing is a form of thinking" is a phrase that constantly pops up in his dialogues with students.

Brinkerhoff has learned through experience that action is indeed a subset of idea. Conceptually, you just *imagine* an image. And really, no matter how eloquent you are, there's only limited information you can verbalize (to an art director or your teacher).

By that same token, Brinkerhoff thinks it's sometimes difficult to get students to talk about the ideas behind their work. This can become a source of frustration for the learner, shifting attention from the heart of the matter: actual drawing, painting, and observation. "When your focus shifts to the *message,* it becomes even more difficult to balance it all," Brinkerhoff considers. "People who do it the best are going to be the better illustrators."

Figure 16-5: The work of Brinkerhoff.
© Robert Brinkerhoff

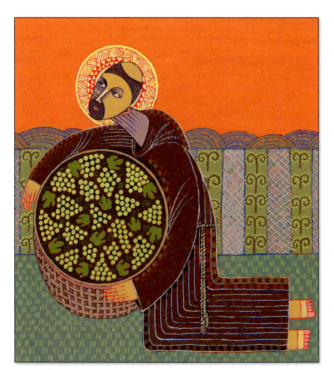

Figure 16-6: Meganck's point of view captures the essence of the idea.
© Robert Meganck

Why, Why, and What

Robert Meganck says that illustration is really just drawing to communicate an idea. "Illustration is drawing with a point; a point of view," he tells you, "communicating the theme behind that story, an essence of a play, a political slant to an editorial piece. You try to communicate the author's intent, and take it beyond words with an image."

Meganck has been teaching for over 30 years, the last 27 at Virginia Commonwealth University. He tries to get his students to think, analyze information, and express ideas. For him, *the* questions to ask are: "Why are you doing this? Why are you drawing this way? What is it you hope to accomplish with this form or this style?"

"Robert made me far more attuned to the way *I* work," Meganck's former student, Julia Melograna comments. "Through Robert, I found a lot of creative identity." Melograna says that Meganck's critiques concentrated more on the basics. Less "nit-picking" meant that such projects could really be about *community*.

To which another part of that community, his former student Tin Salamunic adds, "At the heart of the matter were drawing skills. Without this foundation, nothing works. You can be a genius, but if you can't put it down on paper, the exercise is meaningless."

And Meganck recognized that Salamunic could draw. For his part, Salamunic drew constantly. "I was allowed to keep screwing up over and over, until I got my artwork right," he says. "And now that I am out," Salamunic grins, "the real learning experience is going to start."

The Lingo

Andrea Wicklund tells us that mechanical and conceptual skills go hand and hand. "You can't express yourself if you don't know the language," she says. Wicklund employs many different media—graphite, acrylic, paint, sometimes collage—to talk that talk. "It's just much more fun," she states.

According to Wicklund, it makes problem solving somewhat out of control as well, but also creates more options. "It keeps me interested," she comments. "Problem solving process is what makes the result a little more fascinating.

"I have people tell me my work is somewhat surreal," Wicklund says. "My imagination definitely takes over my daily life as I daydream and imagine, so it must come through in my artwork a little bit. It's just the way I picture things in my head.

"But I cannot sit and draw things *out of* my head," she balks. "I can devise composition and design shapes, but I always need to be looking at something—it's so much easier for me to draw an accurate drawing of a shoe if that shoe is in front of me.

"It's all about those different categories of the imagination, I guess."

Expert Texpert

Wicklund's illustration is about the depiction of people, places, and things from a somewhat conceptual viewpoint. "Is this an accurate documentation of anything?" she asks. "I don't know, but it's certainly a record of my observation of the current scene." And Wicklund loves that research. "It offers me the opportunity to become an expert on any given topic," she says, "It gives me an excuse to know things other than the art. I'd label my artwork as intelligent fine art."

Figure 16-7 © Tin Salamunic

Figures 16-7 and 16-8: Meganck comments that in a class of 16 students, you'll have 16 individual personalities. "In such a class, you get certain students who are just driven," he says. "Instruction for these folks is almost secondary—they know what they have to do, and they pull it off with real passion. They love it. The more you throw at them, the more they flourish.

16-8 © Julia Melograna

Figures 16-9 and 16-10:
Wicklund never quite knows how an illustration is going to turn out, but she understands that "predictable" and "safe" don't usually translate to "fresh" and "exciting."
© Andrea Wicklund

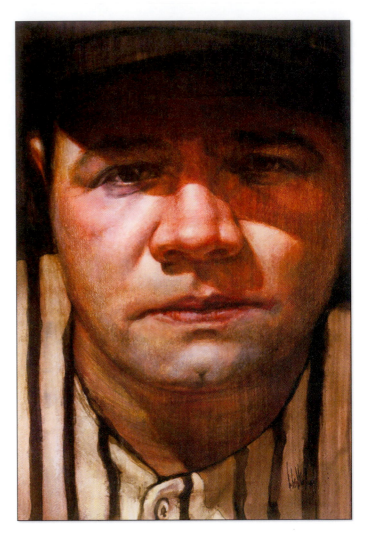

Her mixed media approach is definitely not the safest way to go—it's a little bit riskier since it's less predictable. But for this illustrator, that's precisely the appeal. "I get a kick out of that," she smiles. "I like not knowing exactly what is going to happen."

"I used to do really detailed color studies and I would exhaust myself," she tells you. "The color study always looked better (than the final). And I'd think: what am I doing? Why don't I simply do the color study *on the illustration*?"

All in the Family

Fred Lynch teaches at Rhode Island School of Design as well as the Montserrat College of Art. "My work now is definitely an outgrowth of my teaching," he states.

A comparatively young institution, Montserrat was started in the late 60s, and overlaps its departments more than most. Students take a great deal of courses outside the illustration department. The school is interdisciplinary; departments are interdependent. Because the school is so small, Lynch says that personal attention is "possible and doable."

Audience Award

The Montserrat way of the world is to simultaneously stress the message of the picture and the corresponding professional issues—a total application of that art. Every student is pushed to develop his or her own vocabulary. So, for instance, your illustration doesn't need to look a certain way—it needs to *act* a certain way. No preconceived notions of how illustration "should" be. Not a lot of time obsessing about technique.

"We do talk about picture-making necessities while we guide the transition from making pictures for ourselves to making pictures for others," says Lynch.

"Because you are making picture communication, everything is set out on the table (as far as how you want to express yourself), *as long as you can apply it clearly to an audience.*"

That's a cool—and crucial—idea: master your watercolor (make that any media); take control of your time; achieve a consistent result. While I hardly endorse and applaud good fortune and happy accidents, the most successful way to do that is by having a steady process.

Energizer

"Fred Lynch's intense illustration and vivid brush, his rich imagination and driving curiosity, are perfectly conveyed in his passion for teaching," says his former student, Nate Walker. So knowledge combines with wisdom (gained only via actual experience) to enlighten a classroom that is an open and nurturing forum (as well as a challenging, professional environment where students must defend their ideas and their art).

"What sealed my seat in Fred Lynch's classroom was that Fred energized the class to become a family," adds another former student, Heather Newton. Newton says that Lynch urges his family "to look for their joy. To get a firm grip on your materials and technique.

"Then he'll 'make' you get the best out of that media and style," she smiles. "So while he's a huge supporter, Fred constantly pushes students to think above and beyond. He helps you grow by building on both strengths and weaknesses."

Figure 16-11a and b: Lynch warns that the process of fine art is different from the process of applied art. "When you're a fine artist, you're creating an image or a piece of art that asks a question of the audience," he says. "An illustrator, more often than not, creates an answer for the audience. You need to understand how those things are different. This answer doesn't have to be in the form of a declarative. It can be in the form of a question, but a question answered by an audience. That's what happens at Montserrat."
© Fred Lynch

Play It as It Lays

"My school sports background plays a role in my style of teaching," Lynch considers. " I hear myself acting as much as a coach as a teacher: Pep talks from the sidelines. A lot of signals. Drills. Talking strategy. Figuring out positions; how to focus (and where), what to address; the idea of working together. Building each class as a team. I draw on the board a lot, too.

"Only recently have I realized how much that background has affected me. Let's just hope I don't walk in with a whistle this next semester. I'm not sure my students would like to run laps!"

New Toons

As far back as the second grade, Newton declared that her college major would be illustration. And she actually kept that focus. But she wasn't that kid with the crayons anymore.

As a young adult dealing with the rigors (and stress) of an illustration education, Newton's coping mechanisms in college would unfortunately compromise her childhood ambitions.

Figure 16-12a and b: "Heather Newton's bright and worked very hard on her work," her teacher, Lynch, recalls. "Naturally artful, but not a natural illustrator; she made works that only she understood." In time, one of Lynch's repeated mantras took hold. Which is that—at least for the applied arts—something about your work has to be user friendly for the viewer.

"Exciting architecture must still boast the most basic functions," Lynch tells us. "People need to find the entrance easily as well as the fire exit! In illustration, a clear entrance is necessary too. If one's work is challenging in form, it helps to make the content easy to grasp. The reverse is also true. If the content is challenging, delivering that concept clearly is crucial.

"Heather's approach was unusual, and simplifying her concepts made a big difference in her success. Clarifying her ideas allowed her to continue to create personal paintings without the confusion."

She'll candidly tell you that her priorities were all over the place. A lack of focus and no appreciable self-confidence combined to agitate big delivery issues. And this negative mix seriously impacted both her emotional and physical well-being.

Hers is a cautionary tale, but comes complete with a great ending. With help, Newton gained strength, control, and confidence. "Students who have issues to any degree need to recognize that you have to feel good about yourself," she says. "Staying healthy and sleeping properly enable you to handle deadlines, to create truly personal illustration, and to grow as a creative person."

✔ Check Point: In Response to the Real

For our hot list this chapter, Tom Garrett and five former students—Jason Greenberg, Carrie Hartman, Matt Mills, Charlene Smith, and Ulana Zahajkewycz—think back to their student days at Minneapolis College of Art and Design (MCAD), and consider their process:

1. It takes real skill and grace to be truly fresh and spontaneous. And that actually means *practice*. Technical proficiency means little if the message is something that's seen time and again. Masterful illustrators present truly novel ideas *and* offer some simple use that the audience understands. If not, there's a problem. (TG)

2. I spend a lot of time asking the painting what colors it needs. Sometimes the paintings take a long time to answer. (UZ)

3. You must guide students without crushing them, like the way you would hold an egg—gently, but with purpose. The idea is not perfection at this stage, but to gain understanding; skills come later. (UZ)

4. Being creative *on demand*, 9 to 5, every day, can be daunting. Get away from a stalled project (and work on something else) to hotwire better solutions. Brainstorm. Inquire. Interact. Gather information. Trust your instincts. Connect. Everybody has these abilities, and school strengthens all that. (CS)

5. It's almost as if one sees an idea more clearly when you *don't* get caught up in the minutiae of "perfect" drawings. I'll grab stuff not knowing what the connection is. . . *yet*. I just know that it feels right. The end process is arranging those elements in a way that tells a story for me. Whether the audience really "gets" that end result exactly isn't the issue. Does it mean anything to them? That's what counts to me. (CS)

6. It's about inspiration, then application. It's asking yourself, "What do I want?" It's *focus*, pure and simple. (CH)

7. One of your main concerns as a student is to think and expand your ideas. (CH)

8. I personally needed art school. Yes, I was (and am) a social being. Formal art education was a way to motivate me, expose me to what is out there, and what other people are doing. And I needed guidance. While the desire to *be* creative came naturally to me, the road map of *how* to get there successfully did not. I needed someone to see something in me and to affirm my abilities. I needed the nurturing environment that allowed a self-conscious young artist to morph into something a little more confident and a lot more talented. (MM)

9. Be a jack-of-all-trades. Dive into a subject. Research is key. Always learn new things. (MM)

10. Find (and speak in) your own voice, but don't limit yourself by only seeing things with your perspective. So, really listen to what people have to say about your work. (JG)

11. Practice makes perfect, they say. And then you hear that nobody is perfect, so you may be tempted to stop practicing. . .but *always* practice. Experiment all the time; it helps with your personal growth as an artist. Notice I said *growth*, not *success*. Success can be misleading. Success pretty much tells us what we are doing right, but can leave you living in a tiny little box of thought, afraid to come out. So much depends on what *you* want out of art school. Be ready to *go*. Come to the party motivated." (JG)

© Charlene Smith

© Tom Garrett

© Ulana Zahajkewycz

Garrett calls *realness* and *response* two concerns that should speak to values students (hopefully) already possess. As shown here, Garrett, as a professional, remains curious about what makes his view of the world special. "Now, the job of the educator is to pose questions that promote that inquiry," he tells you, "and push for the answers that create a visual vocabulary." Two of his former students provide answers to that query here.

© Carrie Hartman

© Matt Mills

© Jason Greenberg

Garrett's students are approached with professionalism, patience, and understanding; they are guided to trust their instincts, sense the connections to strengthen skills and focus. The illustrations here showcase the potential of each student's particular voice. Garrett develops this crucial aspect by advocating for the student's approach and *not* stressing how he would do it. "Because it isn't about me," he says. "I look at my students' art and I realize why this profession is truly thrilling for me."

Comic Relief

Marc Rosenthal lives and works in Lenox, Massachusetts. He tells you that "communication in illustration is not only key; it's really what separates illustration from what we call 'fine art.'" Rosenthal continues by saying that an illustration should be visually arresting. But then, like a good joke, it must have a satisfying punchline. That punchline should add to the story, not merely visually repeat what's already said in words.

"Even a complex story can often be boiled down to a simple, illustratable concept," Rosenthal states. "An emphasis on concept means removing distracting or confusing elements. Any opulent detail or vast perspective should always be in the service of the concept."

Straight Man

Line is *the* basic element of drawing for Rosenthal, who says, "Line is the most immediate means to describe an object on paper, to communicate an idea (or even, to formulate an idea). It is direct and expressive and, for me, it is still always my first step."

Rosenthal's relationship with line as a finished graphic element always seems to be changing. He grew up loving comics, and his first experience with drawing was copying comic strips. "This was almost entirely a linear medium," he says, "and when I started illustrating, that remained my approach. I was also very much under the influence of Milton Glaser. I did crosshatched drawings to which I then applied flat color.

"I still love the economy of line," he comments, "and I like the idea of a finished drawing that can be faxed, and still retain its integrity. However, I've been playing with removing line, letting color and value describe the boundaries of objects."

Flat Out

"I'll talk about color and value together because, to me, they are linked," Rosenthal considers. "One fully appreciates color only when the values are *close*. When the values are extreme, the art tends to become graphic (which I actually like), and color is secondary. So I keep finding myself attracted to images with limited color. I have been trying to see how much color I can eliminate.

"Plus, as both color and especially value describe form, I've recently been playing both against line to flatten the image, using strong, flat shapes that contradict the linear drawing."

Lately, Rosenthal has also been trying to use color more abstractly—divorcing it from the real world of local color. "I hate having to make a blue sky, and green grass," he says. "With color I tend to pay more attention to its graphic impact. A red sky will pop forward. Here, it becomes a more powerful element, not sitting too comfortably back behind the horizon—although one does have to check the emotional component: are you sending the wrong message? Does the sky look 'threatening'?"

Figure 16-13a and b: "I am attracted to flattened images; more medieval, without deep perspective," says Rosenthal. "Thus, I naturally look for conceptual solutions that fit into my pictorial preferences. And that is why I hate it when clients have an image in mind before they call me. It almost always clashes with the way I like to set up a picture.

"And there are occasions when no brilliant concept presents itself," he considers. "Then one can attempt to make up for it with composition, color, and dazzling artwork."
© Marc Rosenthal

What's the Point of Time and Space?

From West New York, New Jersey, Robert Kogge says, "Line is a point in time and space. Line is where positive and negative space meet in communicating what can't be spoken or heard. Line moves us in mysterious ways, generating the nature of an image. In more practical terms, it is the primary vehicle in constructing, editing, and finalizing thoughts to a material form. But *mystery* (for us to ponder and celebrate) is what generally should be communicated through drawing and painting."

I get it. In terms of time and space, that means that value is more the *distance* from light to dark. "Yes, it provides a decipherable profile of all that is visualized," Kogge says. "Line is created by way of contrasting value."

Bringing Up Baby

"For me," Kogge continues, "value is the primary means to not only bring forth an image, but to carry it beyond my original expectations. To take that image to places of its own design and effect. The farther my work gets from my ego, the better (and closer) it comes to universal inclusion. At some point, like children, the work needs to stand—if not rise—on its own terms and reconnect to its source . . . until then, the best we can do—as with kids—is to rear them."

"Along those lines, a grasp of the fundamentals is only the beginning," Kogge tells you. "An artist needs to customize this grasp to best suit, if not enhance, articulating their aesthetic vision. To name a few: Seurat, Cezanne, Picasso, Pollack, Chuck Close come to mind."

Weave It Alone

In a great spin on fundamental practice, Kogge actually offers a class that challenges the boundaries of painting and drawing by joining them as a single process. "This is an alternate or extension of more traditional methods," he explains. "This approach will demonstrate the significance of personalizing one's materials and methods; *how* one creates will be highlighted as well as *what* one creates."

The spotlight in this course will be on art media—the heavy weave of the canvas as a dominant but impersonal mark, distilling positive and negative space evenly to render what Kogge labels, "a particulate profile to all. Moreover, the nature of the image is spawned through pigment being penciled to a woven ground."

Figure 16-14a, b and c: "I see color more as a reality than a concept," Kogge says. " I'm really not saying anything in particular and I toil at it endlessly … nothing in particular and everything in general. The key element in my creative process is to get busy and stay that way. I feel I end up with a concept that is helpful as a point of departure for the next piece.

One of Kogge's favorite quotes is from artist Brett Whiteley, who, as Kogge says, gets it right: "Drawing is the art of being able to leave an accurate record of the experience of what one isn't, of what one doesn't know. A great drawer is either confirming beautifully what is commonplace or probing authoritatively the unknown."

Hardly Intangible

"I view creating like I do talking," says Corrine Bayraktaroglu. "It's a means to communicate. I'm not trying to make a specific statement with each piece as much as I want to express something that has moved me. And it's as much about the process as it is about the end result.

"I have a general idea that always evolves," she considers, "and I have this need to put that in a tangible form to explore my feelings.

"The idea arrives first; how I want to express it comes second. Content drives process. My work has a broad range, and technique is always subordinate to the concept. For me, technique is really a tool. I look for materials that best express the idea. So with *Cat*, for instance, I collaged and painted *in reverse* on plexiglass."

Crushed and Raw

"I love graffiti. And I have a mini-obsession with recycling," Bayraktaroglu smiles. "For instance, I like exploiting the actual shape of a found object. You look at the work and ask: Is it modeled or is it the real form of the crushed can or rock?"

Her painting on wood, "Dig Freedom," is a statement about oil and politics and the death of innocents. Color reverses from left to right like a negative: "The little girl was once alive, but now dead," Bayraktaroglu tells us. "It's on wood so as not to get too precious (especially as it's about death); the wood is a raw material that reflects mortality."

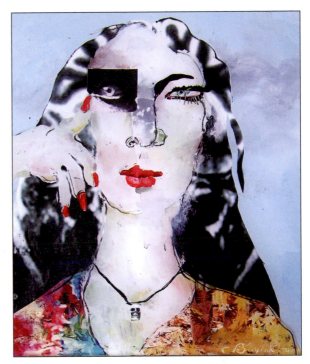

Figure 16-15: Not only is the painting reverse engineered as it were, but in this tale of a medical drama, the woman's hair is fabricated from an actual CAT scan.
© Corrine Bayraktaroglu

Figure 16-16: Bayraktaroglu's "Dig Freedom."
© Corrine Bayraktaroglu

CHAPTER SUMMARY

This chapter was about the power of observation, visual commentary, and communicating concept: it was about focus. We discussed composition and aesthetics that flow from the demands of that content, and that illustration is drawing to communicate an idea. We examined illustration as drawing with a point of view, communicating the theme and the essence of that theme (as answered by certain questions: Why are you doing this? What do you want? Why are you drawing this way? What is it you hope to accomplish with this form or this style?).

This chapter was about the different categories of the imagination, and the record of that observation; gaining understanding, inspiration, and then application. We explored the search for conceptual solutions that fit into pictorial preferences, and the *mystery* of what generally should be communicated through drawing and painting.

Working It Out

1. Foreign Affair

Pick a recent drawing of yours. You're going to seek outside review, but we'll take an interdisciplinary approach. Ask five instructors (or professionals) outside your field of study to critique this piece. What did you learn from this evaluation and different perspective?

2. Look!

What does "Drawing Observes" mean to you? Is there ever a case where drawing does *not* observe? Are *you* an observant drawer? Is there a difference between this act (or process) and "drawing from observation"? Is this the same thing as drawing from *reference*? Based on your answers, do a "drawing from observation."

3. Sequential Stories

Create in a manner that requires you to observe subject matter, style and technique, plus concept from another perspective: for instance, do a "reverse engineered" mixed media piece, in reverse, on plexiglass.

Home and Away

1. Home School

Pick a work *in progress*. You're going to ask your parents, spouse, or friend to do a one-on-one verbal critique of this work as well as a written critique you will share in class. Thanks to Jaime Zollars at MICA who shared this exercise—and an actual assignment from a colleague—with us.

2. Everyone's an Expert

Come up with a concept and ask *every one* of your classmates to advise you on how to do the illustration before you begin. Ask each colleague to be explicit. Do separate illustrations based on this advice (one drawing per "expert"). Compare and contrast.

3. Travelogue

Go on an extended road trip. Sketch the people, places, and things you encounter. Do a series of subsequent paintings or drawings based on these roughs.

Chapter 17

Drawing Takes Off

© Kevin Mack

The Size and Extent of It

Initially this chapter was called "Drawing in the Abstract." Then it was called "Drawing in Other Dimensions." Both titles still work somewhat, but this chapter expands the scope and idea behind those words. Oh, the abstract and non-representational art is still here. And we certainly consider three-dimensional work as well. Plus we'll look at some classical 2-D stuff that could breathe easily enough in previous chapters.

All the artists you'll meet here begin with drawing, and then spin it off—literally and conceptually. From ground zero (drawing), their art takes on different tangents. I think the word dimensions (as in the range covered by our subject—the extent or capacity of drawing) is still viable here. And yes, this chapter regards drawing in the abstract (as in the wiggle room to aim beyond straight depiction or sheer distortion, and shoot at both external and internal structure and form).

So we're going to talk about how drawing practice is at the root of process and how the act of drawing extends the reach of concept (both 2-D and 3-D).

Representing the Abstract (or Not)

Ready or not, here I come: what is the difference between abstract and non-representational art? "Abstract" art is not necessarily "non-representational" art. The words sure are spelled different. And certainly, not all "non-representational" artwork is that abstract (I'm going to make you work for this one: see your dictionary). But by "non-representational," do you really mean "non-objective"?

I've heard "non-objective" defined as "having no resemblance to any real object." And I've seen "abstract" clarified as "real objects that have been changed, simplified, or distorted in some way." Some folks use the words "abstract" and "non-representational" interchangeably. I have—and I've had my abstract chewed out about it by some non-objective intelligentsia.

A game to play: go online and see what you find. Does the mud get any clearer for you? And here's how Webster's weighs in: "[Non-representational art is] art that does not attempt to represent in recognizable form any object in nature; *abstract*; *non-objective*." Oy! If you can't trust good ol' Dan Webster, who ya gonna call?

One could say that discerning the content of "non-representational" art—in whole or in part—lies solely with the audience. The work is "heartfelt" or "deeply moving" (you might even get downright emotional about it). It may possibly make you *think*. Or it simply "looks good to me"—you dig the colors; the "design" is cool, I like the "composition." (And, by the way, what's the difference between "design" and "composition" beyond the semantics that spark debate in some circles?)

You don't have to "get it" or divine the artist's meaning or message (but watch out—if the piece has a title, all bets are off). Is it "good" or "bad"? With non-representational art, you could say that the viewer gets to do the heavy lifting here, as well.

Universal Pictures

At school I found a large backing sheet that someone had trashed in the studio. Multiple layers of textured pigment made for a delightful crazy quilt of rich, serendipitous color combinations and mad brushwork. I loved it immediately, and grabbed it out of the garbage bin with a master plan.

I selected the meatiest bits, the juiciest color passages. I trimmed off the fat, then sliced these remaining board fragments into smaller strips. I rearranged those pieces at will—continuously shuffling as my composition progressed.

Everything is taped together at this juncture—meatball surgery, I know. The next step will be to mount the finals on backing pieces (for a more permanent and archival presentation) and then mat and frame.

Figure 17-1: I was so inspired by all the brouhaha that I worked up these abstracts just for this section. The names of these hybrid paintings are "Frankenstein Meats Vegetables" and "Bride of the Son of Frankenstein Returns." No, I didn't try to hide the seams—what fun was that?

© Michael Fleishman

The Road

"A journey of a thousand miles begins with the first step." This basic precept coming down from the philosopher Lao-tzu has long been the cornerstone of Lampo Leong's approach to both art and teaching. Trained both in China and the United States, Leong's work (academically as well as professionally) is tempered by a multi-cultural vision.

"First, we have that journey," Leong will tell you, "a vision—a long-term goal to make art." That magnitude (and the *worthiness*) of this goal is at the heart of everything Leong wants to communicate as an artist and teacher. "If I have played a role in motivating students to go after this goal for themselves," he says, "I've contributed to this tradition."

Figure 17-2: Leong's own experience—coming from an Asian background into an environment influenced mainly by what he labels as "European aesthetic traditions"—has shown him the value of reinvention. Leong writes classical Chinese calligraphy on traditional rice paper, then literally destroys his creation. Tearing and collaging the shards of line, he then scans and digitally rebuilds the image in Photoshop (incorporating photographic material as well). This hybrid is printed on canvas, then layered with acrylics and oils.

© Lampo Leong

Figure 17-3: Fundamentals are indispensable for artists of every level, and Leong pushes to integrate traditional studio exercises with critical thinking. Analysis becomes just as important as perception and expression.

"What I love is when students really see how artists truly work, *in the here and now*—the rich dialogue arising from an active engagement between artists and experience grounds the classroom experience. This provides a basic understanding of the learning process; the components are integrally related to the total context."
© Lampo Leong

The Clash

Leong sees the collision of different cultures—European, African-American, Latino, and Asian—as a tremendous opportunity for art education. He strongly respects the cultural legacy and ethnic heritage students bring while encouraging each to search for a distinctive individuality. "Only by valuing diversity," he says, "can we best help our students realize their full potential."

"Art, as I see it," Leong states, "is as much about communication, concepts, and language as it is about aesthetics. Art is finding ways to transcend the limits of what has been expressed before."

The Act

"I draw for different reasons and for different purposes," Kevin Mack considers. "Most often to communicate ideas or visual concepts to others. I've found that if I'm explaining something, I'm able to articulate the idea better if I'm drawing it at the same time."

For Mack, the *act* of drawing is really the key. "It actually just helps me express myself verbally," he explains. "Often the drawing itself is of no consequence; other times it is very much about the drawing—showing some intangible that cannot be entirely defined verbally." Mack tells us that, alternatively he practices what might be called "spontaneous" drawing. "Zen" drawing is perhaps a more appropriate description. This drawing style is very much about the character of lines, shapes, and forms. Mostly it's about gesture, and less about making a drawing of some specific thing. It's more about manner and style, and like doodling in a way—but there is nothing sketchy in this approach.

"Marks may be made slowly or quickly, but confidently—with the emphasis on how it *feels*," says Mack. "It is like stream of consciousness (or automatic writing or free association) with the emphasis on random variation. It's the same state of mind as when creating a flow of random non-sequitur words."

Drawing is rather a form of meditation for Mack, a way to clear his mind. "Actually it's akin to dancing," he smiles, "all about free-form movements with little concern for a 'result.' But it is common that the process evolves into a much more directed and considered effort, even over the course of a single drawing.

"If I choose to 'render,' I may start with one of the approaches above but then apply subtle shading—light and shadow—in a value composition. This is usually pencil shading or crosshatched lines. This can be drawing as painting in a way, with numerous gradient combinations and cross applications of different techniques."

Chicken or the Egg?

It is probably safe to say that Ann Smith (Figures 17-5 a and b) draws from the point of view of a sculptor, and that she primarily considers herself to be a sculptor. She will occasionally even use her sculptures for illustrations. So what comes first?

This overlap of concept and mechanics combine to create a delightful product of shared values. It's obvious that lines are a very important part

Figure 17-4a, b and c: For Mack, the act of drawing is really the key. Often the end product is not critical or completely spontaneous—the drawing all about line character or gesture; perhaps shapes and forms take center stage. And while it is much like doodling in a way, there is nothing sketchy in his approach.

17-4a © Kevin Mack

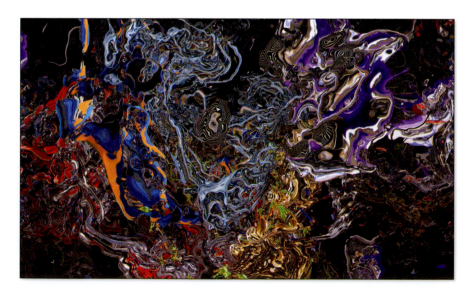

17-4b © Kevin Mack

17-4c © Kevin Mack

of her sculpting process. Lines mean structure. And Smith figuratively and literally constructs her animals from the inside out (just like a good drawing, which is really about anything *but* the surface).

"I'll start with basic curves that define the inner 'skeleton' of a piece," she says. "Many times I start with the backbone. Sometimes I'll build a piece from the bottom up, starting with the legs.

"Either way these first lines determine the size and proportions of the rest of the piece," she continues. From there, I'll add shapes that fill out the meat or muscle of the animal. The final touches are mostly external accents such as streaks of color or textures like hair and feathers. Though the first lines sometimes get buried in the process, the final touches still mimic them in shape and gesture; this helps to keep the piece coherent."

Figure 17-5a and b: "Things need to fit properly," Smith says. In light of that statement, and because of the nature of her work, tone is a somewhat minor component for Smith. Shape is more important; values play out mostly as a result of the materials used and the juxtaposition of those shapes.

For Smith, color defines gesture—an accent runs down a back contour; a bright element creates the curve of the belly. Colors also help define the personality of a piece. "Colors I choose have little to do with actual colors found on the animal in nature," Smith informs. "Instead, they result from the overall impression that that animal gives me. Reds tend to mean 'fast' or 'fierce' (antelopes and raptors); greens and blues are calm and sedate (owls and horses).

"I find that colors carry fairly universal responses from viewers. And whether it's learned or instinctual, color is a great tool for communication."

© Ann Smith

Go Global

Hartwig Braun says illustration is telling a story and that his work chronicles his fascination for the big city, the metropolis—that completely man-made environment. Of course, a city is not only its buildings, but the people who fill it with life. Braun zooms out as far as necessary to portray a cityscape where people—the creators—become less visible and their *creation* catches the eye (and imagination).

Braun loves the design challenge of simplifying complex structures: the juxtaposition of open space and density, artfully crisscrossing all that infrastructure and architectural diversity.

"Finding the right balance," he says, "is what makes a cityscape 'my place.' And that is often given to me by the places themselves: a place will offer a 'natural composition' informed by the actual layout of the city. I just have to find the right position and the best angles; the spots to visually enter and leave the image.

"I play with perspective and freely mix radically different viewpoints. I deliberately ignore all rules of realistic perspective (not unlike a surrealistic or expressionistic painter) but do need to be rather accurate towards the horizon. This angle should remain relatively realistic, gradually shallowing out above and below eye level."

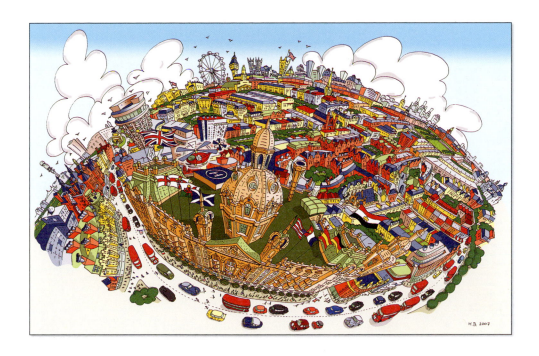

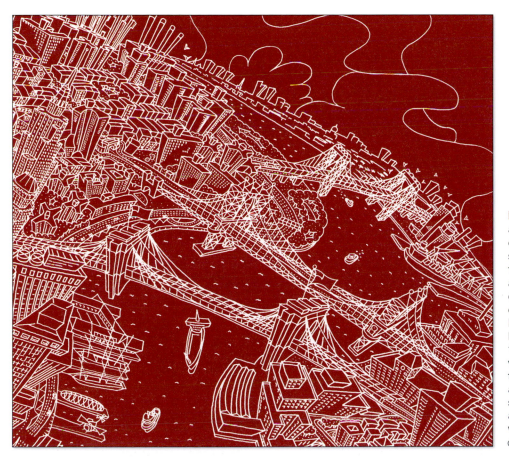

Figure 17-6a and b: "I have a personal connection to an object expressed in the lines," says Braun. "Lines are my foundation. My drawings are, first and foremost, *line* drawings. Lines define the object—they are the object. Lines are the clear boundary between the 'within' and the 'outside': my means to play with perspective, to squeeze, to stretch, to distort an object, and to exaggerate. Lines are simultaneously the essence— and the quirkiness—of my work."

© Hartwig Braun

Figure 17-7: Dunlavey points out that "pure" line was avoided in these drawings. "Some shapes are very linear," he says, "but hopefully, they are read as shapes, not line. The drawings are intended to be a compositional exploration of shape, repetition of shapes, and the spatial tension between shapes. This formal tension is what gives the completed drawings their sense of movement, balance, energy, and life."
© Rob Dunlavey

For the Little People

Rob Dunlavey's *Little People* is a series of 208 drawings done in magic marker. Working from August 1994 to August 1995, the drawings were made on loose sheets of cream laid paper and subsequently punched and added to a 3-ring binder as the project progressed.

Generally, markers used were from those inexpensive box sets geared toward kids, and marker brands varied over the duration. At the time, Dunlavey was frequently commuting by train into Boston and the little people grew up on those rides.

In creating his cast of characters, Dunlavey only followed a few rules:

1. There was no pencil sketching or formal planning before he drew the first shape on the paper.

2. The design had to fit on the paper and look pleasing in that page space.

3. There was no limit on the number of colors (but Dunlavey found that limiting the palette for each drawing made for a stronger piece).

4. Somewhat inspired by stencils and silk screen techniques, Dunlavey tried not to overlap shapes.

Dunlavey tried new schemes to keep his interest up. And as such things seem to have a natural life span anyway, his rules were relaxed towards the end of the project.

No Serial for Me, Thanks

"The question 'does practice make perfect?' amuses me," Brooke Cameron tells you. "It depends on what you call practice. You need to keep your hand in the process, whatever that may be." Repeating ideas or serial motifs are of no interest to Cameron, but she says there are consistent *themes* in her art: social concern, family matters, travel, as well as experimentation with new techniques.

"My work stems from these sources," she states. Cameron's "Is Blood Thicker Than Water?" is technically a print. Yes, it did start as a photo collage with added lettering and other design elements, but this vinyl photogravure (or, as its sometimes called, a solar plate) is a photo-based print. And at its heart, the piece is about the whole question of what constitutes family.

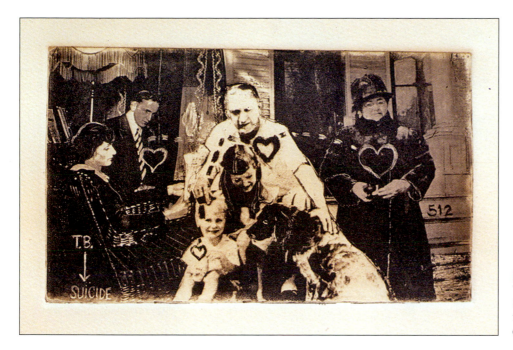

Figure 17-8: What's family? That's the deep (and deeply interesting) question posed in this work by Cameron.
© Brooke Cameron

Puppets in His Game

"Yes; yes!" exclaims Chris Sickels emphatically, "sketches are the best way to communicate. My roughs are always sketches. I don't send 3-D roughs because the final product is a 2-D photograph. Seeing a sculpture/puppet in progress doesn't show the whole concept in context. The approved sketches are my blueprints to build from. If I can't build it like I draw it, it doesn't work."

"I am a firm believer that the concept is the core/ foundation of any image," he continues. "Without a good concept an image will lack substance, and not communicate what it needs to for the viewer. Most of my work that 'works' seems to deal directly with a character striving or reaching, looking or pondering … for something. It helps to have some conflict for that character to deal with, that conflict helps create the dynamic that can pull a viewer in."

Red Knows

Most folks know Sickels' creative enterprise as Red Nose Studio. Sickels states that there is a fundamental concept of line in 3-D practice. "Very much so," he says, "working in 3-D for print, you have to keep the 2-D photo in perspective the entire time, because it's how the thing looks on the page or in the layout that matters. The piece has to work as a flat image. You have to keep the composition in mind—how you use the edges, negative space, etc. Being trained as a painter is why I am so rooted in those fundamentals."

He also says that mass and form are obviously expressed through his process. Spatial (and shape) relationships are critical; a viewer's perception of whole and partial forms—even edges—are enhanced through both gesture and details. "The gesture and motion that comes out in the sketches approximates what I try to capture in the final image. Working in 3-D can be very static. but I find that an active sketch helps me keep that movement in my final images. Again, this goes back to why drawing is so important."

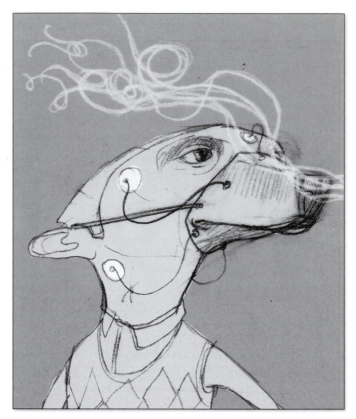

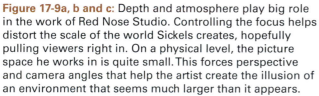

Figure 17-9a, b and c: Depth and atmosphere play big role in the work of Red Nose Studio. Controlling the focus helps distort the scale of the world Sickels creates, hopefully pulling viewers right in. On a physical level, the picture space he works in is quite small. This forces perspective and camera angles that help the artist create the illusion of an environment that seems much larger than it appears.

What about value? "This I try not to address in the sketch stage," says Sickels, "because the light does all the work with the 3-D forms. It's my job when I light a piece to light it like I was taught to paint."

Color is a tougher nut. And as such, Sickels keeps his palette simple and limited. "It's hard for me to control too many colors," he clarifies with some candor. "Also once a painted surface is photographed, it can take on other colors due to the type of lighting, gels, and surface texture. I always seem a degree or two removed from the color—which can be also be hard to deal with."

© Chris Sickels

Be Animated

We've said it before, but every artist has a specific visual vocabulary that distinguishes his work from another. Technique, style, and aptitude all combine to form *your* artistic identity. "It's at least partly indigenous to personality and inclinations," says Louie del Carmen. "My approach to line and space is completely capricious and open," he tells us. "In my personal work I tend to go by feel. I churn ideas and feelings with inherent and developed personal preferences. The result is hopefully something honest and natural. I keep working it out until I draw something I like." He adds, after a meaningful pause, "*I have to like it.* Before anyone else does."

For an animator (del Carmen's day job), action is necessary to communicate emotion. This can range from broad, gag-oriented (what might be labeled "cartoony") pacing, to fluid, yet minimal staging. Shapes and space are at the fundamental level in animation.

"The whole basic concept of animating characters and objects is determined by how shapes are inter-connected and constructed," del Carmen informs you. "While line work helps solidify and communicate the overall theme, good designs will use contrasting shapes," he says, "and always look dimensionally sturdy and well constructed."

Hand in Hand

Wrangling light—value in terms of light (or lack thereof)—is also important in communicating emotion. "I like visual drama and expressing mood by figuring in the dominant values," del Carmen says. "Often times an idea will come to me as a lighting or value concept: hot and cold colors. The dark tones of film noir. Cinematic vignettes. Comic book stylization. Silhouette; shading.

"Adding tone to clothing or skin brings clarity to a drawing. Appropriate lighting schemes (rim light, cast shadows, and so on) are a healthy way of extracting drama in each drawing. In the end, it's all about clarity and intention— how the use of value will help effectively communicate one's message."

del Carmen points out that line quality, value, and color all go hand in hand; one dictates how the other is executed. But color is core to the idea. "The burden is on me to use a palette that clearly conveys the message," he states. "You may not prefer my color sensibilities, but we can at least agree as to the context of those choices."

A perpetual student of color, del Carmen bases a lot of his color choices on gut feeling. That's pure savvy: good artists tend to have good instincts. "Most of the time, the choice of what color to apply is as important as the reason for applying it," he says, "so I do what feels right for me."

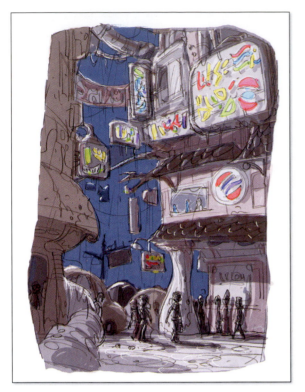

Figure 17-10 a, b, and c: del Carmen leaves you with this excellent advice: "Managing line, color, and value, as well as composition, is a subtle yet highly important process. It takes time to master. The keys are drawing mileage and experimentation, patience and perseverance, setting standards (especially in your work ethic and process). It's absolutely necessary to improve skills and fight complacency. Take classes, read books, attend lectures, research … and most of all, draw!

"Being an artist is a 24-hour proposition," he states with conviction. "Keep one's senses keen and current with the state of the art, as well as the state of life."

© Louie del Carmen

✔ Check Point: One Wild Hair

Jing Wei attended the Rhode Island School of Design and is currently living in Brooklyn. She supplies our hot list for this chapter:

1. Line is my *final* element to pull an image together (concept is the first, by the way). It's important that the line really activates the space and reinforces the mood of the piece. Yes, color can stimulate, but the foundation of a successful illustration is the drawing.

2. Since I work with flat colors, I can really use line to describe form through variations in line weight.

3. Color is the opportunity to bring a drawing to life. Color can ground an image and make it believable to the viewer. You begin by creating a color palette that is familiar and recognizable, then subtly introduce one or two unexpected colors to spin a unique twist. Value can be troublesome.

Ironically, my process is structured by value. I print from the lightest value to the darkest.

4. Value is what makes a piece readable (and that begins in the sketch phase). I have to know exactly where to place my lightest lights and darkest darks. I try to establish a hierarchy of value before I establish a hierarchy of color.

5. Lack of value contrast is a reflection of indecision. Don't be timid when it comes to organizing an image. If value relationships are unclear (at the planning stage), it very likely will remain that way right to the final.

6. An illustration without a concept is like a tool that does not function. Never lose sight of what you are trying to communicate. Find your prompt—maybe a line or two in the text that you can really grab onto—and then make your kind of image.

Wei lets you know that the details matter. She advocates using reference and advises you to truly engage in what you are drawing. "It is no fun drawing something you are not interested in," she asserts.
© Jing Wei

© Jing Wei

7. Brilliant concepts are often the most simple. Complexity can follow in the execution—and concepts can exist through formal elements (such as color, composition, and texture).

8. Compositionally, it's often easier to know what to avoid rather than what to add. You can quickly spot an awkward or distracting compositional element. The best compositions make it easy to enter the image. The viewer immediately understands what is going on. But in order to keep the viewer's interest, there needs to be a visual reward, some substance. Keep the composition very simple and direct, so the concept comes across without any confusion.

9. I use a method called reductive woodcut, where the illustration is cut entirely out of one block. You must consider how colors will interact (and look) when printed on top of one another.

10. Color intensity can help pop out certain parts of an image. Often, a highly saturated color put next to a homogenized area of color will draw the eye to that specific part of the image. If there is no color range, the viewer will not know where to look.

It's About Time

"Line changes constantly but never ends," Aliza Lelah will tell you. "In my drawing I use line to create the movement of time. Time literally crosses from one figure to the next, transforming and growing. I draw with thread. I sew by hand in a way that moves cautiously. I use the sewing machine in a way that moves freely and passionately. Together my stitches tell a story, not just of the people they portray, but of all of us.

"Line is the driving force of art-making," Lelah states. "It unleashes the dancing and the laughter and the tears. For me, line expresses an unwavering confidence. My hand stitches are timid, but when I let the machine guide me I become swept up in the marks and freedom of authority."

Just Breathe

"Color brings me out of my black and white world," Lelah smiles, "the magic really happens here." Indeed, Lelah often works with black and white photographs, drawing and creating, weaving color into the grayscale, all the while coaxing concepts to new levels. She says this literally gives her figures the breath of fresh life.

"And in addition, it gives purpose; value is extremely important in the 'painting' of my work. The bits of fabric come from such different sources," she remarks, "so it's not like I can just mix a little white to get a highlight! Value allows for my figures to exist in their world. It is the most important building block for me because it lays the foundation and gives a common balance between the figures and space."

And concept? "Without concept there can be no art," she asserts. "Concept is the key element of the creative process, but I don't think concept has to bear the weight of a work in the way we often think."

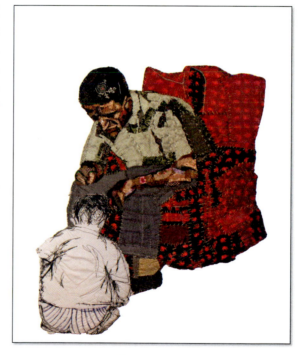

Figure 17-11 a, b, and c: Lelah says that drawing is about telling a story and expressing ideas. It's a way of communicating that everyone can understand, regardless of language or semantics. For this artist, drawing crosses boundaries; it transcends time and space.
© Aliza Lelah

CHAPTER SUMMARY

This chapter expands the scope and idea behind the labels "abstract" and "non-representational" art. We considered three-dimensional work as well. And we looked at some classical 2-D stuff that could work in other chapters.

All the artists met in this chapter begin with drawing, and then spin it off—literally and conceptually, some rather broadly. We talked about how drawing practice is at the root of process and how the act of drawing extends the reach of concept (both 2-D and 3-D).

Working It Out

1. Non-Objectivity

What *is* your definition of the words "abstract," "non-representational," "non-objective"? Come to class prepared engage in a lively discussion (and maybe debate) about this complex topic.

2. Abstracted

After our dialogue, and over the course of the next four class days, we will be doing four abstract drawings (or paintings). These are to be four versions of the same composition, and you have four initial parameters:

     a. Grayscale (black and white with grays)

     b. Monochromatic

     c. Full-color

     d. Black and white (no grays)

3. Redux

Same as above with the same four initial parameters; however: four *different* compositions.

Home and Away

1-3. Another Dimension

One project each:

     1. Fabrics (needlepoint and appliqué)

     2. Classical sculpture materials (wood, clay, metals, plastics and resins, wire, found or junk objects)

     3. Printmaking: wood or linoleum cut, silkscreen, intaglio, lithography. Lino and woodcuts can easily be accomplished at home without much bother or expense. Silkscreen too for that matter (with perhaps a bit more fuss and muss). Intaglio and litho will be best accomplished as part of an actual printmaking course in an adequately equipped and ventilated studio.

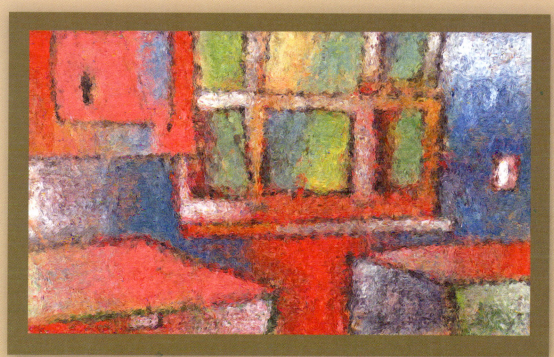

© Michael Fleishman

The Creativity Killer

What does it mean to be a "digital illustrator"? It's not much of an argument to qualify the computer—and the art generated at (and by) this creative tool—as our era's breakthrough innovation. You may agree or disagree with this assertion. And you might just believe that only skills make the real difference. And here you would be right—it's not the tool that makes the art, it's the artist.

But whether you shun new gizmos or embrace technology as the end-all/be-all, in today's creative environment, you simply can't reject the computer out of hand. As illustrator Elwood Smith remarked to me, "Technology doesn't kill creativity, a closed mind does."

Modern illustrators, whether traditional or digital, tackle an ever-growing laundry list of creative, technical (and tactical) challenges. "Today's artists," illustrator David Julian will tell you, "succeed by being original, brilliant, and memorable—as well as savvy and resourceful."

In this chapter we'll discuss the relevance of digital illustration, and examine the connections of the digital illustration process to traditional practice. We'll compare and contrast traditional and digital illustration and do a general overview of digital image-making, hardware, and software.

Has a Ring to It

I hear a common complaint amongst illustration teachers. In this digital age, many students shun traditional ideas, techniques, or skills. Commonly, color theory and figure classes are looked at with apathy or downright contempt. The mindset is: "Why learn this ancient twaddle—I can do it all on my Mac."

Well, cartoon swearing aside, misinformed line weight still compromises perspective (even though you can infinitely tweak that vector stroke in Adobe Illustrator). Photoshop won't save you: the millions of colors at your disposal will always add up to ugly if you don't understand color relationships. Hey, pal—any solid high school junior will be able to draw rings around you if your last real figure studies were in the 10th grade.

It's a Poor Workman …

It bears repeating: it's not really about the hardware, folks, it's the guy working the device—and his understanding of how to work it. As Craig Sellars (Figure 18-1) says, "The fundamental understanding of composition, line, shape, value and color are absolutely essential in the creation of appealing and affecting visual imagery."

"Each element here is integral to the success of the others and ultimately the success of the image being created. Fundamentals teach us as artists to learn to see, design, edit, and solve problems," Sellars tells it. "Without a solid grasp of the fundamentals, no software, plug-in, or filter can help.

"While I believe that the greatest artist needs only a pencil to express a beautiful idea or create a compelling image, if these fundamentals are understood and used to great effect, the artist is limited only by their imagination."

By Choice

"I choose to work digitally," says Giovanni Da Re. "I am quite happy on the computer, but at the same time, I experience a sort of detachment. I truly miss the real pleasure that a stroke of a brush offers, the unique marks made by traditional media.

Figure 18-1: Sellars says that line is the structural building block of an image, and value largely fosters interest, focus and, yes, the *story* of that image. So he'll use carefully constructed value relationships to create mood and drama.

Subtle value describes form and adds depth by defining the play of light across a surface, but it's overall value relationships that truly move the eye. "The eye is drawn to contrast, and value can be used to design those areas of contrast (both high and low). This enhances the narrative of an image."

In this digital piece, done in Photoshop, the woman is in the area of highest contrast and therefore the viewer's eye is drawn to her first. The distinctive robot is mostly in a spot of lower contrast—not the greatest draw to the eye. The woman thus becomes the primary focal point. The robot is discovered only after the viewer examines the image further. "The robot lurks in the shadows and this creates a sense of foreboding and mystery," Sellars says. "This is an example of value composition adding to narrative."

© Craig Sellars

"I've always tried to get the computer to simulate traditional tools— which, in my opinion, avoids that 'plastic' look of digital creations, and is a good way to up the emotional impact of digital media."

"And I'm just about completely digital," considers the artist from his studio in Castelbellino, Italy. Da Re does his roughs digitally as well. "When I started out, I used to sketch with pencils on paper," he tells you. "I was wasting a lot of time scanning detailed drafts into my computer. I realized I could streamline my entire process by eliminating this phase.

"Sketching in a digital environment fits my finished layout better (and gives me freedom to build and rebuild the composition)."

Feel It

"I had to practice," Da Re continues. "A graphics tablet has a different feel from pen on paper. I first fill my digital canvas with a 'guide' color and then start working out a draft as a 72 dpi JPEG sketch that I send as email.

"Art directors want your sketches (and the finish, of course) as soon as possible. As the ability to make quick adjustments is vital, working on the computer, then delivering via email and the Internet, helps to speed up the entire process."

Figure 18-2a and b: Da Re is just about 100% digital. He works hard to get his computer to simulate traditional tools (even sketching digitally) as well as delivering the final via the Internet or email.

90 Percent of this Game Is Mental, and the Other Half Is Physical

Pixel or not, here I come. First we should say that you can still work as a "traditional illustrator," pure and simple. Some assert that traditional techniques are actually the new wave. As Yogi Berra remarked, "It's Deja Vu, all over again."

Figure 18-3: You choose the right tool for the job. In terms of the final product, regardless of format, you must get exactly the same end result: a great illustration. And as Loughran points out: "It actually all happens in your head, anyway."

© PJ Loughran

And with all the timeless tools of the trade, illustrators often combine digital and traditional techniques. This syncopation may begin with a scan: comp drawings or roughs (in just about any media), generic line work or brush strokes, real-world patterns and textures, actual fabric or 3-D elements. Indeed, scratchboard and collage artists, printmakers and photo-illustrators: all go digital to their distinct advantage.

PJ Loughran began his career doing illustrations for the Op-Ed pages of the *New York Times* while attending Parsons School of Design. He says that for this present generation of students and professionals, it just may be that the computer has always been *the* creative tool. But he's quick to note that "new technology doesn't mean a change in the creative process. It provides a different method by which you make the delivery—a faster means of getting there; more convenient, more controllable."

Tickle Me

So is the computer really just another tool in the art box? And will paper and print disappear (as has been wildly and widely threatened for years)? I hope not.

There's a small tickle you get from scratching a sharp nib on crisp paper. I've been known to wax poetically on the primal intimacy of holding—and studying—your illustration in both hands (and let's not forget to mention the rush of seeing that finished piece in print).

We Can Work It Out

"I'm still completely smitten with digital illustration," Randy Wollenmann says. "But it is too easy to just switch on the computer and start drawing away without the eraser mess, or charcoal dust all around. But as time goes on, you feel more disconnected with the true process of drawing," he cautions. "And there is a difference in the final product—subtle, but different."

And while he has by no means forsaken his digital tools, Wollenmann notes, "I've been moving toward doing more 'real life' drawing now. I've just re-established a full working studio in the house after 5 years without. Getting back in touch with that whole tactile experience is wonderful, and I had no idea how much I've missed it."

Nail, Bounce, Noodle

"I originally began using acrylics because they dried so fast, and I figured this would really speed up my process. It did ... but it wasn't always fast enough," Justin DeGarmo tells us. "So I adopted digital media for some of my commercial work. Working in layers, erasing, undoing, color adjusting ... it's so convenient. But even that is based on the look of my traditional paintings, and the process over-all is pretty similar."

Here, Matt Hammill chimes in, "When I've nailed what I want to draw, I'll usually whip up a black-and-white comp in Photoshop on my tablet, maybe with a bit of shading. The computer lets me change the scale of things, rotate or move characters around and stuff like that.

"I've been bouncing between different media lately," Hammill says, "but often, most of the piece will be done traditionally. The computer will be used to add color, tweak areas, or fix mistakes."

To which Dice Tsutsumi adds, "And these days, with digital media, we may make unlimited mistakes without any cost. We can fall into a trap where we don't even think at all when painting and we end up 'noodling' too much."

"However, I'm a strong believer that the more mistakes you make, the more you learn," Tsutsumi states. "Of course, you try your best to 'get it right' and it's okay if the result turns out flawed."

"There's a parallel here with winning a game," he says. "Winning isn't everything, but the player should still play his best and try to succeed."

Figure 18-4: "I'm doing the River Dance between cyber and real-," Wollenmann laughs, "constantly shooting back and forth. I have the computer studio set up on one side of the house and the traditional studio set up on the opposite...adds to my physical workout as well!"
© Cokesbury

Figures 18-5, 18-6, and 18-7: Working digitally can speed up your process in general (even when that process is similar to, or the result actually parallels, an analog product). Part of this whole scenario is making mistakes. Flaws come with the digital territory, too, although recovery—and recovery time—is not as painful as in the "old days" before the computer.
© Justin DeGarmo

Figure 18-6
© Matt Hammill

Figure 18-7
© Dice Tsutsumi

Apples and Oranges

I can't assume what you know, reader, so forgive me if we do a little Digital Illustration 101 here.

Digital illustrators work in pixels (a.k.a. bitmapped or raster images) and/or vectors (also called object or shape-oriented imagery). The "bits" of a bitmap image are arranged on a grid. These pixels (picture elements) are squared dots of color or tone that convey the information about the picture seen on your monitor.

Programs like Adobe Illustrator and Photoshop are continually evolving in some similar directions, but we can ballpark the difference between vector and raster images by considering the imagery itself.

Bitmapped images generically offer the opportunity of photographic realism, a smooth blend of tone (often continuous tone) and the subtle (or painterly) variation of color and texture. Smooth, solid (but not necessarily flat color) vector graphics are resolution-independent and mathematical in origin (but not pixel-based). Lines, curves, and geometric shapes can be manipulated and scaled without a loss of quality. A stamp-sized vector object (or entire illustration) bumped up to gargantuan proportions remains crisp and clean on your monitor and the page (even at billboard specs).

Floormats? No—Formats

Currently, the most common file formats include:

- AI (.ai—Adobe Illustrator document)
- BMP (.bmp—the basic DOS or Windows bitmapped file format)
- GIF (.gif.—Graphics Interchange Format. I've heard both the interchangeable hard or soft g. A basic format for images on the Web)
- EPS (.eps—Encapsulated Postscript. Handles both vectors and bitmaps)
- JPEG (.jpg—Joint Photographic Experts Group. High-quality and compression range)
- PDF (.pdf—Portable Document File. This file will look exactly the same on any computer, any system)
- PICT (.pct—the stock Mac designation)
- PSD (.psd—Adobe Photoshop image format)
- TIFF (.tif—Tagged Image File Format. Bitmap files that can contain black and white, grayscale, color and photography. Great format for scanning images. High fidelity can mean huge files, though)

Color Models: What's the Diff?

"Well," says Mike Maihack, "besides the Web using light-based RGB (Red, Green, Blue) color channels and print using ink-based CMYK (Cyan, Magenta, Yellow, Black), the only other real difference you might consider is how art generally looks darker on the printed page (paper stock has a lot to do with this, too).

autumn

spring

summer

winter

Figure 18-8a, b, c and d: Our colorful model for this evening's program: the great work of Mr. Maihack.
© Mike Maihack

"So when I get ready to make an illustration ready for print," Maihack tells you, "I almost always bump its saturation levels anywhere from 10 to 20 percent. I guess this is yet another advantage to working digitally…or maybe it's a disadvantage, since you never will have a perfect print representation of your art on your computer screen, either!"

We Now Continue Our Standard Programming

Adobe Photoshop and Illustrator have set the standard and continue to mature with each upgrade—real workhorses that keep improving with every version. But there are other fine programs to consider. The following apps are also feature-laden, and each is powerful, sophisticated, and effective in

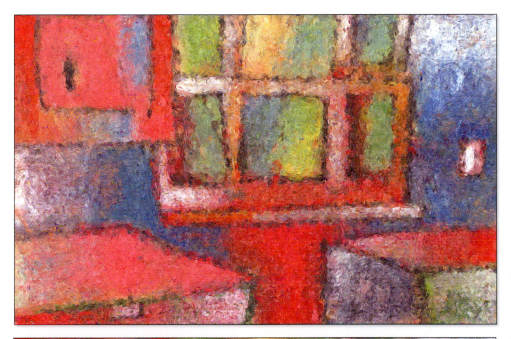

Figure 18-9a and b: Digital paint sketches done on a Wacom Intuos tablet (with a stylus, of course). I worked in Synthetik Studio Artist 3.0 and exported the files to Photoshop, where I did some color correction and lighting tweaks. By the way, no filters were harmed in making these pictures. These studies tap into Studio Artist's standard patches (a.k.a., brushes) off the program's default Paint Synthesizer preset. Here, powerful software combines with the responsive, pressure-sensitive hardware to produce some lovely painterly effects.

A note: the strokes are perhaps *too* digital in spots—to my eye it looks a smidge artificial here and there—but overall, the tandem drawings (of a corner in the garage) were grand fun to play with, and brought out the junior Monet in me.

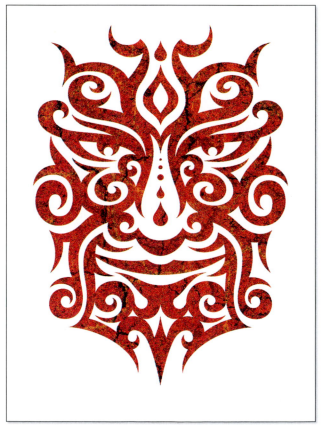

Figure 18-10a and b: Vonster spoken here.
© Von Glitschka

its own right. See if the following titles offer you an ideal production environment and experience: Corel Painter (and its baby brothers, Painter Essentials and Painter Sketch Pad); Corel Paintshop Pro; Corel Draw; Synthetik Studio Artist 3.0; Art Rage; Autodesk SketchBook Pro.

Decisions Decisions

You may have to make a professional (or personal) choice—PC or Mac? I am without a doubt, biased—I have used and owned Macintosh computers since 1986. And most art professionals I know or talk to prefer the Mac (a limited focus group, no doubt, but the majority of my world). But of course, a patriotic PC user will dispute and debate any Mac advantage. The argument over which system is better or "best" is ongoing.

Our industry is largely geared towards the Macintosh, and I don't think that's going to change. But over time, lines will continue to blur. The Mac and the PC will move closer. Great software will be available for both; new, powerful systems will always be just around the corner. As sleek product development pushes ease-of-use, sophisticated interfaces, and slick graphics, the hardware will evolve constantly and consistently.

It's a win-win. I love the Mac, but you may not. It's a big world; there's room for both platforms.

Making Degrade

Von Glitschka has been in the communication arts industry for 22 years. He now refers to himself as an "Illustrative Designer." His work reflects the symbiotic relationship between design and illustration. In an age of digital illustration where computerized perfection is easily attained, Glitschka adds an organic flair to his illustration via textures. "I take my vectors into Photoshop and then use varied textures controlled by layer blend effects to subtly—and not so subtly—degrade my art as I see fit," he says.

The Vonster, as Glitschka is known, does delightfully patterned art that is also very shape-driven. One of his primary inspirations (and a timely, terrific reference here) is the wonderful art of the late Jim Flora, whom I also recommend with gusto.

"I have pseudo 3-D looking elements," Glitschka comments, "but nothing that is true 3-D. As I create my artwork, I normally think in terms of shapes and how negative and positive areas balance and affect one another."

✔ Check Point: Have Some Backbone

Charlene Chua provides our hot list for this chapter. Chua (pronounced "choo-wah") grew up in Singapore, started her working life in 1998 as a Web designer, and eventually pursued illustration as a career in 2003 (going full time in 2006). In 2007 Chua moved to Toronto, Canada, and now spends her time illustrating and working on comics. She specializes in digital and vector illustration.

1. Line forms the backbone of every image I create. I've been more comfortable with a pencil than a brush throughout my life; I tend to think in terms of line rather than color. Whether drawing from memory or looking at a reference, I always "see" the lines first. Straight lines, curves, dots, dashes . . . I look for the various marks that have the right amount of intricacy.

2. Color—values, palette, lighting—all serve one purpose: to enforce the mood of a piece. What is this piece about? I'm more literal than conceptual, and I try to build little stories around the drawing itself.

3. My approach to color is very simple, it helps me focus on certain elements within the picture. I tend to think of color in broad and general terms: "happy" seems yellow; "sad" is blue. "Trouble" appears a dull gray; maybe purples here.

4. To be terribly honest, I sometimes wish we weren't quite so responsive to color. I enjoy messing with the colors and seeing what works out. Quite often I end up using a set of colors that doesn't match what I originally had in mind.

5. All art should be about communication. What's the point otherwise? What's the point of the "artist"? Perhaps any debate comes down to the definition of communication. For communication to "work," the message transmitted must match the message received. But the arts don't require such a linear interaction. Be it dance, music, or the visual arts, the objective is to communicate an idea that the viewer or listener will eventually draw their own conclusions on.

6. It can be argued that commercial artists are obliged to "make sense." Okay, that's fair . . . sometimes a very specific idea must be transmitted clearly through the image itself. Think of medical and technical illustration here.

7. But illustration doesn't have to be visual summary—need not be so literal. If anything, we lament illustration that communicates (and interprets) a little too literally.

8. Illustrators who focus on concept have to take charge of the message to be communicated. Not everyone can—or ought to—be a conceptual thinker. You need an illustrator with a creative yet flexible approach.

9. I worry about those novice illustrators with little classical education, particularly when it comes to digital, vector-style art. There is a very apparent glut of folks with absolutely no training in basic draftsmanship. They claim to be competent artists because they use software to trace out a photograph.

10. I'm self-taught. One's career should not be penalized for any lack of formal training. But a good grasp of the basics allows you to grow as your career develops. The concept of "fundamentals" is rather open-ended in this day and age, but I advise you to get a handle on the foundations of illustration.

© Charlene Chua

© Charlene Chua

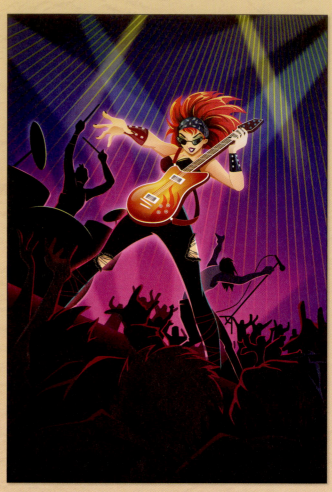

© Charlene Chua

For Chua, "The line is what makes or breaks my image." And for her, the sketch stage is the hardest part of any project. She typically works in Adobe Illustrator, a program she says is "pretty much an upgraded form of line work anyway, since I am virtually redrawing my elements."

Photo(shop) Finish

While most of Jesse Kuhn's work begins by traditional means (pencil, pen, & ink on paper), it is always finished digitally. "I learned all the traditional methods in school and through my own experimentation," he tells you. "One thing that drove me away from some of the more material-heavy techniques is that it required too much stuff around to do the deed. And once it was done, I had to figure out where to put it. I have many paintings, scratchboards, and prints that all hang in my parents' living room (or are in storage now)."

Your Choice

All this to say that the execution of an illustration should be what feels the most natural to you, the creator of the work. Certainly, the very idea of all that intensive "stuff" Kuhn worked around may ardently quicken the pulse of another illustrator in his same zip code. Yours too, maybe.

Kuhn's style and technique was formulated years back, at the inception of his first illustration gig. Time was of the essence, preplanning a necessity. He chose the computer for easy color correction and efficient press-ready production.

"Digital illustration allows me to work anywhere in the world that boasts electricity and an Internet connection," Kuhn tells you. "The idea of being a 'nomad illustrator' has always excited me. And I've always maintained that your environment impacts your work greatly too. I think it would be really cool to take a year or two in an RV and travel the country in my mobile studio, illustrating one week on top of a mountain and then the following week next to the ocean."

Kuhn views his process as the best of both worlds. "I'm able to satisfy my appetite for working with the organic—and sometimes unpredictable—line forms that result from my shaky hand plus the pen and ink; all the while fitting my entire office in a laptop bag that gives me the freedom of mobility and the ability to change my environment whenever I see fit."

Figure 18-11: "Through my personal experience (and conversations with other illustrators), I see turnaround times continuing to get tighter," Kuhn laments. "Unfortunately, that applies to the pay too."

"I keep a minimal amount of materials on hand for the initial pen and ink drawing. I'll do color digitally, and then FTP printer-ready art: all in a fraction of the time it would take to do a traditional painting that then has to be hustled to a photographer, shot and digitized, and now forwarded onto the client."

"And about that traditional painting...if that client then realizes they now hate the color of a character's shirt, and wants it changed? Hey, no thanks."

© Jesse Kuhn

CHAPTER SUMMARY

In this chapter we discussed the relevance of digital illustration, and examined the connections of digital illustration process to traditional practice. We compared and contrasted traditional and digital illustration (and what it means to be a "digital illustrator") and did a general overview of digital image-making, hardware, and software.

Working It Out

1. Tah-*may*-toes; tah-*mah*-toes

Loughran says, "New technology doesn't mean a change in the creative process. It provides a different method by which you make the delivery." Do an "analog" illustration, "by hand," with traditional materials via a classical process. Now do that same illustration digitally. Compare/contrast process and product.

2. A Riot of Variety

Whether it's analog or digital, you choose the right tool for the job. Do an illustration in Photoshop. Do that same illustration in Illustrator. Do it again, this time in a third application. Compare and contrast all three: How does concept, process, style, and technique (and ultimately the final product) differ from application to application?

3. Morph

Most of Kuhn's work begins traditionally and is finished digitally. That's the job here: begin the assignment by hand, with traditional materials via a classical process. You'll have to decide the juncture, but finish (and print) the illustration digitally.

Home and Away

1. Pah-*tay*-toes; pah-*tah*-toes

If you're a Photoshop kind of guy, only use Illustrator for one month. If Illustrator is your thing, it's Photoshop for 30 days (with no parole)!

2. Lite Me Up

To compare and contrast workflow and process between big and little sisters, use only the *light* versions of various applications: Photoshop Elements,

Painter Essentials. Do this for a month; at the end of the month have a small exhibition and do a workshop/lecture about the experience (call it something like "Out of My Elements" or "Getting To Know Hue" that plays up the duck out of water concept).

3. Talk to Me

What does it mean to be a "digital illustrator"? What does it mean to be a "traditional illustrator"? Give a series of lectures and workshops (at libraries, Senior Citizen Centers, elementary and secondary schools, etc.) about your work in particular and the field in general. This is not only great practice in portfolio presentation and preparation, but also a fun way to pay it forward and accomplish some community service.

Chapter 19

It's Just Business

© Esther Pearl Watson

Business Class

Many illustrators I talk to complain that if there is one thing they never learned at school, it was, well, the *business* end of the business. "What I would have given to be able to know so much of what I learned the hard way," says Rick Tulka, now based in Paris. "For example, how to bill, contracts, payment, copyrights, etc. That was all learned as I did it. Actually, every art student should have a business class."

Business Before Pleasure?

As you wander your career path, keep in mind that there is a difference between being a commercial *artist* and being a *commercial* artist. Illustrator Brian Zick hails from Los Angeles. "The job of 'commercial art' and producing works of creativity are not mutually exclusive," he says, "but they are separate things."

To sort it out, identify the distinctions. Know yourself. Be at the top of your game (which means understand the craft *and* the business).

A No Grunt Zone

For a young illustrator right out of school, the challenge may be motivation: continuing to market and promote in the face of little (or no) work; maintaining a steady focus to stay on task; fending off distraction (all the while, multi-tasking with grace, efficiency, and speed). And of course, not feeling too overwhelmed by rejection—now, there's a good one.

Even seasoned artists deal with these demons. I don't think it is naïve to hope that you are personally motivated to stay in business

Figure 19-1: Tulka is a veteran illustrator who shows *a lot* of business class.
© Rick Tulka

Figure 19-2: Zick feels that our English language may need more words for the term "art." "There are all different kinds of art," he qualifies, "many genres, schools (and styles), and all have intrinsic *value.*"
© Brian Zick

Figure 19-3a and b: Kuhn, relatively new to the world of business, labels his business practices as "still in trial mode." But he actually accepts the challenges (and his mistakes), doesn't shy away from the paperwork, and welcomes the change of hats in his work day.

© Jesse Kuhn

because you love *creating*. Your zest for your work should be the bedrock of your business. Lose that passion and this could all be pure grunt work (as Michael Cho elaborates on later in this chapter).

Take It Out for a Spin

Jesse Kuhn recently went out on his own to work full time at his design/illustration studio, so he labels his business practices as "still in trial mode. I personally like being a part of the business side of things," he tells you. "It shakes up the work week and allows me to do something during those creative blocks or moments when I'm not so inspired.

"This is when I typically do invoicing, estimating, research, self promo, etc. I don't particularly care for doing taxes, but a necessary understanding of this is *essential*. Also key: making sure you properly keep track of earnings/expenses and paying estimated taxes in a timely manner—I learned the hard way on this one."

Commerce and Art

Art (with a capital "A") is the labor of "pure" creativity. And we should point out that certain fruits of this labor—the rewards of fame and fortune, perhaps—are not guaranteed in the creator's lifetime (statistically speaking). "On the other hand, 'Commercial' Art," Zick states, "can be quite handsomely rewarding, if artistic gratification may be measured by the size of the checks deposited into an author's bank account."

How true. A paycheck is a wonderful source of inspiration! And by definition, "professionals" enjoy such motivation all the time. Work produced and sold—whether it's for advertising or a gallery—may correctly be described as *commercial art*.

Historically, there are very few "pure" or purely self-indulgent artists. Art History is all about marketing, isn't it? Michelangelo's Sistine Chapel was a hired gig. Van Gogh had a rep (his brother), and a lamentably lousy sales/exhibition record that contributed to his depression. DaVinci, Rembrandt, Lautrec, Warhol—hey, they were all commercially viable artists.

"Successful artistes—in any venue—become masters of their particular style," Zick says. "Style (and success) results from the combination of distinctive vision, a dedicated passion to explore, plus working assiduously to excel in the craft."

Essentials

There may only be four things you—the student of life, art, and business—need to know:

1. Understand that you must be a craftsman. This is not a bad thing. Practice. Practice. Practice. *That* is not a bad thing, either.

2. Be self-aware. Understand your weaknesses *and* know your strengths. Appreciate your limitations. This does *not* mean you go around broadcasting your failings (nor does it mean obnoxious displays of ego).

3. It's okay to be honest, even forthright, that you make a living doing your art. Customers are paying you to—hopefully—deliver (hopefully) valued technical skills. They are hiring you for your given talents. So when you provide a creative service, your client expects to get a particular product when/as agreed.

4. Show off what you truly love to do—and what you really can do. "The passion of a creative endeavor is reflected in the quality of the work," Zick comments. "Potential for any employment is always tempting. But the only way to avoid doing the stuff you dislike (and art you'll be too embarrassed to show your mother) is: *don't do it!*"

Figure 19-4: Zick's work underscores our hypothesis above.
© Brian Zick

Grind

The general artistic approach Michael Cho learned at Ontario College of Art and Design was really helpful; it gave Cho a grand overview of the fundamentals. "I appreciated the notion of a 'bulletproof' concept,"

KEEP ON WORKING.

KEEP ON WORKING.

Figure 19-5: If it's "just a job," the daily grind will take its toll and certainly dissatisfy you. And soon, that will show up in the work. Ultimately, this cheats you (and your clients) out of a job well done.
© Michael Cho

he says, "and that you understood why you draw what you draw."

Coming out of OCAD, Cho remembers one instructor's good advice. "He told us to have an absolutely unwarranted confidence in your own abilities for the first five years after graduation, otherwise you won't make it."

Cho worked a variety of day jobs after graduation, which left him little energy to paint in the evenings. However, he wanted art to be his main focus, and the self-labeled "somewhat illustrative" artist ultimately discovered the field of illustration. Then Cho quickly realized he needed an attitude adjustment about "illustration" as a "career." "There's personal work and there's client work—very different animals," Cho says realistically. "Regardless of my mindset, I saw if I treated illustration as just a job, I would never be very good at it."

"If I was going to be an illustrator, I should be the very best illustrator I could be. Otherwise I would just be cheating myself; it would be merely another dissatisfying day job—a grind."

How Can I Help You?

It's called "commercial art" for a reason—the bottom line being that you have to ultimately satisfy clients who pay the bills. But that's not really a negative. As a paid professional you are in a service field, with the freedom and right to pick and choose your gigs. The power of that little word "no" is very enabling.

So how 'bout that you are actually in the business of *potential* and *opportunity*? Consider the potential of fulfilling (and valued) work as well as artistic challenge, career achievements; the opportunity to "do good/make good"—and, yes, the perks of financial reward and/or recognition: maybe even some fame and glory.

Bottom Lines

But notice I place those last side benefits at the bottom of the list. It's healthier—mentally, emotionally, physically—to welcome such outcomes as gratifying byproducts of your art—not the other way around. Certainly, it is advisable not to summarily equate "success" with fame or glory, reward and recognition. That "do good/"make good" thing (i.e., a superior product, great inspiration, positive change, a real difference) is the better qualifier.

A Well-Oiled Apparatus

This is a business of people, potential, and opportunity. Valued (and valuable) work and artistic challenge are not mutually exclusive; same with career achievements and the chance to "do good". Financial rewards (and recognition) are possible, but should not be the priorities. It's healthier in all respects to accept these potentials as byproducts of your art and craft, and not vice versa.

Your freedoms come with some risk—and plenty of external factors to deal with—but there are real rewards as a result. Location, schedule and calendar, challenges, the speed, style (and philosophy), plus growth of your business are up to you ultimately. Remember that word, "no"? The phrase, "That's it … I'm done" (for good, for now) is always right at the tip of your tongue.

Balance is important—a personal life and family obligations are key. Discipline and fun are necessary sisters to know and respect. Hard work will be a given but play hooky when you must. Smarts are nice. Savvy is good. Study and learn for a lifetime. Be ready. Be game. Be prepared. Go for it.

Figure 19-6: The art of being in business can be a satisfying and stimulating counterpart to the business of illustration.
© Michael Fleishman

And We're Off

Set goals—surviving that first year will probably at the top of the list—and declare your independence. You're going to make or break it on your own conditions and values. So it's okay to fail. And it's fine to succeed (and both for that same reason: don't be ashamed of either outcome, if it's on your terms).

There will be sacrifice: time, energy, funds. Break a few eggs and enjoy the omelet. There must be an equilibrium of earnest desire and perfectly good sense. Skills and talent are a given, but pure talent doesn't necessarily equate to business success. Discipline, structure, and planning, as well as a budget, are important.

Know what's happening (for all aspects of your operation) at any time; definitely keep close tabs on your costs: this may be the most important part of operating a business—and hey, you *are* the business. Think and act just that way—in other words, taking care of business is taking good care of yourself.

Basics

Where will you work? Home studio or outside office? Wherever the location, it must be an environment that promotes your creative side while fostering the business end.

Get in touch with your inner accountant. Come out of the closet as a bookkeeper. Document everything: correspondence, proposals, estimates, contracts, invoices. Indicate the relevant dates and times. Know the right names (and spelling). Get signatures *before* doing a lick of work and definitely before sending the job.

Be articulate—clarity and communication are important. Be eloquent, but plain speaking is underrated. Illustrator Bill Mayer says it well: "Give them a good firm handshake, look them in the eyes, and just be yourself. Most of the time your work should sell itself. Answer any questions, but remember you're not a car salesman."

Have a Heart

Follow your instincts about your work. You can't please everybody, don't even try. Please yourself first. *Sell it; don't sell out.* You are marketing work that really shows you off—the work you love, the way *you* see things.

Self-promote with zeal. Market like clockwork. Network, network, network. Think like an entrepreneur, act entrepreneurial. Remember that whole "opportunity and potential" mindset I advocated above? Jump on opportunities. Create potential. It's not taking advantage *to offer help and solve a problem.* Look for a connection and plug into it.

Love your work. The finished product should shout that right out loud. But remember—you are more than your wrist. As Mary Thelen says, "Love your clients, too. Express your concern; demonstrate that you care. Show your respect. You'll get that all back in return. People like to give work to people they love and respect."

Figure 19-7: Your smart commerce generates bigger and better business. There should be a natural flow in both the business and practice of illustration (and *between* your practice and business, too). Why are you selling your work otherwise?

The multi-talented Mayer is a respected and seasoned pro. The busy illustrator understands the people skills, communication base, and work ethic needed to succeed.

© Bill Mayer

Figure 19-8: Love. Respect. Care. Concern. These can be business practices too.
© Mary Thelen

✔ Check Point: Bits of Business

Ostensibly random thoughts you may not think are about Business (with a capital B), but actually are:

1. Know yourself. Be aware of what you do; what you like to do; why you do it.

2. Be rather self-critical, be honestly objective about outside critique.

3. The debate about being a generalist or a specialist rages on. I hear lucid and sharp arguments from both sides, and there will be exceptions to both rules. What feels good, what makes sense to you?

4. Start small because it's reasonable. Stay small by choice. Pace yourself. Be in it for the light, not the heat (that's good advice for practically anything, actually).

5. Sure, we all know it's smart business to keep abreast of hot market trends, but know yourself first. Be aware of what you do; what you like to do; why you do it .

6. Buzzwords and catchphrases: It's about excellence (of course; you knew that). Quantity is not as important as quality. Pay attention to details. Consistency counts. Be unique; be original. This all applies to life, business, and your portfolio.

7. Three important business tips everybody should practice: Be real. Be nice. Be yourself.

8. There may be no small jobs (particularly to the client), only small illustrators (especially at the beginning of your career).

9. What is beneath you? A decided, but polite "no" takes only a half second of your time, a mere instant of your karma.

10. Express your gratitude. Show your appreciation. During lean times, down turns, or slow days, ask this question: "Why is this the best thing that's ever happened to me?"

So why is being in business the best thing that ever happened to you?

© Michael Fleishman

Figure 19-9: Here's a sample of Osiecki's product placement and development. The lively Max showcases her company's interest in character development as well as the illustrator's sparkling illustration style.

© Lori Osiecki

Get Happy

Lori Osiecki worked for Hallmark, but left after eight years to freelance. Eventually lamenting what she deemed a lack of opportunities plus unfortunate directions for creatives (a.k.a. stock art), Osiecki ultimately established her own company, Beati Productions (pronounced "bee-ahhtee," the word means "happy" in Latin).

"There were so many things I wanted to do visually," she says, and I wasn't getting those jobs. So I went into business for myself."

"You must have some business sense," Osiecki tells you, "and you'll have to wear all the hats. But it's a troubling time; we're all trying to figure out how to make a go of it in this field. How *do* you monetize it? I don't think there's a definitive, solid answer," she says with candor. "However, two things never go away, even in a recession," she points out, "people need entertainment, and stimulation. And that's where the artist comes in. That, and food—an art in itself, actually."

Makes Sense

"I would never show my digital work in a gallery setting," Mark Todd tells you. "I think if you're buying a piece of art, you want something that's actually *painted.* The subject matter is different, of course. But this is just me," he states.

"I have so many other things that I want to say in a gallery setting. It's more the subject matter, less of the style. A paid gig that is closer to my gallery work would be the ideal. Now saying that, I do love my illustration. I have fun with this work, it's not just a mere job. I try to make even the mundane assignments *interesting*—something you actually want to look at.

"There are pieces I could advertise that might get me more—even better paying— jobs; but I usually promote my personal work, the stuff that is uniquely *me*. Money is important of course," he reflects. "You have to make a living; it's just not the only priority." And here Todd smiles pragmatically. "Now, when that kind of work does come in," he says, "I definitely don't turn it down."

Eggs on the Path

"Students tend to gravitate to the gallery world as a potential career path," Todd states, "as if being a 'gallery artist' means 'let me do what I want.' That's a bit naive: 'I can make money from home and no one will tell me what to draw.' But this is a hard road to go down and not for everybody. It's a tough way to make a living."

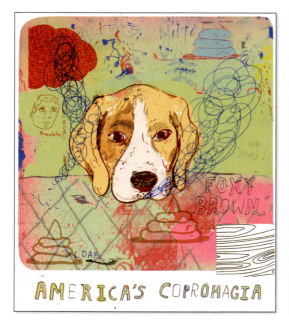

19-10a © Mark Todd

19-10b © Esther Pearl Watson

Figure 19-10a and b: In both concept and execution, the husband and wife team of Todd and Watson balance home and family with commerce and art.

Referring to his wife, Esther Pearl Watson, Todd says, "We jump around, we're definitely not putting all our eggs in one basket … I'm a hard worker, but Esther is me *times ten*. She will not stop, she doesn't take 'no' for an answer. Esther will give a thousand percent with no complaints. Two to three book ideas in her head *and* a gallery show in mind; some TV show bubbles up *plus* a film version of her book—Esther opens doors that I will walk away from. I'll maintain the attitude that we can't do everything, but Esther will say, 'Yes, Mark, *we can*, why not?'"

You Can Do It All

PJ Loughran graduated from Parsons with an Illustration degree, but as far back as high school, Loughran had a modest goal. "I just wanted to do *everything* that I wanted to do," he smiles. "I had a lot of different interests and I didn't want to give up any one of them for the others," he says. "I had a teacher who told me: 'You know, you're going to eventually have to choose *one* of these things and commit to it if you ever want to be successful at something.' I never really understood why that was."

Loughran is a consummate renaissance man so he switches gears at will. "There's a certain pleasure I get out of drawing that I don't get from anything else," he comments. "But there's a distinct satisfaction I get from writing and performing music that I don't get from drawing. There are professional and business skills you hone working with a team that are really fulfilling in ways far different from music or illustration. I like the constant range of challenges, the stimulation I get from all these different pursuits. I feel content—very satisfied—doing them all."

Figure 19-11: In addition to doing exciting illustration, Loughran is an accomplished songwriter, lyricist, and working musician with three albums to his credit and steady gigs. "Songs are like little stories," he explains, "and parallel the other disciplines I'm working in as well.

"At the core of it you are trying to tell a story and express a point of view. A song is a three- to five-minute story. While an illustration is a more immediate narrative; it all sort of carries over into one another."

© PJ Loughran

Fired Up

Loughran owns a small creative agency called Kerosene. "As a freelancer, once I started doing movie projects I thought, 'Wouldn't it be great if I had a firm where I could do illustration, music and any other related projects under one umbrella.'"

So he did his research and homework and literally studied up on how to make it happen. "Somebody's out there doing this," Loughran figured, "why not me, why can't I give it a shot? So I bought a book about creative businesses, and realized that I didn't need a business degree to do this. I got some ground rules from this book—and followed them—and they work."

"Running a business means there are a lot of little tasks you need to constantly stay on top of ... this multitasking was something I was very used to, " Loughran states. He feels that business is actually an intuitive kind of thing. It hinges on common sense and following very basic, rational rules, like people skills, reliability, and follow through: delivering on your promises (which should certainly be about handing over a quality product). Do the core values right, and you'll definitely increase the odds that your business will grow and nurture return clients.

It's also about marketing sense: sales; public relations; accounting and bookkeeping; overhead and profit margins. If you don't know about these things, you find help. "I'm new to this," Loughran points out, "but I simply follow my head and my gut." He's honest, too. "It can be difficult and frustrating at times, exceptionally challenging," he admits, "but I really enjoy it. I think part of the satisfaction is seeing it work and knowing that I was able to navigate all the challenges along the way to get it there. It's very fulfilling."

Figure 19-12: Illustration—like any discipline in which you sell a product—has a clear business component to it, and Loughran still does a lot of illustration assignments. "I don't feel obligated to just take anything that comes in," he says. "However, I guess sometimes I do, just because I want to keep drawing—I love drawing and solving problems; it's still so fundamental to everything I do."
© PJ Loughran

Solving the Problem

Out of Seattle, Washington, David Julian is an illustrator and photographic artist who also works in mixed-media assemblage. Julian feels we need to get back to the analog world of human solutions. He tells you that the competition is out there, that the pool is *huge*.

"Technology enables us to compete on a higher level; it's no longer about talent alone," he says. "I suggest you may have to sell more by selling *different*. However, the classical business model of hard work and perseverance is not dead: choose your jobs; direct a style at certain buyers; identify your target audience (not to mention clients and markets). Follow that formula to success."

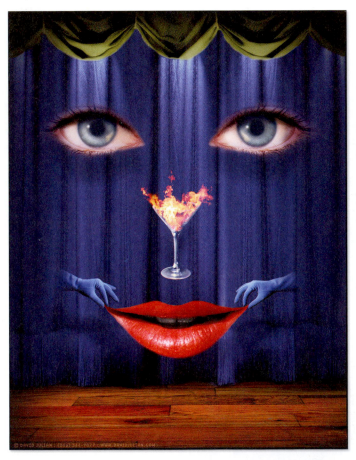 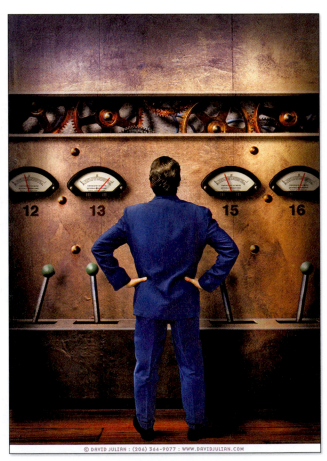

Figure 19-13a and b: Julian's fine skills translate multi-media in decidedly human terms. A master digital artist, he nonetheless feels that analog solutions provide the best answers to business problems or creative concerns.
© David Julian

CHAPTER SUMMARY

This chapter discussed the *business* end of the illustration business: the challenge of motivation, marketing, and promotion. We looked at the difference between a commercial *artist* and being a *commercial* artist; that it's okay to be honest (even forthright) that you are making your living doing art. We discussed that you must think of this as more than "just a job"; that you are in the business of people, potential, and opportunity. We examined the freedoms a freelance business offers, the risks, and the rewards (and the balance of same). We explored the idea that discipline and fun can co-exist, and that the art of being in business can be a satisfying and stimulating counterpart to the business of illustration.

Working It Out

1. What's the Deal?

An upcoming project has an added element: business paperwork. In addition to the illustration itself, you will also write up (and present at the appropriate juncture in the life of the assignment):

a.   An estimate based on job specs and parameters

b.   Confirmation of Agreement (and get it signed)

c.   Invoice upon delivery of final art

Before this happens, look for our in-class unit on writing this business package as well as handouts, document samples, and templates.

2. Identification

You will create a logo, business card, and letterhead (for stationery and envelope). These marketing and identity materials will be used in the business paperwork you'll be creating.

Before this happens, look for our in-class unit on designing logos and marketing materials for your business package (including handouts, document samples, and templates).

3. Financial Report

You will research and do a (written and oral) report—not with a famous artist or popular illustrator, but with an accountant or business/financial advisor! This report is not about the accountant, but should cover business, financial, and tax practice/advice for artists. Look for our in-class handout for further information.

Home and Away

1. Homework

We're going to read a few business books (please see reading list in syllabus). These books and scheduled readings will be assigned and discussed in class (see schedule).

2. Meet and Greet

Think of (or find) an artist you'd like to meet—someone whose work you admire and respect. Contact that person via an introductory email, mailed letter (you remember how to do those, right?), a phone call (prefaced by an email or letter), or even face to face, as the opportunity presents itself.

These days, comments at a blog or Web site, Twitter, Facebook, MySpace are some other ways to go about this, as well.

Now, Network! This isn't a job hunt; you're not looking for leads (or work) or references/recommendations—it's shop talk.

3. Challenge

Do you enjoy testing your limits? Let's find out. Pick a task or discipline that is out of your comfort zone and/or expertise: work up a screenplay, throw a pot, learn to play the tuba, write a song, write a play, make a quilt.

Challenge yourself. Like Loughran, you may find that there's a compelling stimulation you get from chasing different pursuits, and the cross reference of artistic side projects is often just what you need to maintain a creative edge with your main event.

Chapter 20

Words and Pictures

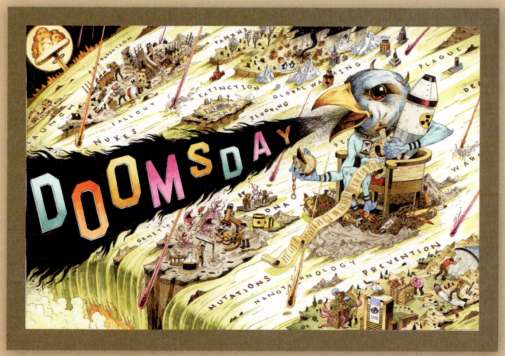

© John Hendrix

What Are You Looking At?

In a book about connections, it made sense to have a chapter that discussed the relationship between letterforms and visuals, calligraphy and art, typography and illustration. We'll take a look at how words and pictures combine to link people, techniques, tools, and concepts, and offer creative opportunities to advance the art of illustration.

20-1a © Ilene Winn-Lederer

Figure 20-1a and b: The work of Ilene Winn-Lederer and Peter Arkle. The combination of words with pictures offers rich creative opportunities to play style and concept off tools and techniques.

20-1b © Peter Arkle

The Relationship

"Illustration is a relationship between text and images," says John Hendrix. "In the classic sense, without text, we don't have illustration. So, said a different way, illustration is about communication."

But as Hendrix cautions, don't confuse expression—or organization, for that matter—with communication. "Compositions are not to speak to themselves, but to serve the content of the image. They must, in a word, communicate," he says. "And a drawing that functions clearly, functions efficiently. That is to say that all the visual elements inside it (value, shape, color) quickly aid the communication to the viewer. Remember that an illustrator *always* has something to say, be it about form or concept."

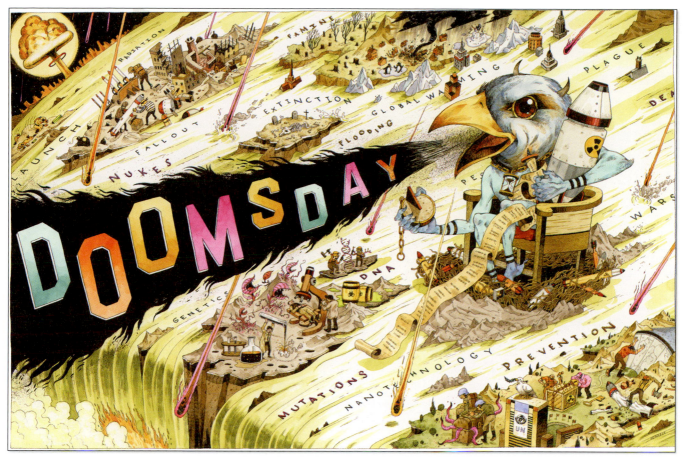

Figure 20-2: Linear elements are some of the most important nuances of how Hendrix communicates the relationship between text and images.
© John Hendrix

Figure 20-3: My logo. My initials form the face of the character that creates the logo itself.
© Michael Fleishman

The Very Fabric

"Type is everywhere," says Allegra Agliardi, "it's part of our life. Few images are without text. And an illustration, most of the time, refers to a text. So why should the text *not* be part of the image?"

Fact is, Agliardi often considers the text as part of the illustration. "Most of the time I think that words and images are one; and unique," she says. "Dialogue and art work so well together, that in a sense, the text is somewhat visual to me."

For this reason, Agliardi regards text in much the same way she works with images. Take her *Le Parole Magiche*, a children's book that inspires readers to discover and write poetry. "I found a perfect solution," Agliardi smiles. "The text becomes the protagonist. The words were really lively and onomatopoeic, and the concepts very visual. So I illustrated the letters themselves (making sure that's all readable), plus I used the letters as part of the actual illustrations: for instance, the giraffe is made with a reflected letter f."

Figure 20-4: A page from Le Parole Magiche.
© Allegra Agliardi

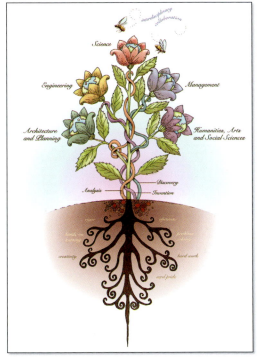

Figure 20-5: If "illustration is writing with pictures," perhaps prose is drawing with words? Brinkerhoff encourages students to define their own formal and technical solutions to visual communication problems; to realize that they are developing a visual vocabulary of their own.

© Robert Brinkerhoff and Massachusetts Institute of Technology

Writing with Pictures

Robert Brinkerhoff tells us that "illustration is writing with pictures." Brinkerhoff ran across this line some years ago, and it adds some interesting dimensions to our thinking about what we do as illustrators and how we, as illustrators, communicate. The straightforward little quote carries plenty of meaning for Brinkerhoff, who has the utmost respect for teaching based on formal and technical issues.

He never frames an illustration problem with the formal labels of "drawing," "color," or "type"; he has his students explore the communication concepts of context and metaphor instead. "This is a different set of considerations," he tells you, "and all my classes fall into what our department calls the 'illustration concepts' category. So while issues like drawing, color and typography are certainly discussed at length, these designations are rarely at the center of any student assignment."

Madam, I'm Adam

Adam Lehl is a graphic designer currently living and working in Madrid. And he collects alphabets. Lehl's collection (now boasting some 7,000 handwritten submissions, collected from people all over the world) is a grand social experiment that is based on the act of collaboration.

"I want to showcase this idea of *collecting* alphabets," says Lehl. "It's the interaction; the relationship with the individual writing their alphabet. It has nothing to do with graphology. I use the alphabets as personal and artistic inspiration as well as a typographic dialogue."

Some Words About Type

It has been almost 600 years since the first book was printed. As I write these words, the newspaper and book publishing industries are weathering extremely hard times. It's more than a little scary out there. For years, we've heard that the paper medium is breathing its last, but I've been hearing that for a long time—ever since I started working digitally. And you are still reading these words in book form, on a printed page. That's good; so we'll take a deep breath and paraphrase Mark Twain: with some hope, the reports of print's demise are—and will be—only exaggerated.

I'm not a gamblin' man, but it's *very* tough out there today. As I write this chapter, books, newspapers, and magazines are literally folding, shrinking, cutting back delivery or distribution. But I'll make an optimistic, albeit conservative bet that paper will still have some kind of edge in the foreseeable future—cutting or otherwise.

Typecast

From ancient times to modern day, people have been representing speech sounds as typographic information—graphic marks absorbed on parchment, carved in stone, imprinted on paper, and now dots on a screen. With the advent of desktop publishing—for better or worse, according to some—and the revolution of digital design and production, typographic jargon has almost become part of our everyday lexicon.

As an illustrator, you will be closely associated with words on a page: typography, calligraphy, letterforms. For me, what separates the designer from the desktop publisher are the *details* of typography. And by that same

Figure 20-7: A great comic page by Michael Cho. This fake ad has nothing to do with the demise of print, but has *everything* to do with how to deal with changes to your markets: learn to draw and draw inspiration from there. Hey, that has a ring to it, don't you think?
© Michael Cho

token, a savvy illustrator needs to know how to effectively (and gracefully) draw around type. And in some instances, it will be how to draw *with* type (a cool hybrid indeed).

Come to Terms

Terms like *typeface*, *bold*, *italic*, and *indentation* are good examples of our shared typographic language. Anyone who has ever sat down in front of a computer (or word processor) knows at least some of that vocabulary. This section can only be a beginning primer for understanding typography. What we want to do here is to provide a little overview and review some definitions. We're not a Typography book, so we won't go too deep here:

- The *Baseline* is the invisible line upon which all the characters sit.

- *Body Size* refers to the font's *x height* (roughly, the size embodied by that font's letter x, excluding ascenders and descenders). So, some fonts appear bigger than other fonts because their x height is larger.

- *Characters* are each individual letterform.

- *Contrast* refers to the disparity between a font's thick and thin strokes.

- *Font* is a set of letters, numbers and punctuation designed to work as a unified group (a.k.a. the weight, width, and style of a particular typeface).

- *Form/counterform* refers to the figure ground (or positive/negative) quality of a letterform. Counterform (a.k.a. *counter*) is that white shape created by negative spaces within an individual letter or between grouped letters. My absolute all-time favorite example of form/counterform at work—and to my mind, maybe the smartest brand ever—is the logo for Federal Express™. But I'm not going to show it to you—that would be way too easy. Instead I'll simply ask your homework question for tonight: can you spot the arrow in the Fed Ex™ logo?

- *Italic* typefaces refer to that right-hand lean. In a true italic, the glyph (or shape) of the letter character is different than the *roman* version. *Oblique* typefaces are modifications to the roman version of a font that just slant at an angle to the right.

- *Kerning* is the adjustment of spacing between letters. It generally refers to balancing *a pair* of characters (letterforms) optically. Kerning removes space. *Letterspacing* adds space between letters. *Tracking* is the computer term for adding or removing space between letters evenly, and may be more generic these days. Generally, this refers to space between letters in a word or group of words. *Leading* is the spacing between lines.

- *Typeface* is a unique collection of a unified design for an entire alphabet—letters, numbers, and symbols. A *Serif Face* is a font that has little finishing strokes at the ends of each character. A *Sans Serif* typeface is a font that has clean lines with no serifs. Typefaces are measured in *Points*: 72 points = 1 inch.

- When a paragraph ends in a single last line at the top of a new column or page, it's called a *widow*. You can take this a step further to say that this last line is comprised of one to two words, or fewer than seven characters (not words). An *orphan* is a single first line of a paragraph appearing by itself at the bottom of a page or column (while the rest of the paragraph moves forward to the next page or column).

Parts Shop

Typographic anatomy is extensive—more so than you might realize (and more interesting then you might think). But again, this isn't a Typography textbook. Let's do a marginal intro with the provision that you should do your homework and learn more.

- An *Arm* is a horizontal stroke, unattached on one or either end.

- *Ascenders* and *Descenders* are those parts of letters above and below the x height. The letter p demonstrates a descender, while the letter b has an ascender.

- *Bowl* refers to the rounded shape defining the counter (negative space) of a letterform.

- The *Counter* represents the negative space within an open or closed letterform.

- Cap Height refers to the height of the capital letters.

- A *Stem* is the major vertical stroke of a letter.

- *Stress* refers to the axis at which the contrast occurs. This can be a vertical, or slanted to the left or right.

- *Stroke* refers to the lines that characterize the essential letterform (or character).

Design Legibility and Readability

"Good" design brings together type and visual elements (like Illustration) to complement each other on the page. Typography should *never* be an afterthought. Typography and design go hand and hand. I consulted with one of the best designers I know, MaryAnn Nichols, to discuss some basic typographic concerns. Here are some highlights:

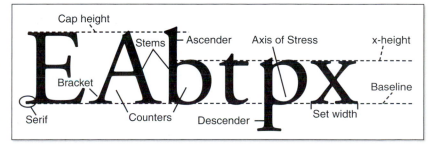

Figure 20-8: Some basic anatomy of letter characters.

✔ Check Point: It's All Greek to Me: A Short Synopsis

I guess I should hedge a few hogs, and say, *at the moment*, we continue to print books (and all sorts of magazines, newspapers, and printed pieces). What all these forms have in common: they all employ typography to convey messages to their readers. The history of typography is a long continuum of progress towards efficiency. Obviously, the methods for passing that message have changed, as well as the vehicles used to produce the message. The so-called labor of handwriting has segued into the ostensible speed and ease of the computer. We have come a long way as we've progressed from the ancient written word to digital typography.

Thus, the hot list for this chapter is our pinhead history of typography.

1. Around 1000 BC, the Phoenicians as well as other ancient Semitic people begin representing speech sounds with graphic signs.

2. The early Greeks develop an alphabet around the 9th century BC that was based on the Phoenician system. Unlike the Phoenicians, who used images to depict sounds and objects, the Greek system was the first to use symbols to represent sounds as part of a word.

3. The Romans conquer the Greeks in the second century BC, and do what all card-carrying, opportunistic invaders do. They raid the cookie jar, taking all the Grecian scholarly work (literature, philosophy, plus government documents) back to Rome.

4. Along the way, the Romans drop a few Greek characters and develop an alphabet with 20 letters.

5. Later in the Middle Ages, the other letters are added to give us the 26 we have today. The Romans unify and codify the letterforms into majuscule (a.k.a. capital or uppercase) letters.

6. Your research may tell you that it isn't until Charlemagne's time (8th-9th century AD) that miniscule (lowercase) letterforms are developed. But I have also heard that the Romans utilized both upper and lowercase, with a surprising variety of unique forms and styles. I guess it's not real history unless it's disputed somewhere!

7. All books are handwritten by scribes (if you think note taking is labor-intensive, think again). Eventually, secular texts are also *illuminated*. The term "illuminated manuscript" refers to the combination of written text, illustration and/or decorative initial capitals. Most of these books are produced for religious purposes: either bibles or daily prayer books. They are incredibly expensive and usually reserved for the wealthy.

8. The Gutenberg Bible of 1454 is the first mass produced book. The advent of letterpress printing meant information could be easily disseminated to many. It quickly spreads throughout Europe.

9. Typesetting remains fairly unchanged for 200 years (from the late 1600s until the late 1800s) when …

10. … the Industrial Revolution brings major innovations to printing technology. From here, new processes snowball—the rotary steam press and photo-engraving; the shift from wood type to metal; the Linotype machine; lithography and the offset press; photocomposition; digital type and desktop publishing—streamline and advance typesetting from the 1800s into the 1900s and right on up to tomorrow.

This Checklist warps you from B.C. (before computers) to A.D. (after digital) in 10 steps.
© Michael Fleishman

- *Readability* is all about lengthy passages of text (a book, for instance) and how easy it is to scan this material. *Legibility* is concerned with how we distinguish short passages of copy (say, a headline).

- Too many fonts spoil the design. Less is definitely more—a general rule of thumb is no more than two type combinations in your design.

- All caps decrease type legibility. Avoid using reverse type in long paragraphs, it's simply illegible.

- Not enough white space can be a big problem. Cramming in as much type as you can fit on a page is definitely a no-no; your eyes need the breathing room. Conversely, too *much* white space presents the other side of the same coin. It's all about *balance*.

- Leading is key. Proper spacing between lines improves readability. Kerning is important. Good kerning between characters also improves readability. And by the way, the secret to good kerning is that it's all visual. Train your eye.

- Study the letterforms of different typefaces. Calligraphy may give you an insight into the beauty of the font (many creative folks—designers and illustrators alike—talk about their love of letters and calligraphy).

Connotation and Denotation

In a book about connections, this chapter examines the thread between words and pictures. Maybe it's more pertinent to talk about the connection between *connotation* and *denotation*. Connotation and denotation impact pictorial image and concept as well as typographic subtlety and communication. But to put it simply: images are pictures, and pictures aren't real.

Imagery—even blatant imagery—still communicates *implicitly*. As opposed to words, which are rather overt (words are "right there" and mainly understood as information). So, denotation involves what is *explicitly* displayed. An apple is an apple—it's red. That's the *denotative* dimension of the thing.

"But what does that 'red' mean," Brinkerhoff asks. "Passion? Violence? Sin? All the hidden meanings buried (or implied) within context are *connotative*. Now, students are pretty savvy, they understand all this. But it helps to discuss this aspect and label it. Here we can promote a better understanding of the scope of communication, and gain a better sensitivity to these dimensions."

"One of the first things I try to do is move students away from getting too explicit in the visual character of their type choices. We can read the word 'Chinese,' right? It doesn't have to be in a novelty Chinese restaurant font for us to understand that it's about something Chinese."

Figure 20-9: "Avoid those unnecessary, easy answers," Brinkerhoff advises. "Try to understand the connotative qualities of type—the delicacy of a particular character; the strength or heat of a specific font (or typographic configuration)."

© Robert Brinkerhoff and Massachusetts Institute of Technology

Creating Visual Messages

Verbal/visual interplay—combining words with images to promote both physical and/or conceptual realms—can express different ideas or the same ideas differently.

Robert Meganck teaches in the Communication Arts program at Virginia Commonwealth University. "We're not folk artists, we're communicators," he says. "My work is about design and illustration. I teach *drawing-based* visual communication. Most programs would call it illustration, but we also include typography, type and image, and art direction classes in our curriculum—it's more than just illustration."

"My course, *Basic Typography*, is a prerequisite for our *Type and Image* class," Meganck tells us. "*Basic Typography* is about understanding letterforms, fonts, and type classification. This course restricts students to using and understanding typography.

"By the way," Meganck adds, "we don't use the computer until the second half of the semester. The first half is all done by hand (however, this does not change my opinion that drawing letterforms is key to understanding them).

"*Type and Image* is about creating visual messages. It's a junior level class," Meganck says. "In this class, all the assignments are essentially combinations—theater posters, menus where you use images and type. In a *Type and Image* project, every element is integral to the communication," Meganck tells you. "Take away one of those two components, and the solution won't be successful; you can't just create an illustration and caption it underneath. The type doesn't necessarily have to be in the illustration itself, but if you remove it, you'll lose a big aspect of the whole statement."

Secret Identity

So, should students think more like a typographer who can draw, as opposed to an illustrator who knows type? "That's a good question," Meganck considers. "Drawing is basic to typography. Drawing is also basic to design.

"Many graphic design programs do not have drawing as a major component, and I think that's a big mistake. It just results in students going right into the computer and simply moving things around. If you can sketch, draw, and conceptualize a piece before you ever sit down, you're much better off.

"I feel typographers should understand drawing. And if you really want to get students to know a letterform, don't just get them to key it in, ask them to pick a font, sketch it out—draw it.

"There are students graduating from schools now who just illustrate," Meganck comments. "But the market has changed, and illustrators who shy away from design are closing an awful lot of doors."

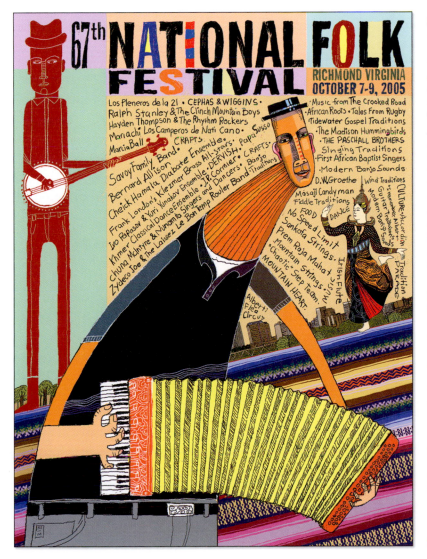

Figure 20-10a, b and c: "You need conceptual skills in both design and illustration," Meganck advises. "The concerns are identical for both disciplines: picture elements (*which could be fonts*). Do you want stability in the layout, are you looking for action and chaos … what's the message? It's all the same thing," Meganck states. "The conceptual components are no different for a designer or an illustrator. If somebody can draw an image *and* understand type, if you know how layout interacts with the drawn image, you're much better off."

How do you get students to look at type as more than just letters? "You have to regard all aspects of the assignment," Meganck tells you. "Why use this font to communicate this idea? Why this size? Why do you set type at a certain column width? What does the negative space do? That's layout."

"Now: how can you create an expressive image that communicates an idea? You have to look at how your message is going to be decoded, interpreted. You have to step out of your own personal tastes and look at it from the audience's point of view."

20-10a © Robert Meganck

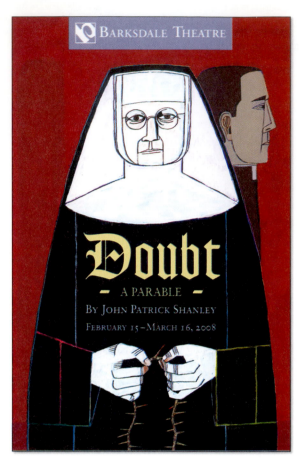

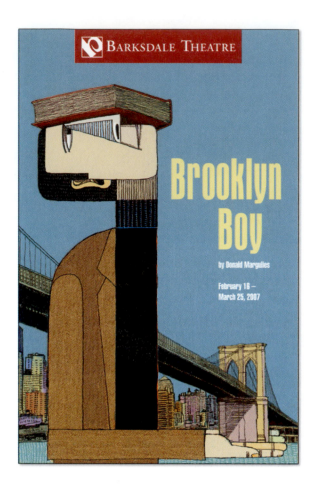

20-10b and c © Robert Meganck

Tell the Tale

"I'm a story teller," says Esther Pearl Watson, "I definitely want words in my paintings. And I am very much inspired by the interaction of those words with the picture."

"But at first glance, I want to only hint at the whole story. I want you to *read* a contrasting story rather than what you visually *see* off hand. Then when you take in the text, you go, 'What? This is very different from what I thought when I first looked at this.' The words should really take you to another place. The words hint to the personal; they suggest the humanity of the piece.

"Words are design elements," Watson states, "but not just decoration. Words become picture elements, pictures are story elements (and not necessarily more important than the other). The words and pictures must work together."

"I am concerned with pacing and rhythm . . . you see the image, read the words, go back and forth; something changes. Words and pictures exchange a dialogue and spark a tension that alters your perception of the painting after you read the text. In my comics I am playing with the whole tension of what you read first (and next). I want to disrupt the sequence of how you read, what you are supposed to read and when. Even the idea of using 'perfectly' spaced and 'clean' lettering."

Speak to Me

For Ryan Loyko (Figure 20-12), "Composition is king and line is the vehicle through which good, relevant composition can exist. I've seen paintings on gallery walls that I hated and cereal boxes that I love."

"There is a very fine line between lines that work and ones that don't," Loyko states. "The slightest variation in a curve or the way a shape sits up against another can make or break an entire work. The eye needs to flow effortlessly through a piece; sometimes it takes very little to throw the illustration off entirely."

"Color sells," Loyko continues, "but black & white *speaks*. I use color and try to think like a letterpress or woodblock artist. My background in screen printing has been invaluable in helping me use a spare palette, using color when and where necessary, to accentuate and balance, rather than to confuse the actual message."

Figure 20-11: "My comics are about the collapse of all order," Watson laughs, "how far can you push the legibility here?"
© Esther Pearl Watson

Figure 20-12: "Drawing is as much about communication as it is expression," Loyko says. "But saying 'drawing is about communication' sells it a little short," he considers. "You communicate a concept: for personal work or for a client; the creative process is dictated by the required means or a desired end. I can doodle with no deep purpose; I can scribble roses over junk mail while doing my taxes. There is no need for concept or communication or meditation—it's just an intellectual, creative, constructive way of passing time—but it means nothing other than helping the wheels turn."

© Ryan Loyko

Opening Doors

"I'm untrained," confesses Whitney Sherman. "Maybe I should say *not formally trained*, in illustration and design." Yet these are the things that Sherman, Chair of Illustration at Maryland Institute College of Art, connects deeply with.

Sherman tells you that the use of letterforms in illustration is on the rise. "It's part of the Luddite-style environment of the 21st century," she says, "yet this counter-revolution is not counter at all! This time the revolution embraces opposing philosophies, the new and the old; the technically crafted and the handmade. These things are juicy and invigorating. Doors are open for taking the text that used to sit *next* to the image and placing it *within* the image—or making it be *the* image."

Sherman isn't saying lettering in illustration—in or with imagery—is new, but its purpose is. "Historically," she informs us, "lettering itself has been illumination, as in a manuscript; it has been identification as in the name of a person of status applied to a Renaissance painting; it has been decorative and informative as in an Art Nouveau poster, or a manifestation of precision as in an Art Deco advertisement"

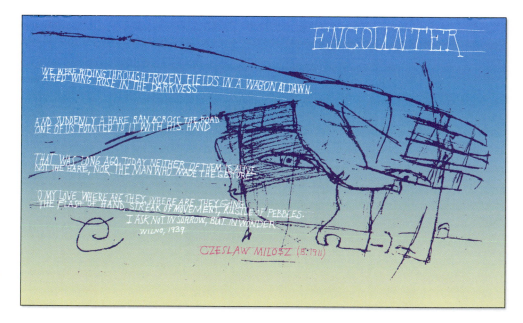

Figure 20-13: After 25 years of accomplishments, activism, and advocacy, Sherman says she maintains a passion for art and a driving interest in the profession. Her self-training, experience, and observation have found her blending numerous practices, including the use of lettering in illustration.

© Whitney Sherman

CHAPTER SUMMARY

In this book about connections, it made sense to have a chapter that discussed the relationship between letterforms and visuals, calligraphy and art, typography and illustration: words and pictures.

We looked at how words and pictures combine to link people, techniques, tools, and concepts, and offer creative opportunities to advance the art of illustration. We said that type is everywhere and illustration is writing with pictures.

We offered a beginning primer for understanding typography by providing a little overview of terminology, and we examined letterform parts.

We stated that "good" design brings together type and visual elements and provides the thread between words and pictures. We explored verbal/visual interplay as storytelling.

Working It Out

1. Play's the Thing

Theater posters are wonderful vehicles for drawing-based visual communication—great opportunities to artfully merge type and image. In class we will create posters for a series of plays mounted by a real or fictitious theater company. These productions can be related by theme or writer or genre—or not. Each member of class will be assigned a different play for their poster. See handout for further guidelines, technical specifications, and specifics.

2. Narratively Speaking

Create a painting or drawing that integrates words and visuals in a thoughtful or provocative manner (technically and/or conceptually). See handout for further guidelines and technical specifications.

3. Illuminate Me

Create a modern illuminated manuscript. See handout for concept and production notes, further guidelines, and technical specifications.

Home and Away

1. Sequence of Events

Write, design, and illustrate a graphic novel (a.k.a. comic book) that tells a story in a sequential format. Your comic book should integrate words, visuals, and panels in a thoughtful or provocative manner (technically and/or conceptually). The graphic novel may be done traditionally or digitally.

2. What's It All About, Alpha?

Steal a page from Lehl's guidebook: create your own alphabet (A–Z, upper- and lowercase; 0–9. Now go out and collect alphabets (at the mall, on the street, in your neighborhood). Certainly, ask friends, family, and classmates to contribute. Compare/evaluate process and product/discuss.

3. Loco Logo

Create your personal or professional logo. Incorporate it in a business package: letterhead and envelope, stationery, business card. Print up a full or sample run of your business package.

21

Drawn Together

© Dorian Vallejo

Tag Teams

The more the merrier, as the old saying goes. In this chapter we'll take a look at teams, collaborations, and, yes, *connections*: how a simple sheet of paper bonds the creative act; the relationships behind a shared space; and the human connection of common experience.

We're Young, but We're Good

As a preface, meet James Bennett and Dorian Vallejo. Vallejo lives and works in Montclair, New Jersey; Bennett is from Bucks County, Pennsylvania.

My connection to Bennett? In sixth grade at the time, the young Bennett took art classes the same years I taught at Armstrong Middle School, outside of Philadelphia (1973–1975, which dates us both, I guess). This was my very first teaching gig. I didn't have Jim in my class, but odds are we crossed paths in the halls frequently, it wasn't a big place. For one 8-week, 45-minute block of his day, we were only separated by a hop, skip, and jump to the other art room.

Figure 21-1a, b and c: But for the luck of the draw, I might have been James Bennett's sixth grade art teacher back in the day.

21-1a © James Bennett

21-1b © James Bennett

21-1c © James Bennett

See Ya Again

What are the odds of this happening twice? Apparently, pretty good. While Vallejo's accomplished career has taken him from illustration to traditional commissions in oil to pencil drawings and intimate life portraits, I knew him (and his younger sister, Maya) when Dorian was 12. Both were campers at The Appel Farm, a great arts camp in New Jersey. I ran the art barn and was one of their counselors for that summer (which would have been about 1977).

Small world, huh?

I'll Do It My Way

Vallejo began working for Marvel Comics while a sophomore in art school. It was his first consistent freelance gig. He grew up immersed in a deeply rich artistic environment (his father is fantasy illustration icon, Boris Vallejo). Constantly drawing, he adored comic books and sci-fi. "Professionally, at first, all I knew was illustration," he says. But he intensely disliked being art directed, and the money wasn't great. He wanted to work larger and it just wasn't practical to do an illustration at the sizes he imagined. It wasn't about selling more of the same and it definitely wasn't about working on the computer.

He *did* want to be challenged and for "my next thing to be better than the last. I sought consistent quality that only improved with the practice of

Figure 21-2: "The personal work you do for yourself is on a whole different plane than work that's commissioned," Vallejo asks you to consider. "And life itself makes it an even more interesting ride. The struggle is to actually do something with your artwork that is poignant and sincere—that touches on life itself."

© Dorian Vallejo

the craft. I love painting and drawing people and I enjoy working from life, so portraiture was an attractive option."

The Weekend in Milwaukee

It began as an impromptu exercise between friends. Hanging out one Sunday morning, Andy DuCett, Ric Stultz, and Michael Joseph Winslow started drawing as a group. "But we weren't really drawing *together*," says DuCett. "Only the surface of the paper unified us. Initially we each worked on a discreet section of the sheet. As space became more limited, in the middle of it all, somebody put a line right through DuCett's contribution. It was refreshing: a wake up call reminding him that this was a co-op, a *collaboration*. "Then the drawing really engaged *us*, and became integrated," DuCett recalls.

Trust

Each collaborator tells me that every time he walks away from a group session there is a strong sense of liberation. "I know I feel that way," Stultz says. "I go back to my own work with a renewed sense of enthusiasm. It must have something to do with being freed from making so-called mistakes."

Stultz thinks it's important to build trust in your collaborators. "Besides these two gentlemen, there aren't many other people I would trust to draw on top of my work," he admits. "I've handed my sketchbooks over and allowed them to add things. I couldn't imagine doing that with anyone else. It's the result of developing the relationship over the past five or six years."

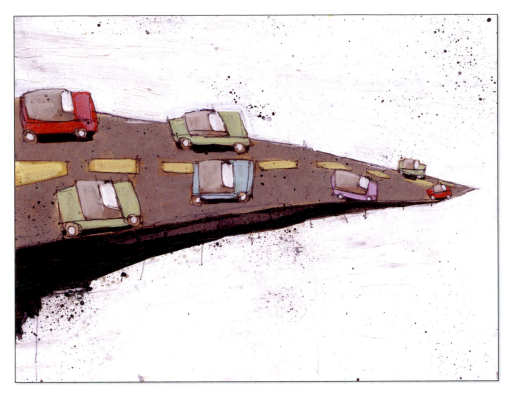

Figure 21-3: Stultz's work is shown here.

© Ric Stultz

The Meat. The Potatoes.

Collaboration seems to work best with *connection*. Long distance was problematic (at least for these guys). "We would meet, bring the supplies, and … rock and roll," smiles DuCett. "Or maybe it's more like jazz improvisation. A jam session. Me working—or reacting—to the material alone never quite made it. The communal aspect of the collaboration was a big part of the meat and potatoes of the whole process. Something this much fun becomes a task or a job when there is no social connection."

Figure 21-4: "You can have it be whatever you want it to be, on the fly," says DuCett, "without planning or formal checklists. But here's a tip: "care just a bit less about the outcome," he suggests. "You may just work right up to the point of success. And if it still all goes to hell, you have taught yourself much more in the process. Mistakes and unplanned occurrences are built right into the methodology of collaboration. It's what the practice *can* be as opposed to what the practice has to be.

"Restrictions only stymie the freedom and flexibility to experiment and create. But drawing is not brain surgery; no one is going to die here. This next mark I make—it's going to be just fine. My idea of a 'mistake'—the supposed ramifications of that—has been tempered through the collaboration."

DuCett's work is shown here.

© Andy DuCett

Figure 21-5: The collaborative work of DuCett, Stultz, and Winslow.

© Andy Ducett, Ric Stultz, and Michael Joseph Winslow

Rules needed to be as minimal as possible (and there were no parameters at all initially). Formal elements of design or concept are introduced, but subtly. "We aren't so delicate, but it isn't all piss and vinegar either," DuCett laughs. "We don't rush it; there's some breathing room. You don't have to think that much. It's reactionary and responsive, and that's great. But it doesn't spiral off into chaos," says DuCett. "We have a keen understanding of our own process and what we bring to the table."

My Marks

You must have the energy to be an illustrator. It takes effort to be a gallery artist. 100 percent dedication either way. Juggling and maintaining dual careers is a struggle.

Around 2007, a combination of factors—including economics—prompted Esther Pearl Watson to move in one direction. She made a conscious decision to stop doing illustration and concentrate on her gallery work. It felt right. "She did fine," says her husband, Mark Todd, "and even though she ultimately made less money, she was having more fun."

Art is the strand of DNA that weaves back and forth between Todd and Watson. "Well, that's how we met," Todd tells you. "I loved her work when we were students at Art Center. Our work was different, but had the same awareness (and still does)."

"Esther at the time was really inspired by children's art, naive art or folk art. Her work had a 'rough around the edges' quality. She'd paint with broken brushes, draw with bits of crayon; her colors were crazy and powerful. Her illustration got a great response, but she was always diluting it for assignments. The work was respected, but perhaps ahead of its time.

"My own work was somewhat more toned down, but still edgy enough to find an audience and buyers. Over the years our styles would criss-cross; we collaborated on occasion, other times we'd split off to do our own thing.

"Artistically, we're very different, but still complement one another. I think Esther's work is more about environment and reactions between people; mine offers more of a 'pop art' and comic book sensibility."

Home

The couple—individually and together—made several migrations between coasts and eventually settled back in Los Angeles, where they've shared a house and home studio since 2003 (they've actually lived together and shared studio space since 1994). They are parents, as well, and find that the dynamics of careers, marriage, and parenthood make for an interesting mix. "Lili has inspired us," Todd says of their daughter. "You start to realize what's important. But kids change everything." Here he smiles. "Sleep patterns, work schedules. You can't just roll out of bed or wait to get inspired. No time to daydream. There's a short open window ... start painting, *now*."

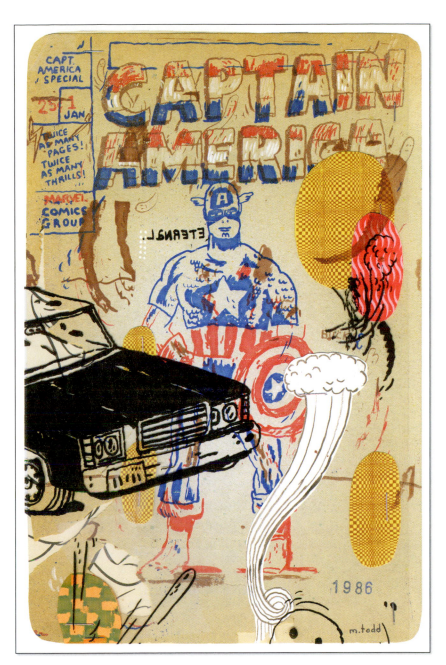

Figure 21-6: See Watson below.
© Mark Todd

The Story of Esther

"If you're constantly with somebody 22 hours a day, you will influence each other," says Watson. Initially we were drawn together because we had similar aesthetics. By now we are absolutely intertwined."

When the couple was younger, they tried to separate that out. In fact, they were somewhat shocked and dismayed when someone pointed out any similarities. "But it's a non-issue now," Watson smiles. "It's really about creating the best piece possible, so it exists in the best form possible."

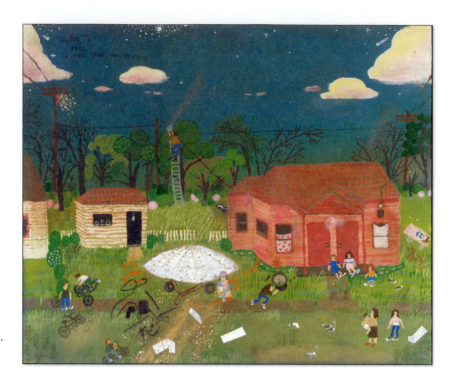

Figure 21-7: See Todd above.
© Esther Pearl Watson

The Acme

Acme Illustrators is the collaborative illustration team of Anthony Freda of Pennsylvania and Daniel J. Zollinger of upstate New York. The award-winning partners became good friends while cutting their illustration teeth at a thriving advertising art studio in New York City. Their career paths varied, but intertwined over subsequent years. Eventually Freda and Zollinger moved on (and out). Separated by geography (and the real world), they fell out of touch for a time.

Fast forward a few years. Freda (now an established figure in the illustration world) came up with the idea of collaborating with his former cohort. The two began to bang about the challenge of melding their individual talents and wide experience into a cohesive, creative, illustration unit.

Location Location Location

At one point, the partners considered a purely analog approach to their artistic alliance. And during their early years in New York City, the guys could obviously work together *physically*. But the distance between the Poconos and the Adirondacks is no easy cross-town commute. However, the Web and the prospects of digital media opened other doors.

The Virtual Studio

Freda scans pieces of old wood, metal, and salvage from flea markets, and Zollinger combines these substrates in Adobe Photoshop. Working with Freda's smart concepts and playful line sketches, Zollinger employs these natural elements to digitally render a final image. Working versions are passed via email between the two artists. All ideas, comments, and brainstorms build and refine the piece into a cohesive, seamless (and ready for print) illustration.

Figure 21-8: "I'm not sure what Dan does in his secret laboratory," Freda smiles, "but I think it involves using one of those huge Tesla coils you see sparks flying out of in the old movies. You have to ask him. He might tell you, but will probably then have to kill you."

"I'm lucky to have Dan as a partner," Freda tells you. "The obvious rule of collaboration is 'team up with the best.' Dan brings a ton of knowledge and a big bucket of skills to the drawing table."

Here's how the sparks fly from Freda to Zollinger; the Tesla coils are absolutely cranked.

© Anthony Freda and Daniel J. Zollinger

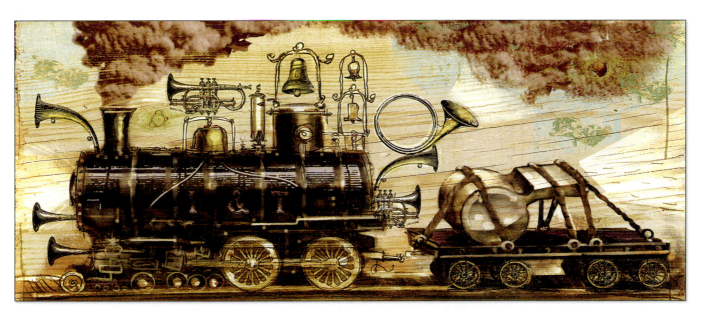

Figure 21-9: This is a job Acme did for a magazine section titled "Bells and Whistles." The art director actually dictated the concept of a train festooned with, you guessed it, bells and whistles. Freda's lighthearted drawing involved pen and some collage. He sent his art (along with a scan of old wood found on the beach) to Zollinger.

It was one of Acme's first gigs, so Freda wasn't exactly sure what to expect. "To this day," Freda says with admiration, "I'm still thrilled with what he was able to create. The limited palette; that interplay of texture; the elements of dark and light—all really sing in this one."

"And that's the beauty of collaboration," he comments. "Two heads can be better than one. I send a sketch to Dan with great confidence that it is in good hands. He respects what I've created and lets the original feeling of the drawing come through, all the while enhancing and strengthening the piece with his digital virtuosity."

© Anthony Freda and Daniel J. Zollinger

On the Bubble

Originally buds at Kent State University, Sean Higgins and Nicholas Rezabek lived together throughout college. Both students in the visual communication program (Higgins received a BFA in Illustration, and "Rez" a BFA in Design), the friends had a like illustration style and a similar sense of humor.

"We were thick as thieves," Rezabek smiles. And indeed, they worked (and played) hard at college. But as it often will, the partners literally went different directions after graduation. Rezabek relocated to New York City, Higgins stayed in Ohio.

But they regrouped via email and sought, as Rezabek puts it, "A dream job that never showed up. We decided to make it happen themselves." This kicked off a long distance working relationship and the electronic pen pals collaborating on professional illustrations and projects.

How do you do this? "We send inspiration and ideas, sketches and work files via our main vein, the World Wide Web," Rezabek says. "Playing tag team on each other's work; we move and manipulate elements; critique; push and shove; agree or agree to disagree; make conclusions that are not always what we originally sought to achieve (but accomplish, nonetheless)."

Despite the challenges of separate locations, they have defined their individual strengths and figured out how to redefine their old team process. "We really like working together, just goofing around, or discovering stuff that simply makes us go *wow*," says Higgins. "We feel we have a great sense of each other—as friends, as well as illustrators and designers."

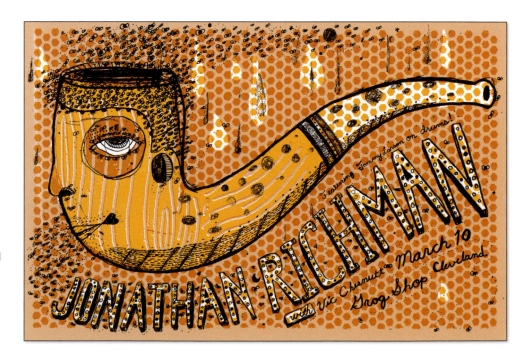

Figure 21-10: "We have learned to play off each other," Higgins says of his creative partner, Rezabek, "to contribute as a unit. To strive. To have fun. And to make posters for a living."
© Sean Higgins and Nicolas Rezabek

Song of Solman

Don Kilpatrick III was taking a class with Gary Kelley at the Illustration Academy during the summer of 1996. Looking at Kilpatrick's portfolio, Kelley suggested his student check out Joseph Solman, a wonderful painter that Kelley had recently discovered (through a volume of Solman's work, inadvertently found at Hacker Art Books in New York City).

"When I got home from this summer session," Kilpatrick remembers, "I went down to my local bookstore and ordered that same book. Joe's art immediately made an impact on me."

Don's Dream

Some years later, Kilpatrick has a vivid dream about Joe Solman. He takes this as an omen to contact the artist, and the gracious Solman readily offers to critique the younger artist's portfolio. Traveling to New York that April, they meet, and from here, Solman becomes Kilpatrick's good friend (and professional mentor). "I saw Joe almost every time I travelled to New York from that point," he remembers fondly.

Figure 21-11: An example of Kilpatrick's illustration.

© Don Kilpatrick III

Gary

Cut to 2005, and Kilpatrick is in Syracuse University's Master of Arts Independent Study degree program—and Kelley is again Kilpatrick's instructor. "I told Gary my Solman story and thanked him for pointing me to Joe's work back in '96," Kilpatrick says. "I wanted to introduce them, and as the next Syracuse session coincided with Gary being in New York City, I gave Joe a call. We set up a time that Gary, Peter Cusack, and I could visit.

"My dream in 2001 sparked one of the most meaningful friendships of my life. And it was one of the most satisfying experiences I ever had to sit back and listen to Gary, Joe, and Peter get acquainted and talk about art."

Pass It On

"Joe Solman," Kelley says, "is a terrific painter most of us have never heard of, but someone whose art meant a lot to me and left a profound impression on my work.

"I was a bit in the middle," Kelley comments, "older than Peter and Don; certainly younger than Joe. My affinity for his work, coupled with a

Figure 21-12a and b: "I loved the way Solman arranged shapes and wasn't necessarily a slave to the formality of figure drawing, the abstract qualities of his composition," Kelley says.

But, as seen here, Kelley doesn't want to do abstract paintings. "Content is crucial," he states. "I'm all about shapes and composition—I just like to find an interesting collection of shapes, enhancing shapes; pushing that forward. Color is important or else I would be doing black and white, but shape is key. There's a very basic quote by Pierre Bonnard, who always said, 'Composition is everything.'"

21-12a © Gary Kelley

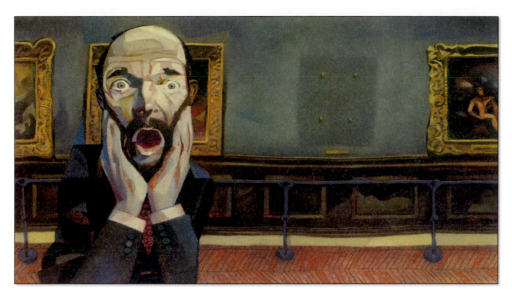

21-12b © Gary Kelley

student's fearlessness in introducing himself to him, made for something to really reflect on. We have these young guys here that want to learn all they can about this older generation of painters. Not many of that era are still around … to actually sit and talk to one of these icons was pretty cool."

Peter

Some years later, Peter Cusack was apartment hunting and actually found himself looking at a vacancy in the building right across from Joe Solman's old place.

"From this apartment, I could see right into Joe's," Cusack says, "and I flashed back to the time I spent there. Someone else was living there again. The painting racks, all the artwork covering the walls; the waft of oil medium, the old easel, his model chair—now gone."

"I remember sitting with him in his kitchen that morning. Above him, on the walls of his kitchen and intimate dinette, hung actual Rembrandt etchings, a Whistler, and more," Cusack recalls. "His spirit was warm; classical music played low on the radio. The smell of fresh coffee brewed the air. He talked about his late wife. I could imagine his sublime daily routine as a painter."

"I loved the feel of his space," Cusack tells you. "This average-size apartment, six stories up, sat on a corner in the East Village, with a dynamic view overlooking St. Mark's Church. It was Joe's home for decades, completely lived-in and totally devoted to the purpose of art, painting, and his voice."

"Joe was overjoyed to have us there. We were free to ask him *anything*. He let us rummage through his painting racks! It was an absolutely amazing and deeply profound moment … advice sent from one generation of artists to another—and passed down again. It's been a few years since we visited Joe that fall morning, but I still repeat his words of wisdom every time I'm in front of my easel, poised to launch into painting the model."

Figure 21-13: "Joe Solman was a work-a-day painter," Cusack says with consummate respect. "You felt in him the values of New York's social realist movement. He had no pretense about himself, his own art, nor the work of other great artists. Although he had a profound commitment to the nobility of being an artist, his thoughts and work projected a very humanist concept." Cusack carries on Solman's humanist tradition in work like this.
© Peter Cusack

Big Ending

Solman died in his sleep on April 16, 2008. He was 99. As a poignant coda to a touching story, Adam Solman Kilpatrick was born on Monday March 9, 2009 at 3:23 a.m. He's happy and healthy. Mom did great, dad reports that the family is fine, and everybody is getting enough sleep, so far.

Pen Pals

Living in separate cities, Aya Kakeda and friends—Nina Frenkel, Fumiha Tanaka, and Tyson Bodnarchuk—have come up with a "good excuse" to collaborate and get together.

While their collaborative art is done with charcoal, watercolor, and ink on paper, Bodnarchuk's solo work is acrylic and resin on canvas or skateboards. Kakeda works in silkscreen, stitches embroideries, and she's an active drawer, of course.

Kakeda (Tokyo/New York) and Bodnarchuk (Montreal) began mailing each other drawings in 2006, and annually set aside a week in January to meet in Montreal as a sort of "Art Boot Camp." During this session, the artists concentrate fully on a larger scale painting, as well as creating some new drawings and adding finishing touches to previous works.

Tickle Me

On their blog, Tanaka and Kakeda (as the "Pao Pao" girls) welcome you to an artificial playground space that employs various mediums: paintings, cloth, sculptures, and digital media. "We are adults," Kakeda says, " yet we never lose sight of our young mind. 'Pao Pao Land' is a magical place where your inner child gets tickled. It reminds you who you are and how to smile."

Sparks

"I think of line as a way to define shape," Frenkel says. "In my practice, I use line to create forms in a flat space—it's an edge that defines the form I am creating. In my collage work, I actually 'draw' these lines with an x-acto knife."

Value is a minor concern for this artist, who says she doesn't usually consider light and shadows in her work. "It's all flat," she tells you, "and highly 'lit'—meaning that all colors are as bright as can be.

Figure 21-14: Kakeda with Bodnarchuk

© Aya Kakeda and Tyson Bodnarchuk

Figure 21-15: Smile with the work of Tanaka.

© Fumiha Tanaka

Figure 21-16: "Process that stems off a good concept generates creative sparks," Frenkel considers. "This good concept becomes the necessary structure to that creative process."
© Nina Frenkel

Occasionally—like with my gouache painting work for *Slate Magazine*—I will use value to help define the facial features on a character or to create shadow and show depth.

"And for me, color is the feeling, personality, and vibration given off by the form assigned that color. I'm trying to celebrate colors I love, and to keep it—generally, technically—simple ... visceral ... alive."

"Drawing is seeing and thinking," says Frenkel. "Sure, sometimes you just want to make something—move your hands around and create, without knowing where it's going. But then there's concept and concept comes later. For a piece to be satisfying ... to stand on its own ... concept is important. Even if the concept is a 'decorative pattern,' there can be a color and/or rhythmic concept to it."

A Good Domestic Whine

"Call us back in two years after we're divorced," Ward Schumaker jokes when asked about the dynamics of being in the same field of dreams as his spouse, Vivienne Flesher. "No, seriously," he quickly comes back, "Vivienne helps me a lot; I help her a lot. But it's difficult at times, for the same reasons it's difficult for anyone to collaborate.

"There have been situations in which Vivienne did the sketch, got busy, and (with permission from the client) passed the finish on to me. And there are times where I had too much work and suggested that the art director hire Vivienne."

"Some clients hire us both, at the same time, to do different elements of a job," Schumaker informs, "and once, we've worked together on the same piece—for an *American Illustration* spread; she created the image, I did the calligraphy, and together we merged them."

"Most often, though, it's simply the matter of one giving suggestions to the other. As we respect each other's work, we value the advice. It's great to have an extra set of eyes."

"The thing that might make it difficult is if one got into more shows than the other, but so far we've been lucky about that. And income discrepancy hasn't hurt either; usually the one doing the better work earns less, so he/she has that to assuage the ego."

21-17a © Ward Schumaker   21-17b © Vivienne Flesher

Figure 21-17: Flesher and Schumaker, at it again!

✔ Check Point: It Bears Repeating

Let's depart from business as usual with this hot list and do a pertinent 10-point review from the various dialogues. Here's a fitting recap to the information and ideas presented in this chapter:

1. Think big (conceptually). Think bigger (technically). Maybe you really want to work larger; is it more practical to do a piece at the size you actually imagine?

2. Drawing is seeing and thinking. Sometimes you just want to make something—move your hands around and create, without knowing where it's going.

3. The older you get, the more you engage your art. Challenge yourself; make the next thing better than the last.

4. Use the collaboration process as a release from the pressures of everyday art practice. What is "drawing" exactly? Collaboration is a way to surrender control in art making.

5. The hope is that you walk away from a group session with a strong sense of liberation, a renewed feeling of enthusiasm; freed from the dread of making "mistakes."

6. Disregard any of the rules that may stifle that freedom and flexibility to experiment and create. Care just a little bit less about the outcome; you may just work to the point of success.

7. Collaboration seems to work best with connection. There is a communal aspect—a group dynamic—that's a big part of the process.

8. You can have it be whatever. You want it to be "on the fly," without planning or formality. Breathing room is important; figure out (through trial and error) what works best for the group.

9. How long can you stay interested in a particular subject? Explore something to an extreme, it will come back around; push to the limit to start doing really interesting things.

10. One obvious "rule" of collaboration is to team up with the best. If you can learn to play off each other, this will facilitate a beautiful scenario: two heads can be better than one.

Off by a hair, Kakeda and Frenkel don't pay lip service to the idea that collaboration can be just pure fun.
© Aya Kakeda and Nina Frenkel

CHAPTER SUMMARY

This chapter examines teams, collaborations, and connections. We looked at how people explore common materials to blend a mutual process; we discussed folks sharing time and/or space (even conquering distance) to bring art to life; we dialogued about a basic human connection bringing peers (and family) together for an uncommon artistic experience.

Working It Out

1. Hand It Over

Artist "A" begins a drawing and passes it on to Artist "B" who passes it on to Artist "C" and so on, and so on (until it circulates through the entire class and gets back to its original starting point). Media: free choice.

2. Squiggle Game

Pick a partner. Draw a doodle for your cohort. That person must now create something out of that mark. First rounds will be free form: anything goes. Establish themes for the next rounds of the exercise. All squiggle creations must adhere to that particular theme until you change that parameter. Media: simple markers (perhaps two different colors, one for each partner).

3. Group

We will do a large group, large-scale drawing. The entire class will work on one drawing as a unit.

You have some decisions to make: rules can be as minimal—or as exact—as possible (even no parameters is okay, should you decide). Formal elements of design or concept can be ignored or as strict and fast as the group deems appropriate. It's up to you if you want to decide about supplies and materials beforehand. If you have a game plan, stick to it. If not, take advantage of trial and error.

Home and Away

1. Free Bird

Find a drawing partner outside of class. Do a team drawing. Rules need to be as minimal as possible (even no parameters is okay). Formal elements of design or concept should be lightly discussed, if at all. Decide about supplies and materials on the fly. Figure it out (through trial and error) as you go.

2. Rules of Engagement

Same partner. Do another team drawing. This time the rules need to be established and fixed. Formal elements of design or concept should be strict and fast. Decide about supplies and materials beforehand. Have a game plan and stick to it. Try to eliminate trial and error as much as possible.

Compare and contrast product and process of both Exercises 1 and 2.

3. Go Long

Find a long distance drawing or painting partner. Create an illustration that is done without personal interaction (at the same time and/or in the same space). The art exchange can be digital or via the mails.

Appendix

Featured Illustrators

"The internet site references in this appendix are provided as a courtesy to the illustrators. Cengage Learning is not responsible for internet sites not hosted or maintained by Cengage Learning, nor makes any representations or warranties of any kind with regard thereto."

- **Allegra Agliardi** is an Italian illustrator. She won the 2009 "Young Illustrator of the Year" award at the Festival of Illustration in Pavia, Italy. Contact: allegra@helloallegra.it (www.helloallegra.it)

- **Jamie Allaire** graduated from Rhode Island School of Design, and is working as a freelance illustrator for a variety of clients. Contact: jallaire@g.risd.edu (www.jamieallaire.com)

- **Marshall Arisman**, Chairman of the MFA degree program at the SVA in New York City, was the first American invited to exhibit artwork in mainland China. Contact: arisman@sva.edu (www.marshallarisman.com)

- **Peter Arkle** lives in New York City, where he's a freelance illustrator of books, magazines, and ads. Contact: sparkle@mindspring.com (www.peterarkle.com)

- **Patrick Arrasmith** lives and works in Brooklyn, New York. Contact: patrickarrasmith@earthlink.net (www.patrickarrasmith.com)

- **Scott Bakal** is a prolific illustrator from Boston. Bakal has been included in all the major illustration competitions and has won Gold and Silver medals for his work. Contact: info@scottbakal.com (www.scottbakal.com)

- **Corrine Bayraktaroglu** is a "bit of a cheeky Geordie Lass" who calls herself a Jafagirl and is based in Yellow Springs, Ohio. Contact: jafabrit.blogspot.com

- **James Bennett** lives and works in Bucks County, Pennsylvania, and is active on numerous artistic fronts. Contact: jamesbennettart@comcast.net (www.jamesbennettart.com)

- From Montreal, Canada, **Tyson Bodnarchuk** works in acrylics, water colours, and ink. He also works in resin on canvas or skateboards. Contact: tealrobot@gmail.com

- Art has always been **Alex Bostic**'s passion. He's been a professional artist for more than 20 years now. Contact: alex@alexbostic.com (www.alexbosticstudio.blogspot.com)

- **David Bowers** lives and works near Pittsburgh, Pennsylvania and is a former lecturer at the Art Institute of Pittsburgh. Contact: davidmbowers@comcast.net (www.dmbowers.com)

- **Mark Braught's** illustrations for the book *Cosmo's Moon* were nominated for a Caldecott Award. Contact: markbraught@markbraught.com (www.markbraught.com)

- **Robert Brinkerhoff** has been teaching at Rhode Island School of Design (RISD) since 1997. Contact: rob@robertbrinkerhoff.com (www.robertbrinkerhoff.com)

- Internationally renowned artist **Philip Burke** has been capturing the minds and hearts of rock and roll and movie fans, sports enthusiasts, politicos, and the general public for over 25 years. Contact: kari@lbmadison.com

- **Jill Calder** lives in Cellardyke, Fife, in the UK. She is an illustrator, calligrapher, painter, and also a lecturer in Illustration at Edinburgh College of Art. Contact: jill@jillcalder.com (www.jillcalder.com)

- **Brooke Cameron** is the Professor Emeritus of Drawing and Printmaking at the University of Missouri–Columbia. Contact: cameronbb@missouri.edu

- **Scott Campbell** is a painter and comic creator based out of New York City. Contact: scottc@doublefine.com (www.flickr.com/photos/scott-c/ or http://www.scott-c.blogspot.com)

- **Glen Cebulash** is an Associate Professor of Art and Art History at Wright State University (near Dayton, Ohio). His areas of specialization are painting and drawing. Contact: glen.cebulash@wright.edu

- **Ed Charney** is head of the art department at Wittenberg University in Springfield, Ohio. He earned his degrees at Indiana University of Pennsylvania and Edinboro University of Pennsylvania. Contact: echarney@wittenberg.edu

- **Marcos Chin** graduated from the Ontario College of Art and Design, in Toronto, Canada and currently lives in New York City, where he teaches Fashion Illustration at the School of Visual Arts. Contact: marcos@marcoschin.com (www.marcoschin.com)

- **Michael Cho**, a freelance illustrator, cartoonist (and an occasional writer), is based in Toronto, Canada. Contact: me@michaelcho.com (www.michaelcho.com)

- **Charlene Chua** started out as a Web designer, eventually pursuing illustration as a career. She moved to Toronto, Canada in 2007, and spends her time working on illustrations and the odd comic project. Contact: charlene@charlenechua.com (www.charlenechua.com)

- **Fernanda Cohen** moved to New York (from Argentina) in 2000 and graduated from SVA four years later. She's lived in New York ever since. Contact: info@fernandacohen.com (www.fernandacohen.com)

- A professional artist since 1977, the work of **Ray-Mel Cornelius** reflects an interest in the landscape and the mythologies that accompany it. Contact: ray-mel@raymelcornelius.com (www.raymelcornelius.com)

- New Jersey's **Chris Covert** creates his portraits by collaging passages of actual text cut expressly (and directly) from a subject's body of work. Contact: covertcuts@aol.com (www.covertgallery.com)

- **Margaret Cusack** creates stitched illustrations: samplers, quilts, props, and soft sculptures. Contact: cusackart@aol.com (www.margaretcusack.com)

- **Peter Cusack** is an illustrator but thinks it's better to see yourself as an artist first—then you can apply your talents to any field you like. Oh, and he lives in New York. Contact: peter@petercusack.com (www.petercusack.com)

- **Giovanni Da Re** works for international clients using different styles to target different markets (kid's books, magazines, schoolbooks). Contact: info@giovannidare.com (www.giovannidare.com)

- **Justin DeGarmo** was born in New York and raised in California, Washington DC, & Okinawa, Japan. He's currently producing art from a small space in Arizona. Contact: mail@justindegarmo.com (www.justindegarmo.com)

- **Andy DuCett** is a Minneapolis-based artist who works for the Walker Art Center as an installation tech when he's not teaching at the University of Wisconsin-Stout. Contact: andyducett@gmail.com or hello@andyducett.com (www.andyducett.com)

- **Penelope Dullaghan** heads up the weekly creative outlet and participatory art exhibit: Illustration Friday (www.illustrationfriday.com). Contact: penny@penelopeillustration.com (www.penelopeillustration.com)

- Raised in Northern Ireland, **Avram Dumitrescu** works as a scientific illustrator, graphic-design professor, and fine artist in Alpine, Texas. Contact: avram@onlineavram.com (www.onlineavram.com)

- **Rob Dunlavey**, an illustrator and artist from the Boston area, grew up near Chicago, studied fine art in Los Angeles, and has shown his work in Paris. Contact: rob@robd.com (www.robd.com)

- The British illustrator **Jonathan Edwards** started drawing at an early age, inspired by comics and cartoons. Things haven't changed much since. Contact: jonathan.e@talk21.com (www.jonathan-e.com)

- Freelance illustrator **Shanth** (sh-ôn-th) **Enjeti** teaches at Rhode Island School of Design and Montserrat College of Art. Contact: contact@shanthenjeti.com (www.shanthenjeti.com)

- **Susan Farrington** has lived all over the world and says she's never met a medium she didn't like. Contact: the Lilla Rogers studio, info@lillarogers.com

- **Diane Fitch** is a Professor of Art and Art History at Wright State University (near Dayton, Ohio). Her areas of specialization are painting and drawing. Contact: diane.fitch@wright.edu

- **Tim Foley** lives and works in Grand Rapids, Michigan, on the shores of the Grand River. Contact: tim.foley@comcast.net (www.timfoleyillustration.com)

- **Anthony Freda** and **Daniel J. Zollinger** are Acme Illustrators. Contact: Anthony, ambant@earthlink.net (www.anthonyfreda.com); Dan, danzollinger_artist@yahoo.com (www.danzollinger-artist.com); Acme Illustrators, acmeillustrators@yahoo.com

- **Jacqueline Kahane Freedman** has retired as Associate Professor of Art at Cuyahoga Community College, and is now a full-time freelance artist who works with major publishers, national corporations, and private clients. Contact: Jacqsart@wowway.com

- **Martin French** lives and works in Portland, Oregon and currently serves as Illustration Chair at the Pacific Northwest College of Art in Portland. Contact: studio@martinfrench.com (www.martinfrench.com)

- **Nina Frenkel** teaches Animation Design in the Pre-College Program at Parson's School of Design. Contact: nina@ninafrenkel.com (www.ninafrenkel.com)

- **Tom Garrett** teaches at the Minneapolis College of Art and Design. Contact: tom_garrett@comcast.net (www.tomgarrett.us)

- **Von Glitschka** calls himself an "Illustrative Designer." He is principal of Glitschka Studios, a multi-disciplinary creative firm, and has worked in the communication arts industry for over 23 years. Contact: info@glitschka.com (www.glitschka.com)

- **Douglas Goldsmith** has been a professional illustrator and painter since 1981. He received a BFA degree from The Cleveland Institute of Art in 1981 and his MFA from Carnegie Mellon University in 1988. Contact: dgoldsmi@kent.edu or doug@douglasgoldsmith.com (www.douglasgoldsmith.com)

- **Derek Gores** holds a BFA from RISD, hails from Florida, and is best known for torn paper collage portraits. Contact: derek@derekgores.com (www.derekgores.com)

- **Adrian Gottlieb** is a naturalist painter and portraitist. While he has expanded his themes to include more landscape and still life, Gottlieb's passion remains centered on figurative compositions. Contact: adrian@gottliebstudios.com (www.adriangottlieb.com)

- **Jason Greenberg** draws from diverse cultural influences. His philosophy: "to stand as close to the edge as I can without going over. The view is incredible." Contact: Agent, Joanie Bernstein, joanie@joaniebrep.com

- **Art Grootfontein** lives and works in Paris. Contact: grootfontein@gmail.com (www.grootfontein.net)

- **Matt Hammill** is an illustrator, animator, and game developer who lives in Toronto, Canada. Contact: matt@matthammill.com (www.matthammill.com)

- **Carrie Hartman** graduated from the Minneapolis College of Art & Design with her degree in Illustration. She lives in the Minneapolis-St. Paul area. Contact: studio@carriehartman.com (www.carriehartman.com)

- **Jannes Hendrikz**, **Nina Pfeiffer**, and **Ree Treweek** are **Shy the Sun**, a dream-spinning creative troupe based in Cape Town, South Africa. Contact: nina@shythesun.tv (www.shythesun.tv)

- Currently teaching illustration at Washington University in St. Louis, **John Hendrix** received his MFA from SVA, taught at Parsons, and once worked at The New York Times as Assistant Art Director of the Op-Ed page. Contact: mail@johnhendrix.com (www.johnhendrix.com)

- Designer/illustrator **Robert "Buddy" L. Hill** earned his MFA in Graphic Design (from Savannah College of Art & Design) while working full-time for Crayola. Contact: buddy@dahjester.com

- **Paul Hoppe** is an illustrator/graphic designer, children's book author, and an occasional teacher (at SVA). Born in Poland, raised in Germany, he received his MFA in Illustration at SVA and is now based in Brooklyn, New York. Contact: info@paulhoppe.com (www.paulhoppe.com)

- **Margaret Huber** is an artist and senior lecturer at the University of Brighton in the UK. Contact: mhuber@mac.com (www.margarethuber.com)

- **Rama Hughes** was born and raised in and around Florida. He went to school at Maryland Institute College of Art (MICA) and spent several years traveling (and working) from state to state. Contact: rama@ramahughes.com (www.ramahughes.com)

- **Steven Hughes** is an artist out of Kent State University. Contact: steve@primaryhughes.com (www.primaryhughes.com)

- According to the Comics Journal, #14 of **Kevin Huizenga** 's "Supermonster" mini-comic series was named "one of the best comics of any kind released in 2001." Contact: kevin@usscatastrophe.com (www.usscatastrophe.com)

- **Sterling Hundley** is a Professor in the Department of Communication Arts at Virginia Commonwealth University, and one of five core instructors at the Illustration Academy. Contact: (www.sterlinghundley.com)

- **Charlie Immer** is based in Hagerstown, Maryland. He holds a BFA in Illustration from the Rhode Island School of Design. Contact: skeletonslime@gmail.com (www.charlieimmer.com)

- **Susie Lee Jin** was originally on a path to become an engineer or lawyer, but the arts beckoned her, and she took a permanent detour. Contact: susie@susiestudio.com (www.susiestudio.com)

- **David Julian** is an illustrator and photographic artist who earned an MFA from Pratt Institute. He now lives in Seattle. Contact: illustration@davidjulian.com (www.davidjulian.com)

- **Gwenda Kaczor** is a freelance illustrator based in Denver, Colorado. She studied at Art Center in Pasadena, California before moving to New York to work as an illustrator, character designer, and animator. Contact: gkaczor@gwenda.com (www.gwenda.com)

- **Aya Kakeda** lives and creates in Brooklyn, New York; she works in silkscreen, stitches embroideries, and is an active drawer. Contact: aya@ayakakeda.com (www.ayakakeda.com)

- **Gary Kelley** received his degree in art from the University of Northern Iowa, and began his career as a graphic designer and art director before becoming an illustrator in the mid-1970s. Contact: Agent, Richard Solomon, info@richardsolomon.com

- **Don Kilpatrick** has created illustrations for advertising, design, editorial, and motion picture clients, and was involved in the design of the Olympic medal for the Winter Games in Salt Lake City. Contact: Agency, Morgan Gaynin, info@morgangaynin.com

- **Matt Kindt** is a Harvey Award-winning writer and artist who has been nominated for four Eisner and three Harvey Awards. Contact: mskindt@prodigy.net (www.supersecretspy.com)

- **Douglas Klauba** grew up, went to art school, and worked in Chicago before moving to San Francisco and back to his home town to establish his own studio. Contact: Doug@DouglasKlauba.com (www.douglasklauba.com)

- **Matt Klos** is a painter and teacher in the Baltimore, Maryland area. Contact: matt_klos@yahoo.com (www.mattklos.com)

- **Robert Kogge** studied at the Parson's School of Design in New York and studied abroad in Europe as well. Contact: www.neoimages.net/artistportfolio.aspx?pid=3115

- **Geneviève Kote** graduated with a design degree from Ontario College of Art and Design in Toronto. Contact: genevievekote@yahoo.ca (www.genevievekote.com)

- **Dan Krall** lives in Los Angeles. He's worked in the animation industry for many years. He's recently done his first children's book. Contact: dan@dankrall.com (www.dankrall.com)

- Originally out of Boston, **Jenny Kroik** works and studies in Eugene, Oregon. Contact: jennykroik@gmail.com (www.sites.google.com/site/jennykroik/)

- **Jesse Kuhn** currently resides in New York City and works as a freelance illustrator and graphic designer at his one-man studio, Raw Toast Design. Contact: (www.rawtoastdesign.com)

- Illustrator **Boris Kulikov** was born and educated in the former Soviet Union before immigrating to the United States in 1997. Contact: boris.kulikov@earthlink.net (www.boriskulikov.com)

- **Peter Kuper** is an illustrator hailing from Manhattan. His illustrations and comics appear regularly in publications like *Time*, *The New York Times*, *Newsweek*, and *Mad*

- **Aurelia Lange** is Margaret Huber's former student and now works as a freelance illustrator. Contact: aurelialange@hotmail.co.uk (www.aurelialange.co.uk)

- German-born **Matthias Lechner** is an art director, production designer, and visual development artist living and working in Vancouver, British Columbia, Canada. Contact: info@matthiaslechner.com (www.matthiaslechner.com)

- **Ilene Winn-Lederer** is a freelance illustrator and author based in Pittsburgh, Pennsylvania. Contact: ilene@winnlederer.com (www.winnlederer.com/www.heflinreps.com)

- **Adam Lehl** is a freelance graphic designer currently living and working in Madrid, Spain. Contact: www.facebook.com/adam.lehl

- **Aliza Lelah** attended the University of Vermont, and received her MFA in Painting from SCAD in 2007. She now maintains a studio in Washington DC. Contact: alizalelah@gmail.com (www.alizalelah.com)

- **Lampo Leong**, Ph.D., grew up in China and is currently an Associate Professor in painting and drawing at the University of Missouri–Columbia. Contact: LeongL@missouri.edu (www.LampoLeong.com)

- **Susan Loeb** says, "everyone seeks a sense of place." Displaced by Hurricane Katrina, Loeb relocated to Atlanta, Georgia and explores her new environment through landscapes. Contact: info@susanloeb.com (www.susanloeb.com)

- Illustrator **PJ Loughran** is a bit of a Renaissance man who owns a small creative agency called Kerosene. He's worked with Sony Pictures, Twentieth Century Fox, and Warner Brothers/Miramax. Contact: pj@pjloughran.com (www.pjloughran.com)

- **Ryan Loyko** (with wife and business partner Andrea Loyko) runs Rattle 'N' Roll, a company that creates way cool announcements styled after gig posters for rock concerts. Contact: mykid@rattle-n-roll.com (www.rattle-n-roll.com)

- **Rianne Lozano** is an Art Director for a pharmaceutical advertising agency. Contact: riannelozano@gmail.com

- **Fred Lynch** teaches at both Rhode Island School of Design and Montserrat College of Art. Contact: fred@fredlynch.com (www.fredlynch.com)

- **Sac Magique** is British and is a graphic artist based in Helsinki, Finland. Contact: www.sacmagique.net

- **Benton Mahan** lives and works on an Ohio farm, close to the area where he grew up. Mahan attended Columbus College of Art and Design (where he teaches part time). Contact: ben@bentonmahan.com (www.bentonmahan.com)

- **Mike Maihack** lives in Tampa, Florida, and is a full-time illustrator and graphic designer with a BFA from the Columbus College of Art and Design. Contact: mike@cowshell.com (www.cowshell.com)

- A graduate of RISD, **Sarah B. Mantell** juggles dramaturgy, playwriting, and collage in Philadelphia. Contact: sarahbmantell@gmail.com (www.sarahbmantell.com)

- **Bill Mayer** is regarded as one of the best and most industrious illustrators in the business. Contact: bill@thebillmayer.com (www.thebillmayer.com)

- Illustrator **Steve McInturff** lives and works in Springfield, Ohio and has been teaching since 1987. Contact: kdsturff@yahoo.com (www.stevemcinturffstudio.com)

- **Robert Meganck** is a partner in Communication Design, Inc. and teaches in the Communication Arts program at Virginia Commonwealth University. Contact: robert@meganck.com (www.meganck.com)

- **Luc Melanson**, a graduate from the University du Québec à Montréal, is an illustrator with a whimsical, engaging style. Contact: luc@lucmelanson.com (www.lucmelanson.com)

- **Paul Melia** is a much published, much honored, internationally known illustrator and painter since 1952. Contact: paul@paulmelia.com (www.paulmelia.com)

- **Julia Melograna** graduated from Virginia Commonwealth University and is an illustrator and art director in Richmond, Virginia. Contact: juliamelograna@gmail.com (www.juliamelograna.com)

- Illustrator **Ken Meyer, Jr**. recently received his MFA from SCAD and is hoping to teach. Portfolio: www.kenmeyerjr.com/port

- Inspired by architecture and dinosaurs, **Matt Mills** was born and raised in Kansas City, Missouri, and educated in Minneapolis. Contact: NicelyDrawn@yahoo.com (www.nicelydrawn.com)

- Illustrator **Julia Minamata** is based in Toronto and a graduate of Sheridan College. Contact: julia@juliaminamata.com (www.juliaminamata.com)

- **Jay Montgomery**, a part time illustration professor at SCAD Atlanta, received his BA from LaGrange College, then attended the Illustration program at Portfolio Center in Atlanta, graduating in 1994. Contact: (www.jaymontgomery.com)

- **Kathy Moore** earned her BFA in Painting from Wright State University (near Dayton, Ohio). She still resides – and teaches – in the Dayton area, as well. Contact: kathyamoore@hotmail.com

- **Kelly Murphy** is an award-winning illustrator and animator working predominantly with traditional and mixed media. Contact: kelly@kelmurphy.com (www.kelmurphy.com)

- **Robert Neubecker** freelanced in New York City for 20 years, moving to Utah in 1994. He's been a regular contributor to Slate.com since its inception in 1996, and his first children's picture book, *Wow! City*, was published in 2004. Contact: www.neubecker.com

- Out of Massachusetts, **Heather Newton** graduated from Montserrat College of Art with a Bachelor of Fine Arts in Illustration. Contact: www.heatherlnewton.com

- A graduate of Cooper Union, **MaryAnn Nichols** is a graphic designer living and working in New York City. Contact: ngd80@aol.com

- From Sydney, Australia, **Christopher Nielsen**'s scratchy retro images have been used by clients around the globe. Contact: chris@chrisillo.com (www.chrisillo.com)

- **Jacqui Noll** graduated from Edison Community College and is working as a designer and freelance illustrator in the Dayton, Ohio region. Contact: jsnoll@windstream.net

- **Tim O'Brien** is an award winning illustrator who works for clients in magazines, books, and advertising. Tim lives and works out of Brooklyn, New York. Contact: www.illoz.com/obrien

- **Lori Osiecki** worked for Hallmark, but left after eight years to freelance. She then established her own company, Beati Productions. Contact: lorio@beatiproductions.com) (www.loriosiecki.com)

- **Susanna Pitzer** is a New York City writer, illustrator, playwright. Contact: susanna@susannapitzer.com (www.susannapitzer.com)

- Currently residing in Wyoming with his wife and son, **Zachary Pullen**'s character-oriented illustrations are seen in numerous publications. Contact: zak@zacharypullen.com (www.zacharypullen.com)

- After graduating from UCLA School of the Arts, **Mike Quon** launched his career as an art director and illustrator with a mission to "help clients stand out from the crowd and tell their story." Contact: studio@quondesign.com (www.quondesign.com)

- **Celeste Rapone** is a 2007 graduate of the Rhode Island School of Design and currently resides in Brooklyn, New York. Contact: celesterapone@gmail.com (www.celesterapone.com)

- **Melanie Reim** is an illustrator, full-time professor, and chair of the MA in Illustration program at the Fashion Institute of Technology in New York City. Contact: melreim@nyc.rr.com (www.melaniereim.com)

- **Jon** and **Rachel Reinfurt** are talented brother and sister. Contact: Jon, jon@reinfurt.com (www.reinfurt.com); Rachel, mail@rachelreinfurt.com (www.rachelreinfurt.com)

- British illustrator **Michael Renouf** currently lives and works "in the deepest suburban jungles of North-East London." Contact: michael@michaelrenouf.co.uk (www.cathill.com)

- **Nicholas Rezabek** and fellow classmate **Sean Higgins** call their professional collaborative effort "The Bubble Process." Contact: info@thebubbleprocess.com

- **Martha Rich** graduated with honors from Art Center College of Design and obsessively paints underwear, wigs, lobsters, and Loretta Lynn. Contact: martha@martharich.com (www.martharich.com)

- **Don Rogers** is keenly interested in the creative aspects of problem solving and the effective use of design. Contact: drogers@scad.edu (www.donrogersonline.com)

- **Marc Rosenthal** is an editorial and children's book illustrator who has worked on many books. Contact:marc@marc-rosenthal.com (www.marc-rosenthal.com)

- With 30+ years of experience, **Bill Russell** studied at Parsons and presently lives and works in San Rafael, California (just north of San Francisco). Contact: bill@billustration.com (www.billustration.com)

- **Tin Salamunic** was born in Bosnia, grew up in Germany, and finished his BFA in Communication Arts in Richmond, Virginia at Virginia Commonwealth University. Contact: Salamunic@aol.com (www.salamunicart.com)

- **Zina Saunders**' father was pulp cover icon **Norman Saunders**. Zina lives and works in New York City, and has been a writer-illustrator for more than 15 years. Contact: zina@zinasaunders.com (www.zinasaunders.com)

- **Ward Schumaker** is married to **Vivienne Flesher**, living and working in their house on San Francisco's Potrero Hill. Contact: Ward, ward@warddraw.com; Vivienne, vivienne@warddraw.com (www.warddraw.com)

- **Rick Sealock** is an instructor at both Sheridan College and the Ontario College of Art and Design. Contact: sealock@rogers.com (www.ricksealock.com)

- **Bob Selby** is an illustrator and professor at Champlain College in Vermont. Contact: bobselby@vtusa.net (www.bobselbyillustration.com)

- **Craig Sellars** freelances as a visual development artist and currently works in the video game industry as a concept designer. Contact: sellarsart@hotmail.com (www.greensocksart.com)

- **Jenny Sue Kostecki-Shaw**'s children's books are *My Travelin' Eye* (2008) and *Same, Same but Different* (2010), both published by Henry Holt. Contact: coloredsock@mac.com (www.dancingelephantstudio.com)

- **Stan Shaw** teaches and provides illustration and visual design for advertising, comic books, and editorial markets. Contact: drawstanley@harbornet.com (www.drawstanley.com)

- Illustrator/designer **Whitney Sherman** is Chair of Illustration at Maryland Institute College of Art (MICA). Contact: ws@whitneysherman.com (www.rappart.com)

- Illustrator **Yuko Shimizu** was chosen by Newsweek Japan as one of "100 Japanese People the World Respects" in 2009. Contact: yuko@yukoart.com (www.yukoart.com)

- **Terry Shoffner** holds a Master's degree from Syracuse University and a B.S.Ed from the University of Arkansas. He is an associate professor at the Ontario College of Art & Design in Toronto. Contact: tshoff@rogers.com (www.terryshoffner.com)

- **R. Sikoryak**, author of *Masterpiece Comics*, is a cartoonist and illustrator based in New York City. Contact: rsikoryak@earthlink.net (www.rsikoryak.com)

- From Glenageary, County Dublin, Ireland, **Steve Simpson** has been creating award-winning illustration for major ad & design companies for the last 15 years. Contact: mail@stevesimpson.com (www.stevesimpson.com)

- **Mike Slattery**'s work combines video, photography, and drawing. While it starts out as an image based solely in technology, it ends up as something quite traditional.

Contact: mslatter@bju.edu (www.michaelslattery. carbonmade.com)

- **Charlene Smith** graduated from MCAD. She's now a freelance designer & trend consultant and is always looking for new challenges. Contact: Charlene@ paisleypickle.com (www.paisleypickle.blogspot. com)

- **Britt Spencer** currently resides in Los Angeles where he continues the task of recreating reality one ink stroke at a time. Contact: britt@brittspencer.com (www.brittspencer.com)

- An innovator for over 30 years, **Chris Spollen** is both a productive illustrator and a vibrant teacher. Contact: cjspollen@aol.com (www.spollen.com)

- **Nancy Stahl** lives and works and plays in New York City. Contact: www.nancystahl.com or www.illoz. com/stahl

- **Petra Stefankova** is a London based award-winning illustrator and art director. Contact: info@ petrastefankova.com (www.yetanotherface.com)

- **Akiko Stehrenberger** is an Art Center College of Design alumnus, was an editorial illustrator in New York City, and is now an illustrator and art director in LA. Contact: akiko1024@gmail.com (www.akikomatic. com)

- **Katherine Streeter** lives in New York City and illustrates for various clients globally. Contact: dollhead@ mindspring.com (www.katherinestreeter.com)

- **Ric Stultz** is an artist from Milwaukee, Wisconsin. Contact: ricstultz@gmail.com (www.ricstultz.com)

- **Maggie Suissman** is a painter/illustrator based in Brooklyn, New York. Contact: maggie@maggiesuisman. com (www.maggiesuisman.com)

- **Tina Sweep** is an illustrator who was selected as the Society of Illustrators' very first Zankel Scholar in 2007. Contact: tina@tinasweep.com (www.tinasweep. com)

- Born in Poland, **Gabi Swiatkowska** immigrated to America at age 17. As an adult, she lived and worked in New York for many years and currently lives in France. Contact: gabi.swiat@gmail.com (www. chocolateforgabi.com)

- **Shaun Tan** grew up in the northern suburbs of Perth, Western Australia, and currently works full time as a freelance artist and author in Melbourne. Contact: www.shauntan.net

- **Fumiha Tanaka** works in mediums from paintings and ceramics to crochet, using nature related themes.

Contact: fumiha1@mac.com (www.FMTishere. com)

- **Mary Thelen** is a freelance illustrator, writer, and life-long book lover. Her favorite books, of course, are those with pictures. Contact: info@lindgrensmith. com

- **Mark Todd** graduated from Art Center College of Design, moved to New York City, then moved back to southern California with his wife and fellow artist, **Esther Pearl Watson** (and their daughter Lili, an avid artist herself). Contact: funchicken@verizon.net (www.marktoddillustration.com; www.estherwatson. com)

- **Jack Tom** lives and works in Connecticut. After graduating from college, he made his way to New York and various full-time gigs, eventually starting his own company in 1985. Contact: jacktom@sbcglobal. net (www.jacktom.com)

- **Huan Tran** is a Toronto-based illustrator/designer. Contact: huan@leakingfaucet.com (www.leakingfaucet. com)

- After a seven-year run at Blue Sky Studios, **Dice Tsutsumi** recently signed on as an art director for Pixar Animation Studios. Contact: dice@simplestroke. com (www.simplestroke.com)

- Living in Paris, **Rick Tulka**'s caricatures and humorous illustrations have appeared in numerous American and European magazines, newspapers, and books. Contact: rick@ricktulka.com (www.ricktulka.com)

- **Edwin Ushiro** graduated from Art Center College of Design and since then has been wearing a number of creative hats. Contact: ed@mrushiro.com (www. mrushiro.com)

- Inspired by his father, the fantasy artist and illustrator **Boris Vallejo**, **Dorian Vallejo**'s passion for drawing was hard wired at an early age. Contact: d-vallejo@ comcast.net (www.dorianportraits.com)

- **Kurt Vargo**'s illustrations have appeared in books, magazines, annual reports, children's videos, and as posters in the United States, Europe, and Japan. Contact: kvargo@scad.edu (www.vargoart.com)

- **Nathan Walker** is a freelance illustrator and sculptor based in the seacoast of New Hampshire. He also teaches illustration at Montserrat College of Art. Contact: nwillustration@yahoo.com (www.nathanwalker.net)

- **Andy Ward** is an expatriate Englishman living (and illustrating) near Venice, Italy. Contact: andy@ andyward.co.uk (www.andyward.co.uk)

- **Kyle T. Webster** once trained with a world-class card magician. He's an advanced origami folder, speaks fluent French, and is the Original Design Gangsta. Contact: kyle@kyletwebster.com (www.kyletwebster.com)

- Award-winning illustrator **Ellen Weinstein** is a native New Yorker. Her work appears in major publications, and she is currently in a show traveling in Italy. Contact: ellen@ellenweinstein.com (www.ellenweinstein.com)

- **Andrea Wicklund** lives in Seattle, where she works as an illustrator and videogamer. Contact: aewicklund@gmail.com (www.andreawicklund.com)

- **Martin Wittfooth** was born in Canada, studied at Sheridan College in Canada and the School of Visual Arts in New York, and now lives in Brooklyn, New York. Contact: info@martinwittfooth.com (www.martinwittfooth.com)

- In the 1980s, **Randy Wollenmann** worked as a staff artist for 10 years at Abbey Press. From there he moved to the southwest and has been developing illustrations and designs for a broad range of markets. Contact: randy@randywollenmann.com (www.randywollenmann.com)

- **Erin Brady Worsham** is fighting ALS (amyotrophic lateral sclerosis). She creates her work with the assistance of a computer connected to a tiny wire taped between her eyebrows. Contact: erinbradyworsham@bellsouth.net

- **Ulana Zahajkewycz** received both her BFA (Montclair State University) and MFA (Minneapolis College of Art and Design) in illustration. Contact: ulnanaz@yahoo.com (www.ulanaland.com)

- **Vincent Zawada** is a illustrator based in Colorado. Contact: vzawada@yahoo.com (www.vincentzawada.com)

- Illustrator **Brian Zick** hails from Los Angeles. Contact: zick@brianzick.com (www.brianzick.com)

- **Jaime Zollars** is a freelance illustrator who's inspired by fairy tales and Flemish painters. She teaches at Maryland Institute College of Art (MICA). Contact: jaime@jaimezollars.com (www.jaimezollars.com)

Illustrator's Index

Index

D

N

M

O

Sketch Pad

Sketch Pad

Sketch Pad

Sketch Pad